Modern Paraguay

Modern Paraguay

Uncovering South America's Best Kept Secret

Tomás Mandl

McFarland & Company, Inc., Publishers
Jefferson, North Carolina

Library of Congress Cataloguing-in-Publication Data

Names: Mandl, Tomás, 1979– author.
Title: Modern Paraguay : uncovering South America's best kept secret /
    Tomás Mandl.
Description: Jefferson, North Carolina : McFarland & Company, Inc.,
    Publishers, 2021 | Includes bibliographical references and index.
Identifiers: LCCN 2021019252 | ISBN 9781476684680
    (paperback : acid free paper) ∞
    ISBN 9781476642895 (ebook)
Subjects: LCSH: Paraguay—Description and travel. | Paraguay—
    Economic conditions. | Paraguay—Politics and government. |
    BISAC: HISTORY / Latin America / South America
Classification: LCC F2676 .M34 2021 | DDC 989.2—dc23
LC record available at https://lccn.loc.gov/2021019252

British Library cataloguing data are available

ISBN (print) 978-1-4766-8468-0
ISBN (ebook) 978-1-4766-4289-5

Front cover image: The Asunción skyline and Paraguay River
(© 2021 maloff/Shutterstock)

Printed in the United States of America

McFarland & Company, Inc., Publishers
  Box 611, Jefferson, North Carolina 28640
  www.mcfarlandpub.com

To Laura

Table of Contents

Acknowledgments   viii

Time Line   xi

Introduction   1

I—The Echoes of Paraguay's History   9

II—Politics: The Old and the New   54

III—An Emerging Emerging Market?   78

IV—Paraguay's Way of Doing Business   101

V—Labor Forces: Mennonites, Brasiguayos,
Indigenous, and the New Urban Class   127

VI—Big Agriculture Versus the Green Energy Utopia   155

VII—Island Diplomacy   177

VIII—Epilogue: Modern Paraguay and Its Challenges   193

Chapter Notes   205

Bibliography   229

Index   233

Acknowledgments

My first thanks go to Sandip Mehta and Angie Mizeur, who in the early stages of doubt and second-guessing the whole book-writing enterprise provided the cheerleading I needed to take the plunge. Elizabeth Knox gave me early guidance on how to write a book; her timely and frank advice, based on her own experience as an author, set me straight right from the beginning.

I am grateful to Christopher Saenger, who volunteered to read the book's proposal and its early drafts. His masterful editing set the bar high, lighting a path forward for the remainder of the book.

I count my blessings for having met Alfonso Velázquez at the time when I was doing the book's early research in Asunción. Alfonso's encyclopedic knowledge of Paraguayan history, its politics, and culture, which he selflessly shared with me over many conversations, was a crucial stepping stone for the book. Furthermore, Alfonso's deep Rolodex, together with his extensive list of family members and acquaintances, allowed me to meet many of the individuals who contributed their knowledge to this book. Alfonso also found time to read draft chapters and share his thoughts. And that is not all; some of the pictures he took in his many travels appear in this book as well. Aguyjé chera'a.

Many thanks to historian Milda Rivarola, who opened the doors of her house and hosted me—a perfect stranger—for two days to learn about Paraguayan history. The history chapter's structure and themes stem largely from those two days with Milda.

I owe a debt of gratitude to the following individuals, who shared their time with me and whose deep knowledge of Paraguay greatly enhanced the book's material: Diego Abente, Sebastián Acha, Alberto Acosta Garbarino, Victor Raúl Benítez González, Georg Birbaumer, Alfredo Boccia Paz, Martín Burt, Eduardo Bogado Tabacman, Dionisio Borda, Pilar Callizo, José Cantero, Santi Carneri, Miguel Carter, Javier Contreras, Emily Creigh, Liliana Duarte-Recalde, Hugo Estigarribia, Wilfrido Fernández,

Benjamín Fernández Bogado, Camilo Filártiga, Marcello Lachi, Magui López, Fernando Masi, Henry Moriya, Alfred Neufeld, Andrew Nickson, Javier Pérez, Adelina Pusineri, José Tomás Sánchez, Leila Rachid, Kate Raftery, and Estela Ruíz Díaz. I was fortunate to meet and spend time with the great Bartomeu Melià, the country's foremost expert on the Guaraní people, before he passed away in December 6, 2019.

I'd like to thank Marcus Carpenter and Daniel Getahun, who read early chapters and provided me with the first quality test; their comments and edits made the book better. I also benefited from many conversations with them about issues relevant to the book. Many thanks to Professor Michael Pisani, who in spite of having met me only once for 30 minutes, agreed to read chapters and provided me with valuable insights. I also thank Kathleen Weaver for providing helpful comments and edits to the introduction.

Thanks to the World Bank, Inter-American Development Bank, and the Centro de Análisis y Difusión de la Economía Paraguaya (CADEP) for their high-quality and timely reports. Without them the book's overall quality and breadth of issues analyzed would have been much limited. The public events they organized to analyze key public policies further helped me produce a better book.

I am also grateful for Luke Gerwe's copy editing and editorial advice. Luke polished the book and brought a keen eye to organize the book's structure and articulate its internal logic.

Charles Perdue at McFarland gave me hope in 2017 and delivered in 2020; this book is out in great measure thanks to him.

Many thanks to the newspaper *Última Hora* and photographer Oscar Rivet for granting me the right to publish their pictures. Muchas gracias.

A big thank you goes to the many Paraguayans I met and interacted with, including my Guaraní teachers Catalina, Joty, and Mariela, embassy colleagues, and soccer buddies, who taught me with much kindness about their country.

Tyler Cowen and Russell Roberts are two economists that I have never met but who have had significant influence in my education. Their writings and podcasts shaped the way I understand and try to make sense of issues related to the social sciences. Just as importantly, their agnostic demeanor, intellectual curiosity, and respect for the views of those who disagree with them are an inspiration. In addition, Tyler not only replied to my emails about the book but was enormously kind to read the book proposal; he encouraged me to finish it with his classic no-nonsense advice, "Writing is its own reward."

I am forever grateful to my parents Teresa and Alfredo, who gifted me with the love of books.

Needless to say, the book's omissions and mistakes are all my own; none of those acknowledged here bear any responsibility for them.

My greatest debt of gratitude goes to my wife Laura. I cannot imagine writing this book without her. She is the reason I came to Paraguay in the first place, but she also encouraged me through our time in the country to finish the book ("just get it done Tomás"). She was my lead editor, proofreader, and reality checker. She was always there when I needed her through the many times I was typing away and missed being with her and our children. For all of the above and more, I dedicate the book to her.

Time Line

1800 BCE–10 CE—First Indigenous groups settle in what would later become Paraguay.

1524—Aleixo García becomes the first European to reach modern Paraguayan territory.

1537—Spanish conquistador Juan de Salazar y Espinosa establishes Asunción.

1542—The Spanish Crown establishes the Viceroyalty of Perú with jurisdiction over Asunción.

1544—Spanish settlers in Asunción carry out their first mutiny against the Spanish Crown.

1558—Asuncenos elect their first governor.

1580—Asunción-based Spanish conquistador Juan de Garay establishes the city of Buenos Aires.

1609—Jesuits establish their first reduction in present-day Paraguay.

1721—First Asunción–based Comunero revolt against Spanish Crown rulings.

1767—The Spanish Crown expels the Jesuits from its territories in the Americas.

1776—The Spanish Crown establishes the Viceroyalty of the Río de la Plata with jurisdiction over Asunción.

1811—Paraguayans declare their country's independence.

1813—José Gaspar Rodríguez de Francia assumes power.

1841—Following Francia's death, Carlos Antonio López assumes power.

1845—Edward A. Hopkins becomes the first U.S. government representative in Paraguay.

1862—Following López's death, his son Francisco Solano López assumes power.

1864—Triple Alliance War commences.

1870—Paraguayans approve the country's first constitution.

1878—U.S. President Rutherford B. Hayes, in his role as international arbitrator, awards Paraguay lands located in the Chaco region that were claimed by Argentina.

1887—Foundation of the Colorado and Liberal parties.

1904—Liberal Party triumphs in civil war and assumes power.

1926—First Mennonite settlers arrive in Paraguay.

1932—Chaco War commences.

1936—Febrerista uprising installs Coronel Rafael Franco as president.

1937—Liberal Party overthrows Franco and installs Felix Paiva as president.

1940—Liberal Party president José Estigarribia dies in an airplane crash and General Higinio Morínigo assumes the presidency.

1944—Paraguay introduces the "guaraní" as the country's first national currency.

1947—Following a five-month long civil war, Morínigo in alliance with the Colorado Party defeats an alliance of Febreristas with the Liberal Party.

1954—General Alfredo Stroessner wins his first (fraudulent) presidential election.

1965—The Friendship Bridge, connecting Ciudad del Este to Brazil's Foz do Iguaçu, opens to traffic.

1966—Paraguay and Brazil sign the Act of Iguazú.

1973—Paraguay and Argentina sign the Yacyretá Treaty.

1975—The military governments of Argentina, Bolivia, Brazil, Chile, Paraguay, and Uruguay establish the Plan Condor.

1979—Paraguay hosts the World Anti-Communist League's XII Annual Conference.

1984—Itaipú Dam begins producing hydroelectric energy.

1989—General Andrés Rodríguez emerges victorious from a military coup and sends Stroessner to exile in Brazil.

1992—Paraguayan lawyer Martin Almada leads investigation that uncovers the "Archives of Terror."

1994—Yacyretá Dam begins producing hydroelectric energy.

1996—General Lino Oviedo threatens a coup d'état against President Juan Carlos Wasmosy.

1999—Following Vice President Luis María Argaña's assassination, clashes among police, opposition, and government supporters trigger the "Paraguayan March," resulting in seven casualties.

2008—Fernando Lugo wins the presidential elections, ending the Colorado Party's 61-year rule.

2012—Congress impeaches Lugo and Liberal Party's Federico Franco assumes the presidency.

2017—Protesters burn the Congress building to protest a constitutional amendment allowing presidential reelection.

2019—Colorado Party's Senator Víctor Bogado becomes the first legislator to be convicted for crimes committed during his congressional tenure.

Map of Paraguay (CIA World Factbook).

Introduction

On the afternoon of March 31, 2017, I was dozing in a hammock in the warm spring breeze of Asunción, Paraguay, when I received a frightening text message from my wife: "turn the TV on." My wife's text message sent me racing inside expecting disturbing news. Sure enough, live footage showed the Paraguayan Congress in flames, one of its members shot in the face, and tear gas–filled street battles between police and protestors. Later that night, a group of police in hot pursuit of alleged vandals forced their way into a nearby opposition party's office and killed a young activist on the spot. The whole city went into lockdown, and the warm spring breezes suddenly felt ominous. It was just three months after I had moved to Paraguay and my parochial tranquility was over. Why the sudden commotion? The proximate cause was a proposed constitutional amendment to end the president's one-term limit and allow for reelection, but there were deeper problems underneath the turmoil.

Unfortunately, there was neither a book (in either Spanish or English) nor a single long-form article that could offer much insight into why the protests were happening, let alone provide a broader perspective on modern Paraguay. As an international affairs analyst by trade, I look for tools in the written word, especially that of travelled experts (even the stuffy types). As I was preparing to start work in my third American embassy, I was hoping to find something similar to a "Scene-setter," the concise yet thorough document I helped draft many times explaining to senior U.S. government figures the key aspects of a country's politics, economics, and society. After surveying the literature, however, I corroborated what the foremost English language expert on Paraguay, Andrew Nickson, said about the country: "[It is] the least known and least researched country in Latin America," one with an "unusual history" that has given rise to "much mythologizing and romanticizing."[1]

I had come to Paraguay in December 2016 following my spouse's assignment with the U.S. Agency for International Development (USAID).

1

To be quite honest, although I grew up in nearby Uruguay, my knowledge of Paraguay was largely limited to soccer stats. I could recite the national team's starting lineup, recall the Paraguayan club Olimpia's achievements, and tell you everything about the sport's greatest goalkeeper ever, José Luis Félix Chilavert. Generally speaking, Uruguayans are naturally inclined to anything European and consume mostly Argentine culture, while paying some attention to what happens in Brazil. But Paraguayan affairs? Nada. I also knew that my Jewish great-grandfather and his family, including my grandfather, had escaped Austria right before World War II, boarded a boat in Hamburg, and headed to Paraguay. For reasons that remain unclear,[2] they stopped in Montevideo and never looked back, except to reclaim their luggage, which had continued its route to Paraguay; years later it would return with a big German encyclopedia that belonged to some other itinerant family. But beyond thinking about what could have happened if my family had actually made it to Paraguay, I had never thought carefully about the country.

My first deep dive into Paraguayan data took place in my post-college years when I was working for Canada's congressionally funded Mercosur Economic Research Network, a non-profit organization dedicated to academic research with a Mercosur[3] perspective. The network's sole Paraguayan member was the Centro de Análisis y Difusión de la Economía Paraguaya (CADEP), which to this day remains Paraguay's leading and most prestigious think tank. At the Mercosur Network, I watched Paraguay's slow economic transition away from the dark cave built by strongman Alfredo Stroessner toward greater intra-region trade and investment. In those early 1990s days, Paraguayan policymakers were gung-ho about market-oriented reforms taking place in the region, but almost no one outside Paraguay seemed to be paying attention to the country's transformation. The view from my little world was that "Paraguay was being Paraguay"; that is, slowly changing but keeping its old political instability and failing to get a handle on violence. As it happens, the reality was far more complicated and interesting.

~~~

Unfamiliarity with Paraguay is not new. Back in 1954, in the foreword to the first serious academic study of Paraguay, U.S anthropologist Julian Steward was already claiming, "The people of Paraguay are among the most interesting and least understood of Latin America."[4] Almost thirty years later, U.S. political scientist Ronald McDonald (his real name) could still plausibly argue, "no country in Latin America has received less attention from social scientists than Paraguay."[5] The country was for a long time an isolated territory, far from the world's economic metropoles and earning nicknames such as the "Albania of South America" and the "South American Tibet." Even the Paraguayan government not long ago called the country "South America's best kept secret."[6] Since the advent of international media, Paraguay has not suffered from the kind of human and natural tragedies that put a country on the developed world's radar. Indeed, non-academic books available in English about Paraguay present a picture of an exotic country and describe journeys to a land where magical realism is alive and kicking. "Wrapped in a layer of clichés"[7] was how one of the many hit-and-run foreign journalists described the place. Sometimes the scribes are not so amiable. For example, a *New York Times* review of a popular Paraguay travel book in 2004 ran under the headline, "You Don't Want to Live There" and called Paraguay, "the strangest country on the planet."[8] Or as Homer told Marge during an episode of *The Simpsons*, "You can thank your lucky stars we don't live in Paraguay."[9]

There's an argument to be made that Homer was onto something. For most of its history Paraguay was poor, plagued by wars, dictatorships, and economic stagnation. Paraguay was also remote, land-locked, and walled in by wastelands and jungles. But starting in the last decade of the twentieth century, something started to change. The depressing indicators started to reverse. Prosperity grew and hope began to emerge. Yet the familiar risks have not gone away: political crisis, economic mismanagement, corruption, and, increasingly, environmental damage, are all lurking behind the encouraging Paraguayan story of the past few decades.

My aim in this book is to provide the reader with tools to move past the clichés and better grasp modern Paraguay. It is the book I would have liked to read when I first moved to Paraguay. For over three years I traveled through the country, read the limited extant literature (both academic and fiction), closely followed traditional and social media, and sifted through reams of data. I had the privilege of speaking to the country's leading intellectuals—more than forty in-depth interviews with historians, political scientists, economists, journalists, and diplomats—but also learned Guaraní and heard the views of regular citizens. I even experienced dengue fever for a couple of weeks. I also worked at the United States Embassy in Asunción as a political analyst and was actually paid to understand the country's political and economic changes. In all my experiences, I sought the Paraguay reflected both in the statistics and the stories supporting the numbers. Reader, be warned: the book does not uncover new research findings or unpublished records, but it does bring together all the different pieces scattered around in books, the Paraguayan press, academic articles, reports, and in the heads of knowledgeable Paraguayans. I relied on strong empirical regularities when possible, trying to identify causal mechanisms and avoid misleading correlations or circular arguments; when the data was not sufficient to make a claim, I relied on relevant theoretical tools and the experiences of countries that either already achieved or are on the path to high-income status. And when none of the above was possible I tried to convey my skepticism and lay down all the reasonable explanations at hand. The subjects I explore in the book stem both from my professional bias and what I gathered from my research to be the most important issues. I set off to understand the country's "political economy," the amalgamation of political, economic, legal, and cultural relations that explain its current circumstances.

I take the Merriam-Webster's definition of "modern" as "of, relating to, or characteristic of a period extending from a relevant remote past to the present time." The overall focus is on the *perennial* rather than the latest. In this sense, the book is not a handbook for the country's famous-and-notable or a "how to invest" type of book. I tried to avoid naming names as much as possible, focusing instead on the macro trends, the long-standing institutions and behaviors, and developments that explain modern Paraguay beyond the sitting finance minister or successful entrepreneur. Likewise, I quoted some of the many voices that informed the book, whether cultured or streetwise, enlightened or crass, Paraguayan or foreign, to shed light onto specific phenomena, but avoided the character-driven distractions or personal memoir digressions that affect many books about international affairs.

In sum, I sought answers to the following question: "What makes Paraguay thrive and what holds it back?" I wanted to explore the journey that some international development experts call "getting to Denmark." That is the multidimensional avenues and roadblocks that mark a country's path to high and well distributed per-capita income, adequate delivery of public services, and social peace. As impressed as I am with Legos and Vikings, the relevant part about becoming Denmark that I examine in the book has to do with achieving tangible results in terms of free and fair elections, living wages, access to justice, good schools, and other markers of societal well-being. Learning about countries' political evolution, economic development, and foreign relations has been a life-long passion; it brought me to Paraguay and, by writing this book, led me out with a better understanding of what it takes to reach the archetypal Denmark. My answers to those questions follow, telling the story of modern Paraguay, its changing institutions and society, and how Paraguayans are seeking prosperity. My quest for answers is divided in nine chapters, starting off with an historical introduction, followed by discussions of politics, economics, formal and informal institutions, human capital, agriculture, energy, and international relations, examinations that are followed by an epilogue that once again takes up the question of Paraguay's options and challenges to reach Danish development.

What About the Nazis?

No other cliché is more relentless, widespread, and mistaken than the narrative of Paraguay as safe haven for Nazis. The 1971 film *Willy Wonka & the Chocolate Factory*, for example, managed to condense in one scene the many misplaced foreign perceptions about Paraguay. The film tells the story of a kid seeking a "Golden Ticket" to visit the mysterious chocolate factory and receive a lifetime supply of chocolate; in a plot twist, a man in Paraguay finds the last ticket. The fictional Paraguayan was a "multimillionaire owner of gambling casinos" and it is later revealed that his ticket is a fake. In the specific scene, a newscast shows the fictional Paraguayan man's picture and it is none other than real-life Nazi criminal Martin Bormann. To an average viewer, the movie paints Paraguay as nothing more than a home for Nazis, gamblers, and scammers. *Willy Wonka,* of course, is not an obscure B movie, but an Oscar-nominated popular film selected for preservation in the United States National Film Registry. Fast forward to 2014 and a more sophisticated proxy for foreign perceptions of Paraguay, the late chef and TV presenter Anthony Bourdain, described Paraguay as, "An empty space on the map of Latin America […] known largely for being a post-war refuge for fleeing Nazis."[10]

This is an instance where the English and Spanish-speaking worlds diverge. In my experience, South American people do not generally associate Paraguay with Nazis, but as soon as I started reading the English-language, non-academic literature on Paraguay and watched popular movies that mentioned the country, it became clear Nazis and Paraguay were inseparable in the foreign popular imagination. There are two different components to the Nazis in Paraguay case.

On one hand, there are some Nazis that fought in World War II and fled to Paraguay after Germany's defeat. In many ways, Paraguay was indeed a good country for runaway Nazis thanks to its remoteness, cultural insularity, and plain demographic emptiness. Most notably, Nazi war criminal Josef Mengele spent time in Paraguay; known as the "Angel of Death," Mengele is infamous for carrying out gruesome experiments with human beings at the Auschwitz concentration camp. Yet, according to Paraguayan journalist Andrés Colmán's meticulous investigation, Mengele lived in Hohenau, a small village in Southern Paraguay, for less than two years (1959–61) under the protection of German settlers engaged in agricultural work.[11] After the war he had gone first to live in Argentina but then moved to Paraguay to escape German post-war trials and the Mossad. After Paraguay, he moved on to Brazil, where he finally settled and died in 1979. The two-year window in Paraguay, therefore, is short in the context of the thirty years that Mengele spent in South America. In addition, there was long-standing speculation about Martin Bormann living in Paraguay, but they ended in 1998 when German scientists confirmed with a DNA test that Bormann had died in Berlin in 1945.

On the other hand, there are the German immigrants who settled in Paraguay in the late nineteenth century and early twentieth century and embraced Nazism from a distance. Friedrich Nietzsche's sister Elisabeth married an anti–Semite ideologue, packed her bags, and went to Paraguay in 1887 to found an Aryan colony called "Nueva Germania"; her adventure ended two years later with her husband committing suicide in a lakeside hotel in San Bernardino, Paraguay.[12] Four decades later, in 1929, German immigrants in Paraguay founded the first Nazi Party outside of Germany and Austria and were seen parading their flags, hosting banquets, and going about their ways without trouble. There were even some Paraguayan sympathizers, like the one police chief who named his son Adolfo Hirohito, after the two Axis leaders.[13] Nonetheless, it is quite possible most Paraguayan residents with an affinity for the Nazi Party derived their views more from affection for the old country than from a consistent belief in the tenets of National Socialism. One hundred years after Nueva Germania's founding, one of the few remaining descendants confessed to British writer Ben Macintyre, "Sure, everything was 'Heil Hitler' […] it was something you did, like supporting the Liberales. It didn't mean much."[14]

While the English-speaking world's perception of Paraguay as a Nazi haven contains a grain of truth, given that a number of Nazis did find refuge in Paraguay, it is an exaggeration in light of the bigger numbers that ended up in other South American countries. According to German archives revealed by the British newspaper *Daily Mail*, around 9,000 war criminals escaped to South America (including Germans and non–Germans) of which they estimate 5 percent made it to Paraguay.[15] The vast majority chose Argentina, Brazil, Chile, and Uruguay (in that order). When it comes to high-profile Nazi fugitives, Paraguay was never a top destination either. For example, of the *History Channel's* "The 7 Most Notorious Nazis Who Escaped to South America," only one went to Paraguay (Mengele).[16]

Likewise, the presence of Nazis in Paraguay serves to explain little of what is relevant to understand modern Paraguay. True, as we will see, the son of a German immigrant (with no links to the Nazi Party) became a central historical figure of Paraguay. But his role in Paraguayan history did not arise from the unique local circumstances under which Nazism existed in Paraguay. Rather, his rise, resilient hold on power, and eventual fall would have happened without a single Nazi stepping on Paraguayan soil. By any measure, Paraguay Nazism's legacy is almost non-existent; the type of authoritarian politics, Manichean discourse, and cult of personality one may ascribe to Nazism were already present in Paraguay at its independence and remained in place for many years after the last Nazis finally bit the dust.

I

The Echoes
of Paraguay's History

When I traveled to rural Quyquyhó, about four hours southeast of Paraguay's capital, Asunción, I could still see the Paraguay of yore: wide-open spaces dotted with small houses while cattle grazed stress-free nearby. It resembled Graham Greene's description of Paraguay as a "land of deep tranquility and the smell of flowers,"[1] even though I mostly smelled freshly baked chipas.[2] While looking out the bus window I remembered the fantastic stories about Paraguay's early development that my high school teachers told me in Uruguay. You see, Paraguay was South America's first country to get electricity, railroads, and an iron foundry. The first three presidents of independent Paraguay built a thriving economy almost in autarky, based on Paraguayan ingenuity and first-class British experts, and implemented an early version of import substitution/infant industry policies still popular among some economists. Moreover, they managed to provide basic education to the whole population, rich and poor. But then Paraguay's two neighbors, Argentina and Brazil, together with Uruguay, launched a big, nasty war against Paraguay that left the country in ruins and forever imperiled its development. Or so my teachers told me.

I went to Quyquyhó to meet historian Milda Rivarola, who kindly invited me to her handsome colonial-style house for two days of deep learning about Paraguayan history. Rivarola is such a committed historian and public intellectual that she managed to amass the country's largest private library on her own dime and efforts. So when I first asked around about talking to a historian, all the replies steered me to her. Although I suspected what the answer might be, I still asked Rivarola whether my high school story about Paraguay was true. She smiled mischievously, took a deep breath, and shot back, "No." She pointed out that Paraguay had never been the thriving nation they told me about in school—just look at the lack of architectural, artistic, or other material remnants of development in downtown Asunción. Rather, Paraguay for most of its history barely scraped along on subsistence levels of income, encumbered by destructive governments, wars, and disengagement from global markets due to both geographic and self-imposed causes.

Nonetheless, as we will see next, these regularities resulted from some incredible historical events, including the almost disappearance of Paraguay as a legal entity, policymaking under consistently turbulent conditions, and a demographic melt of Indigenous and foreign peoples. Modern Paraguay echoes a history of political violence, economic disparities, and institutional unfairness mixed with human resilience in the form of a surviving Indigenous language, growing economic prosperity, and increasing equality before the law.

Geographical Remoteness Meets Strategic Irrelevance (?–1811)

The first *Homo sapiens* to reach modern day Paraguay arrived at least 5,200 years ago.[3] They came after the long march that started out in East Africa and went on to cross the Siberian Peninsula to Alaska some 15,000 years ago. The first inhabitants reached modern-day Paraguay by way of the Amazon basin. These bands of early settlers propagated in a land surrounded by well-defined geographical areas in the form of jungles and wastelands but also large sub-tropical plains. Until the better-armed Spaniards arrived, Paraguay's first societies developed at a snail's pace compared to their northern brethren, such as the Incas in the Andean region. In addition, a Malthusian trap[4] kept those early Paraguayans' demographic growth in check. According to historian Mary Monte de López, the early settlers were similar to those inhabiting the North American plains: small hunter-gatherer tribes connected by family or clan ties.[5] The early inhabitants of Paraguay encompassed a diverse group of tribes that spoke different dialects. The larger group and the one that dominates Paraguay's folklore was the Tupi-Guaraní; they endured harsh and short lives in small hamlets and were harassed by other bands of hunter-gatherers. The Tupi-Guaraní settled in what would later become Paraguay around 2,000 years ago. They migrated from the Amazon Basin and originated from the same linguistic group of the Arawaks and the Caribs, two Indigenous peoples from northern South America and the Caribbean.

A lot of what we know about the Guaraní and the impact of Spanish colonizers on Indigenous people comes from Dr. Branislava Susnik, a Slovenian anthropologist who came to Paraguay by way of Argentina in the years immediately after World War II. Dr. Susnik brought the type of expert human capital that has always been in short supply in Paraguay and went straight to work among the different Indigenous people across the country. Asunción's excellent Museo Etnográfico (Ethnography Museum) bears the mark of her more than forty years of careful scientific work. Dr. Susnik was an early myth buster. Specifically, she shredded the notion of a peaceful coexistence between colonized and colonizers that some twentieth-century Paraguayan historians propagated. As we will see, there was not coexistence but a violent imposition of conditions similar to those practiced in other parts of Latin America.

The first European conquistadors reached modern Paraguay almost by mistake, trying to reach the fabled lands where gold and silver gushed from the mountains in the Andes. Conquistadors were engaged in a mad race to dominate the Inca Empire and its riches; some came from the Pacific and some others from the Atlantic Ocean. In the end, Francisco Pizarro, who entered from the Pacific Ocean, won the race in the 1530s, though explorers from the Atlantic Ocean did not find out until some years later. The story of Aleixo García, the first European to reach present-day Paraguay, is telling. He was a member of the expedition that first "discovered" the lands of present-day Uruguay for the Spanish Crown in 1516. The native people did not roll out the red carpet but killed expedition leader, Juan Díaz de Solís, the moment he set foot in the new territory. Presumably freaked out, the surviving crew set sail back to Spain, but not before catastrophe visited them again. Off the coast of southern Brazil, one of the ships was shipwrecked, leaving Aleixo García behind together with a small number of survivors. García's gold fever and an evident lack of other options for career advancement meant he spent the next eight years scheming how to reach mythological riches. To his credit, García somehow convinced a large group of Guaraníes to undertake the long hike towards wealth and fame. Probably around 1524, Aleixo García finally reached modern Paraguayan territory and went on to cross the Chaco region and trek all the way to Inca territory, becoming the first European to do so. With his sacks full of silver, he decided to return to Spain by way of the Brazilian coast, but misfortune once again assailed Aleixo; as he was making his way back through Paraguayan territory his Guaraní allies killed him. He was survived by his son, possibly the country's first mestizo (mixed race). García and those who crossed Paraguay after him were on the losing side of the race to riches, and once they realized their defeat, some decided to set up permanent camp in or near a new military camp called Asunción.[6]

Founded in 1537, Asunción[7] witnessed its first political mutiny less than seven years later, in 1544, when the local elites expelled the Spanish crown's envoy and chose their own leader to govern the territory. The fact Spain acquiesced to the Asuncenos' gambit is emblematic of the colonial power's long-lasting disregard for a territory far away from trade routes lacking strategic resources. Indeed, in those early days of the colony, for most colonizers "Paraguay" was just Asunción and surroundings (the city's Guaraní name is "Paraguay"). Spain did not acquiesce casually but gave its faraway settlement legal basis to practice political autonomy. The 1544 mutiny and the many political uprisings[8] Asunción witnessed in the colonial period were legally rooted in a royal decree from 1537 called "Cédula Real." The cédula was a Spanish Crown legal document that carried superior legal authority; in the case of Paraguay, it empowered the local residents to elect their authorities in the case the crown-designated governor died and left no legal successor. After the 1544 mutiny and based on cédula guidance, Asuncenos elected in 1558 their governor in the first secret ballot ever in the Latin American region.

The cédula complicates the debate about whether development results from material/institutional or subjective/cultural causes. Seen from an institutionalist perspective, the 1537 cédula—just like the Magna Carta of 1215—could have constituted a milestone for Paraguayan governance. Here it is a legal document setting forth the primacy of local constituents over colonial power and employed in several historical instances to advance a more inclusive government. But unlike the Magna Carta, the cédula did not establish a lasting foundation for a stable order. While it did serve to justify many acts of local autonomy vis-à-vis the Crown powers, it did not become a stepping-stone for inclusive institutions.

Paradoxically, in the years following Asunción's foundation to the early 1600s it looked as if the city and its surrounding territories would become a more central colonial outpost. However, the conquest of Perú, with its colossal reserves of minerals, coupled with a decision to make Buenos Aires the Spanish Crown's Atlantic capital, sealed Paraguay's fate as an isolated, unknown territory.[9] And so, through the early 1700s, settlers hunkered down within a radius of around sixty miles east and south of Asunción; they suffered constants attacks from northern tribes and violent incursions of bandeirantes—fearsome Portuguese/Brazilian colonizers who enslaved Indigenous people in hit-and-run operations deep into Paraguayan territory. Locals survived on subsistence agriculture and limited export of yerba mate via the Buenos Aires port; yerba mate is made from a tree that grows generously in the territory, but in the old days backbreaking labor was required to process its leaves. The highest-ranked government officer was the provincial governor, a position normally purchased by wealthy Spanish families or well-connected individuals.[10] While remoteness and strategic irrelevance meant locals had autonomy to advance their own agendas, these conditions created power vacuums that were more often than not filled with violent clashes.

The U.S. anthropologist Elman Service argues that what made Paraguay different from the other Spanish colonies was the "rapidity and thoroughness" of "interbreeding" between locals and colonizers.[11] The rapid interbreeding made sense: the vast majority of Spaniards were young, adventurous men. Or as distinguished Paraguayan historian Rafael Velázquez summarized it: "Spanish immigration [to Paraguay] consisted of soldiers."[12] Of course, it was not fair to the local women, who were forced to abandon their familiar habitat and suffer through all kinds of mistreatments in the hands of strangers. By marrying Guaraní women, Spanish conquerors had the added political heft of local in-laws. This phenomenon would start a long tradition in Paraguay where familial relations centered on the tovaja (brother-in-law) and the yerno (son-in-law) created long-lasting political dynasties. Paraguayan writer Helio Vera, half-jokingly called it "el braguetazo"[13] and described it as the fastest road to political power. Additionally, Guaraní chiefs traded some of their women to Spanish settlers for protection both from colonizers and from other tribes. As a result, interbreeding took place through a widespread incidence of polygyny, with several[14] women attending to each colonizer. Indeed, like other conquerors in Spanish America, Paraguay's colonizers took advantage of divisions and violent conflicts among the different Indigenous groups. Although the Guaraní might have calculated that sparing some of their women for their colonizers' protection was a price worth paying, they undervalued the violence and bloody methods they received in exchange from their "protectors." Thus, regular Indigenous rebellions against the invaders would materialize, but with little success.

Absent mineral wealth, Indigenous labor became the extractive "industry" in Paraguay. Spanish colonizers instituted a system that legalized the rounding up and coercion of Indigenous peoples called "Sistema de Encomienda" (Encomienda system). The encomienda was not an original idea of the Spanish Crown, but an adoption of a feudal system developed by the Roman Empire. Regardless, the Spanish Crown forced encomienda upon its subjects with traditional callousness, allowing colonizers to monopolize the labor of Indigenous peoples. The crown gave this right to early conquerors and subsequently to well-connected individuals (mostly men); the holder's (encomendero) right was in perpetuity and transferable to two generations of descendants. On top of everything the Indigenous had to pay an encomienda tax! As could be expected, the Indigenous groups were not in agreement with a system that traded their liberty for backbreaking hard labor and rebelled frequently. In response, the encomenderos subjected Indigenous people to extreme punishments and indiscriminate crimes, including torture, hangings, and executions. More lethal still, the colonizers brought with them diseases that decimated the Indigenous population.

The encomienda system would die a slow death at the beginning of the nineteenth century due to a mix of laws, societal changes, and a high mortality among the Indigenous people. The biggest social change was the almost universal process of mestizaje. Either because actual interbreeding had taken place or because the incentives to pass as a mestizo had grown, Paraguayans became a largely homogenous people by the dawn of the nineteenth century, with mestizos outnumbering Spaniards and Indigenous peoples within two centuries of gold fever elapsing. The positive consequence was that no racial or caste-based system developed. As James Hay described it, colonial Paraguay's "porosity" meant "the country never did have racially or ethnically distinct populations which were endogamous and stable."[15] For example, historian Ignacio Telesca estimates the slave population of African origin was around 10 percent before independence and over 7 percent in the post-independence years.[16] Historian Ana Barreto estimates that before independence around half of Asunción's population was of direct African descent, and presumes most of them were enslaved.[17] This population quickly melted in the Paraguayan demographic stew or moved somewhere else starting around 1870 when slavery was officially abolished. Furthermore, the country's lack of economic dynamism and the early governments' tight control on foreign income minimized the type of acute social and economic inequalities found in other Latin American countries. Left to their own devices, the colonial authorities and the local elites engaged in a steady power struggle until independence in the nineteenth century, intersected only by the Jesuit experiment.

In the early 1600s, the Catholic Church's Society of Jesus, whose members are called "Jesuits," set up the most remarkable social experiment in Paraguay's history, one with significant consequences for the local culture and the country's tourism industry. While a Franciscan Order of the Catholic Church had come earlier to take up the task of Guaraní pacification and submission to the crown's rule,[18] the Jesuits had a bigger impact from the moment they stepped into the region. From their beginnings in the 1540s, the Jesuits adopted the martial character and scholarly orientation of its founder Ignatius of Loyola; they would go on to found top universities and educational institutions, including some of the leading secondary and tertiary education institutions in Latin America. The Jesuits' relationship with the broader Catholic Church authorities has been controversial due to disagreements over goals, evangelizing strategy, and autonomy.

Their involvement in the Spanish Crown's possessions in Latin America from the late sixteenth century to 1767 constitutes a symbol of this difficult relationship. The Jesuits started their mission in present-day Argentina, Brazil, and Paraguay, offering Indigenous peoples an appealing social contract: "Come live and work with us and we will give you the

The Holy Trinity Jesuit ruin, one of the few left in Paraguay, was built in 1706 and was characteristically designed for self-sufficiency. Like other ruins, it was left to decay following the Jesuit expulsion from Spanish colonies in 1768 (courtesy Oscar Rivet).

physical and intellectual tools to have a more pleasant life, we will protect you from the bandeirantes, and we will not impose the encomienda system or the Spanish language on you. Last but not least, you need to become faithful followers of the Lord."[19] To implement this social contract, the Jesuits built so-called "missions" or "reductions"[20] in unconquered territories and inhabited mostly by Guaraní tribes. These autonomous rural communities served the Jesuit fathers to enforce a regime of religious indoctrination involving communal work and subsistence agriculture coupled with austere social norms. Although the Jesuits were strict and micromanaged the life out of the Indigenous dwellers, they oversaw a voluntary system regulated by religious doctrine alone. Many of the Guaraní left the reductions, some came back, some went away forever. Historians Livi-Bacci and Maeder note that just two Jesuit fathers administered each mission, which entailed ruling over villages of around 2,000 inhabitants on average.[21] Overall, they calculated, fewer than one hundred fathers governed a territory larger than England with a population that at its peak reached 140,000.[22]

The economic elites of the Paraguayan territories saw the Jesuit reductions as a threat to their wellbeing. These elites simply could not compete with the Jesuits, either economically or militarily. The Jesuits' high production levels brought yerba mate prices down, reduced the supply of labor by giving the Indigenous better treatment, and protected these advantages with large battle-ready Indigenous militias. These elites did not have it easy to begin with; foreign trade in Paraguay was almost nonexistent due to the Spanish Crown's extractionist mercantilism. In order to reach Paraguay, imports had to be shipped from Spain, enter through Panama, where they were loaded onto ships to Lima, hauled by mule to Buenos Aires, then carried back upriver to Asunción.[23] In addition, the crown extracted heavy taxes from Paraguayan exports. As a result, contraband was highly profitable and thus rife across the territory, and most internal trade was confined to barter. The problem with contraband was so bad that around 1620, the sale of confiscated goods had become the Rio de la Plata Viceroyalty's main source of income.[24]

In this context, the Revolts of the Comuneros (1721–35) took place as an attempt by the local elites to counterbalance the Jesuits and royalists' power. The Comuneros were local settlers who felt the Jesuits and the Asunción authorities that protected them posed an unfair threat to their livelihood. More than anything, the Comuneros wanted the Crown to either expel or control the Jesuits in order to protect their rents. The Comuneros also demanded an end to the sale of government offices and to the prohibition of Asuncenos from holding the highest positions. In the end, the revolution lost steam and its leaders were summarily executed, but its effects were long lasting. The revolution's immediate aftermath saw a strengthening of the crown's power, including the dissolution of local institutions such as the Cabildo, and continued autonomy for the Jesuits. But by planting the first seeds of the independence movement, the Comuneros' initial unprincipled aims would later on adopt a more nationalistic character revered by modern Paraguayans.

In effect, the Jesuits lasted a little over thirty years after the Comunero uprising. The Jesuit social contract had not only been embraced but became a victim of its own success. The experiment showed that there was not any intrinsic predisposition toward despotic rule in the Paraguayan territories. When treated with basic human decency and provided with a set of rules that applied equally to all, the local population thrived. Furthermore, by breaking the personal tribe-based component of authority, the Jesuits established the type of higher authority that led in developed countries to rule of law.[25] By the time the Jesuits were expelled from the Spanish territories in 1767—for reasons related to European monarchic tribulations—they had built a little empire with huge territorial possessions, an almost monopoly over Indigenous labor, a thriving yerba mate trade, and after having armed and trained its subjects for battle, the Jesuits were a force to be reckoned with. The Spaniards did reckon with the Jesuits—not by force, but by persuading the crown to expel them from its American territories. The Jesuits' removal in 1767 made plain their failure to empower their subjects for self-government. Once the Jesuits were expelled, the whole enterprise crumbled: missions fell in disrepair, the population dispersed, and most mission infrastructure was ransacked. The physical and human capital painstakingly accumulated in almost 200 years reversed to pre-colonial levels within a generation. The surviving Jesuit reductions ruins, with its carved stones, mix of native styles and Baroque architecture, seamless distribution of buildings, and eerie atmosphere amidst the sub-tropical Paraguayan countryside would eventually become the country's most alluring tourist destination and even a UNESCO World Heritage site.[26] Fundamentally, the Jesuit ruins raise some of Paraguay's most interesting questions in counterfactual history. When strolling around them on a visit, I was overcome with "what ifs"—what could have happened if the Jesuits' social structure had been left in place.

The removal of the Jesuits was followed a decade later by Charles III of Spain's liberalizing reforms for the Spanish colonies. The reforms sought to reduce the crown's bureaucratic weight, lower taxes, and streamline trade within the colonies, as contraband was already getting out of control.[27] As expected, higher trade attracted higher investment, increased yerba mate exports, and the expansion of the market to include more services and other export commodities such as tobacco. For example, economic historian José Cantero calculated yerba mate annual shipments went from 500 tons before the reforms to 4,130 tons in 1798.[28] In turn, the more dynamic economy empowered a new commercial class in Asunción, who would use its financial might to move up the political ladder and educate future independence leaders.

Charles III's reforms also established the Río de la Plata Viceroyalty in 1776 with Buenos Aires as its capital. Established by Asunción-based settlers in 1580, Buenos Aires had steadily gained a strategic status due to its geographic location. With the creation of the new Viceroyalty, Buenos Aires became the Spanish Crown's control center for its Atlantic commercial and military interests. It also meant Asunción was once again overlooked as a power player, with its interests now constrained by Buenos Aires.

From Independence to the Triple Alliance War (1811–1870)

When news broke out that Napoleon had invaded Spain in 1808, Asuncenos reacted with caution, defaulting to a wait-and-see support for the old colonial metropolis. Buenos Aires had almost immediately declared its independence from Spain and the French ruler and sought to bring to its fold the colonial provinces of Paraguay and Uruguay. But the political and commercial subjection to Buenos Aires brought about by the Viceroyalty of the Río de la Plata's creation had worked up the Paraguayans' naturally occurring appetite for autonomy. Indeed, the Paraguayan territory's remoteness and its lesser strategic value had heightened its citizens' independent aspirations. So, when pressed to choose between the old colonial power and Buenos Aires, the future Paraguayos went for the "none of the above" option.

The process of achieving national independence that commenced in 1811 was swift and mostly bloodless, except for two momentous battles against the Argentine government forces bent on annexing Paraguay. From the old house still standing in downtown Asunción where some locals organized, to the immediate shift in military allegiances within the territory, and the formal declaration of independence in 1842, few bullets were fired among Paraguayans. Rivers of blood had already been shed for the past three centuries when the Indigenous and the different mestizo communities (Comuneros, etc.) regularly fought colonial authorities. Still, Paraguay's two big neighbors were reluctant to recognize the small country; Paraguayans had to hold on patiently until Brazil recognized their independence in 1844 and Argentina in 1852. Moreover, they had to wait until well into the twentieth century to settle the national borders. Because the place was so far out from the crown's interests, its boundaries remained unmarked for years until either blood or diplomacy (or both) settled them.

The first leaders of the independent Paraguay inherited all the entitlements of the Spanish Crown, most notably a monopoly over land ownership and overwhelming coercive power. In plain numbers, it translated into the government controlling around 90 percent of land ownership and spending on average more than 80 percent of its budget on the military.[29] The leaders also inherited a highly centralized system of governance with ample room for arbitrary measures and ad-hoc policymaking. Although these first leaders would employ the colonial institutional structure to rule with varying degrees of despotism, they were selected by popular Congresses, seemingly respecting the 1537 cédula's spirit. Following normal practice, once elected, new leaders went after their opponents who inevitably ended up dead, in jail, or in exile.

Thrust upon these circumstances was one of the few formally educated citizens of Paraguay, José Gaspar Rodríguez de Francia, soon to be known as "El Supremo" (the Supreme One). Francia was a typical creole son of Latin America; raised by a European father and a local mother, he studied in Buenos Aires and went on to loathe the colonial powers that brought his ancestors from faraway lands. Setting an example for future Paraguayan leaders, Francia's path to power started under unassuming intentions, emerged out of a governing junta, and proceeded through conspiracy and violence toward absolute power. His political maneuvering was so adroit that he convinced an ad-hoc Congress, whose members included the country's leading figures, to elect him as dictator. Once on top, Francia monopolized power and established a one-man regime fond of comically tragic diktats, such as banning marriages between Europeans or abducting foreign merchants at random. Francia also set a problematic precedent for the two subsequent presidents until the Triple Alliance War, the idea conceived by Louis XIV of France that "L'etat c'est moi (I am the state)."

While Paraguayans' sense of nationality was arguably stronger than

Paraguay's Founding Fathers. Upper Left: José Gaspar Rodríguez de Francia (1814–1840). Lower Left: Carlos Antonio López (1844–1962). Right: Francisco Solano López (1862–1870) (Wikimedia Commons).

little room for political debate, advancement of human rights or principled causes other than national sovereignty. One might suppose that in the aftermath of the Triple Alliance War the turbulence of Paraguay's history might die down, but in the 120 years following the war, Paraguay went from one of the most democratic and politically liberal (existing) regimes in the world to one of the longest dictatorships ever, with another major war in between.

Liberal Attempt, Regular Disorder, and Another War (1870–1954)

So, what do you do if you just lost most of your labor force and foreign troops are stationed in your territory? The first three presidents of independent Paraguay kept ownership of more than 90 percent of lands in public hands. Vast land reserves were the only assets that the government had and so the post-war governments sold the majority of public lands to raise funds and attract foreign human capital and investment. The fire sale of public lands turned over 50 percent of the territory to nineteen landowners by the early twentieth century.[36] In the 1870s the Paraguayan government also tried to tap the international financial markets, but it did not end well, at least not for the country's treasury. It issued bonds in London for 1.5 million pounds ($158 million in 2017 dollars[37]) of which just 600,000 pounds made it to the Paraguayan treasury.[38] The result was decades without international financing for the country's pressing development needs and more reliance on land sales.

The new Paraguayan political leadership brought with it the liberal ideas that were flourishing across the American continent; most of the new leaders had spent years in Argentina and had even proclaimed themselves the government in exile.[39] With Brazilian troops on their side, these leaders formed a new government and passed a new constitution in 1870. Notably, the constitution gave the right to vote to all adult males without distinctions to race, property, or literacy, far ahead most countries in the world. Ungrateful Paraguayan men thought women were capable of rebuilding the country after the Triple Alliance War, but incapable of choosing their own leaders. At any rate, a secret ballot would be introduced more than forty years after passing the constitution; in those early days, voters conveyed their preferences directly to political bosses either in writing or orally. Nonetheless, the 1870 constitution put in place a republican system of government, with separation of powers, and no presidential reelection. Alas, the political reality would overwhelm the constitution; when it was replaced seventy years later, Paraguay still remained a highly unstable and rowdy polity. What is notable about this period is the absence of pure military governments (in spite of several military uprisings) and a general preeminence of civilian rule, under which political parties played a central role.

The small elite that survived the Triple Alliance War, together with the Paraguayan exiles who returned after the war[40] and members of the old regime ("Lopiztas"), engendered two political "clubs" with little ideological differences. They largely agreed on the classical liberal tenets dominant among Latin American elites in the nineteenth century, including laissez-faire economic policies and limited government intervention. Not long after, in 1887, the clubs became what today are Paraguay's main political parties, the Asociación Nacional Republicana (the National Republican Association), also known as "Colorado" (after its red banner) and the Partido Liberal (the Liberal Party, today called Partido Liberal Radical Auténtico, the Radical Authentic Liberal Party). In sociologist James Hay's forthright terms, the parties "represented shifting alliances of powerful individuals vying for the spoils of a shattered nation."[41] In those early days, the spoils dividing the parties were the sale of public lands; Colorados' members were the top beneficiaries and the Liberals represented those negatively affected by the sales.[42] For instance, Bernardino Caballero, a Colorado Party founder and once president of Paraguay, sat on the board of the largest yerba mate–extraction complex (Industrial Paraguaya), whose operations greatly benefited from public land sales. However, many fellow board members would later conspire politically against Caballero and bring the Liberal Party to power in 1904.[43] Although the content of political disputes would vary throughout the years, they would remain centered upon the distribution of government benefits and money from the treasury.

In the course of the first decade after the war, the political parties initiated a cycle that would repeat until the rise of Alfredo Stroessner in 1954. The cycle would commence with a high degree of political intrigue and instability, with presidents lasting no more than a year on average. The plotting would end with one political party overwhelming the other one, establishing a firm grip on power for a long time, and largely governing without opposition until a new stage of intrigue started. Thus, the Colorado Party emerged victorious after the post-war instability and governed until 1904 when the Liberal Party seized power for the next thirty years. However, the Liberals proved to be as factionalist as anybody else and spent many of their years mired in infighting; at one point in March 1912, there were three overlapping governments ruling over Paraguay.[44]

From the perspective of the economy, the first decades of the twentieth century in Paraguay were punctuated by generally modest growth rates, except for the years leading up to and during the World War I (1914–18), when it grew quickly. The remarkable fact is that most of Paraguay's early twentieth century revolutions, although bloody and consequential in terms of the balance of power, did not cause its exports to plunge accordingly. The strong pull of international trade over a small economy explains this disconnect between political crises and exports. However, the country's dismal road infrastructure meant that what happened in Asunción stayed in Asunción, or took too long to reach the rural confines where Paraguayan exports originated. For example, as the Liberals were fighting each other during the 1922–23 civil war, exports kept chugging along nicely.[45]

The Liberal Party–era reached its "golden age" of political civility, according to Milda Rivarola,[46] in the decade following 1923; Roett and Sacks called this period "an oasis in Paraguayan history."[47] Enlightened leadership in all branches of government, cautious policymaking, and helpful global conditions made possible a Paraguay that, seen from a twenty-first century distance, could have turned into a Latin American success story. In 1928, there was even a free and seemingly clean election where more than one party competed. Significantly, the defeated party accepted the victory of the winning party. Alas, Liberals' political missteps and a collective effervescence demanding quick social changes soon brought back the specters of Paraguayan history with a vengeance. But the drop that filled the political glass and first halted the Liberal era was the other war that shaped Paraguayan history: the Chaco War (1932–1935).

Since colonial times the huge Gran Chaco region, encompassing four countries (Argentina, Bolivia, Brazil, and Paraguay) had been a no man's land, where bands of nomadic Indigenous people and random military posts survived in desolated penury. The Chaco's soil and weather conditions without modern technologies and know-how were not conducive to economic accumulation. Plus, the incredibly fertile lands east of the Paraguay River made the Chaco's opportunity cost prohibitively high. But by the first quarter of the twentieth century, the Chaco region's economic calculus started to change in favor of profitability. Rumors of potential oil reserves (which have never materialized) also served to increase the Chaco's value. Meanwhile, the War of the Pacific (1879–84) had left Bolivia without an outlet to the sea and thus successive Bolivian governments had tried to find secure water pathways for the country's exports and to defend the country's sovereignty. This is how control of the Paraguay River in the Chaco's northern confines brought Bolivians in dangerous proximity to what Paraguayans claimed was their territory. In addition, politicians on both sides either sought or were pressed to use the conflict to address their own domestic political challenges and calculated a military conflict would delay other pressing social problems. As the July 1929 issue of *Foreign Affairs* magazine had already made clear, "The inflamed state of national sentiment or political considerations at home have prevented the consummation of a reasonable compromise, whereby each party to the controversy would receive that part of the Chaco which is most vital to its material rather than its sentimental interests."[48]

A Russian émigré, Ivan Belyaev, had mapped the Chaco region for the Paraguayan government; he had pointed to a lake with strategic value, given the Chaco's extreme arid conditions. As fate would have it, the Bolivians also found out about the lake and their storming of the small Paraguayan garrison there would start the Chaco War.[49] Unlike the Triple Alliance War, the Chaco War did not bring about massive physical destruction and loss of human life. Even so, it had a high mortality rate and there was great suffering among soldiers due to the terrain's arid conditions. Soldiers on both sides fought as consistently for water resources as for territorial gain. Soldiers went as far as stopping their own comrades at gunpoint in order to get water, including the boiling water from vehicles' radiators. Carlos Sienra, a Paraguayan soldier who fought at Chaco, vividly portrayed the effects of heat and thirst under the brutal fighting conditions:

> When a man gets sunstroke he loses all control over reality. Some just look for a little shade and don't care about anything, just waiting for the relief of death. The tongue comes out of the mouth, breathing becomes more difficult, and men begin to make strange animal-like noises. I saw many Bolivians shoot themselves in the head rather than meet such a terrible death. In the war I saw so much death, and so many terrible, unbelievable injuries. One soldier in my Company had his lower jaw blown off by a mortar explosion; even though his tongue hung down like a tie, he still survived. But nothing compares to the request "Please, Lieutenant, piss in my mouth." That beat everything. In the end, to see a comrade, a friend, dead or badly wounded, with his lungs collapsed by a bomb, you think, "Well, that could have been me"; but to hear that request, to piss in the mouth of a comrade, left an impression that I will never forget.[50]

In the end Paraguayan persistence, guided by the canny general José Félix Estigarribia, defeated the ultimately demoralized Bolivians trained by the German General Hans Kundt. Subsequent treaties granted two-thirds of the disputed territories to Paraguay, though not enough to regain the size Paraguay had before the Triple Alliance War. Memorials to Chaco veterans sprang up in small towns across the country, and Asunción's streets blossomed with new names honoring those involved in the war. Nowadays, wherever you go in the city of Asunción there is a street for a Chaco participant: medics, chauffeurs, aviators, auditors, chaplains, nurses, musicians, radio operators, the Chaco region itself, and two U.S. presidents who supported Paraguay's Chaco claims; even the country's main soccer stadium was named "Defensores del Chaco (Defenders of the Chaco)."

twelve-year-long civil war (1839–51) in which the parties declared "no defeated nor victors." Likewise, no victorious Paraguayan leader has ever expressed a sentiment along the lines of Abraham Lincoln's post–Civil War message, "With malice toward none, with charity for all." Acknowledging the defeated side's grievances has not been the style among Paraguayan warring parties.

The main victor in 1947 was the Colorado Party, which ended the conflict controlling the state apparatus at will and would do so for the next sixty-one years. However, differences among the Colorados forced Morínigo into exile in Argentina, ending his eight years in power (1940–48) and the longest presidential tenure in the twentieth century up to that point. A succession of palace coups brought Federico Chaves to the presidency in 1950. Although a civilian and aligned with the Colorado faction supporting an eventual return to democratic ways, Chaves's rule opened the door for Colorado supremacy, employing strong restrictions on the press, public assembly, and judicial independence. It also consolidated a transition started under the Febreristas from a largely market-based economy to one with greater government interference. By the end of Chaves's term, there were price controls, state-owned enterprises, higher taxes and regulations, and foreign exchange controls. The mix would prove counterproductive for the economy and an endless source of corruption.

Stroessner (1954–1989)

Like El Supremo Francia, Alfredo Stroessner was also the offspring of an immigrant and a Paraguayan woman. His Bavarian father had come to Paraguay at the turn of the nineteenth century like other immigrants lured to the economic opportunities available in the still recovering country. Young Alfredo joined the Paraguayan military and played an unremarkable role during the Chaco War. Still, service in the Chaco meant rapid career advancement for young officers, especially for those with Stroessner's keen political acumen.

Stroessner first emerged as a political actor during an attempted coup in October 1948, ironically as part of a Colorado faction identified as the "Democrats." The putsch failed and Stroessner barely escaped to the Brazilian Embassy hidden inside a car's trunk.[56] Soon another coup would open the doors to Stroessner's return; back in Asunción, his ascendancy through the military ranks would only stop at the top, when he was promoted to commander in chief of the Paraguayan Armed Forces in 1951. His return to Asunción also meant resuming his plotting against the governing authorities; slowly but surely in 1954, on the heels of a new wave of military uprisings, Stroessner's coalition came up on the winning side and designated a temporary president. Immediately after, new elections were called with only the Colorado Party on the ticket and one Alfredo Stroessner as the sole candidate. It was August 1954 and 35 long years lay ahead for all Paraguayans.

During the Alfredo Stroessner dictatorship (1954–1989) there were elections, but only his vote really counted (courtesy *Última Hora*).

To understand El Stronato[57] it is necessary to disaggregate it into three components: "sultanist" leadership, Leninist political structure, and patrimonialist policymaking. Paraguayan author Marcial Riquelme first explained the Stroessner regime as a case of "neo-sultanism,"[58] even though there is little "neo" about it. The original definition of sultanism can be traced back, as with many a political science concept, to Max Weber. In Weber's definition,[59] sultanism is a type of traditional domination, where the key element is the extent of the leader's discretion in employing his power. The basic idea is that a leader (Stroessner in the case of Paraguay) grabs power, accumulates it, and keeps it without any strong attachment to ideology, religion, or purpose other than the maintenance of power itself. Stroessner easily fit in the sultanist robes; his ample discretion allowed him to create a cult of personality, carry out sham elections (with typical 90 percent plus victory margins), throw his weight behind patronage schemes, and establish an all-powerful secret police able to intervene in all areas of society. Although he went out of his way to keep a veneer of legality by enforcing existing laws and changing constitutions when his "term" was up, legal rules went out of the window when Stroessner wished it. For example, there were working legislative and judicial branches constitutionally attached to the executive branch, but Stroessner had in place a state of siege that suppressed any legal recourse and allowed his subordinates to apply laws selectively. By the same token, Orwellian legislation (one prominent law was titled "In Defense of Democracy") served as the basis for ruthless, bloody pursuit of any whim of opposition. At the end of the day, if a procedure was labeled "Por orden superior (by superior order)" it meant the Sultan wanted it and there was no legal recourse that could stop it. Just like sultans use a weak association with a larger cause such as religion or ethnicity to justify their rule, Stroessner embraced anti-communism and justified his every abuse as part of a campaign to fight real or imagined communists. Indeed, if sultanism evokes images of a mature, mustachioed male with money and young women[60] at his disposal ruling with an iron fist over a territory he treats as his own backyard, you will be rather close to El Stronato's reality.

Yet, there is more to Stronismo than a one-sultan-show. Paradoxically, what also made the Stroessner regime unique was its Leninist political configuration, where the lines between party, state, and armed forces were blurred and the leader on top moved seamlessly between those three spheres. In turn, the Colorado Party became a highly disciplined machine, effective at coopting and repressing enemies, managing patronage, and dispensing political favors as needed. The Party became an arm of the state and its first line of support; most little towns and villages across Paraguay had a Party office responsible for dispensing public largesse, spying on fellow citizens, and implementing public policies.[61] In many districts, the Party also operated militias to enforce policies and terrorize dissenters. Also, it was mandatory for soldiers and government employees to be Party members and only Party members in good standing were able to climb up the public sector's power ladders and thrive in the private economy. Lastly, the Party organized youth, women, student, and professional organizations to monitor loyalty among special interests and to dole out favors accordingly. Even today, Colorado candidates and activists wear a red scarf around their shoulders when campaigning in the style of the communist youth (also known as "Young Pioneers"). Meanwhile, Stroessner remained the commander in chief, espoused military rituals and garments, appointed government personnel, and determined defense policy while also keeping the title of "president" and all its pageants for himself. Furthermore, each government agency directly or indirectly responded to Stroessner's directives.

In addition to sultanism, Weber delineates another type of traditional domination, called the "patrimonial regime"; it is characterized by a blurring of the line separating the public and private spheres. The patrimonial leader acts as if the public sector is an extension of his private assets and encourages such behavior down the totem pole. The renowned American political scientist Francis Fukuyama adds that Patrimonialism is "the natural human propensity to favor family and friends."[62] Under Stroessner, Paraguay was patrimonial in both counts: it had a leader and political authorities acting with contempt for the public-private sector boundaries, and authorities favored family and friends with gusto. Specifically, the Stroessnerian brand of Patrimonialism blended those two components into rampant informal trade. In spite of being generally ascetic in his demeanor and lifestyle, Stroessner allowed a coterie of confidants and family members to get obscenely rich via contraband, drug trafficking, and super-charged rent-seeking.[63] Although the coterie was not always involved in the operational side of deals, they provided cover and protection for a fat fee. The Stroessner regime's basic agreement with his collaborators was not much different from Colombian drug trafficker Pablo Escobar's proposition "plata o plomo (silver or lead)." Plata took the shape of patronage/contraband and plomo became police repression. For example, according to Andrew Nickson, after Stroessner fell in 1990, the assets of thirty-six former military officers embargoed by the government amounted to $550 million, equivalent to 25 percent of the country's foreign debt.[64] When in 1999 Stroessner's older son Gustavo was sued for divorce by his wife, judicial proceedings revealed a fortune estimated at between $500 and $850 million.[65] Another Stroessner spawn, Alfredo Jr., a drug addict of unknown occupation, designed his lavish private residence as a replica of the White House on a 1.7-acre lot in Asunción.[66]

If anything, Stroessner came in to solve one specific problem: political turmoil. From the end of the Triple Alliance War to the start of the Stronato in 1954, there were thirty-four presidents in fifty-four years. What's more, in the seven years leading to Stroessner's ascent to power, seven different presidents had ruled the country. The Febreristas and later President Morínigo had forcefully turned the political debate towards a military solution for Paraguayan development, but could not agree on the torch bearer. In 1954, Stroessner picked up the torch and built a power-structure that would allow him to keep that torch in hand for life. What made Stroessner a leader during those early days was his shrewd command of troops, both to defend his allies and impose his will, combined with a low-profile political maneuvering and an intense work ethic with unremitting attention to details. It would only be in his old age, when these qualities diminished, that Stroessner's grip on power would start to dwindle.

In broad historical terms, Andrew Nickson describes three stages to the Stroessner regime: (1) consolidation, 1954–67; (2) expansion, 1968–81; and (3) decay, 1982–89.[67] Stroessner first consolidated his power by purging the Colorado Party and the armed forces of any potential antagonists. Regime opponents were either imprisoned or sent to exile, their political support networks were dismantled, and those willing to accept the Stronismo rules were left alone, but remained under police surveillance. In the consolidation phase, Stroessner greatly benefited from the U.S. government's helping hand. Stroessner embraced the anti-communist cause with zeal and received U.S. funds in reward. During the first two decades of the Stroessner regime, the U.S. government showered Paraguay with funds that amounted to almost 5 percent of Paraguay's gross domestic product (GDP) during select periods.[68] In addition, the United States became a key trade partner and a major source of foreign direct investment. However, the American foreign aid spigot would be eventually turned off with the arrival of the Carter administration and the post–Watergate Congress; it remained low through the end of the Stroessner years. Bilateral trade and U.S. investment declined too, though not as dramatically.[69]

Stroessner also came in to stabilize the economy; his International Monetary Fund (IMF)–inspired recipe included deep spending cuts, monetary stabilization, and currency devaluation. The short-term pain was significant, but the approach worked, ending the fiscal disconnection from economic fundamentals that had characterized Paraguay since the 1947 civil war. To consolidate power, Stroessner also held on to the economy's commanding heights through state-owned enterprises, including the electric utility, the national airline, and telephone, oil, cement, and steel companies. In addition, widespread price controls and subsidies further tightened the Stroessner hold over the economy. These measures had the expected effect of creating opportunities for patronage and predictable corruption. Similarly, Stroessner blessed contraband as "the price of peace" and soon it became a way of life for regime officers, political allies, and anyone with the right connections.

By the start of the expansion stage, Stroessner was in full command of Paraguay's power trinity: the state, the armed forces, and the Colorado Party. In 1968, the world was under deep political stress, with millions of youth contesting their parents' rules and the political world they inhabited. In Latin America in particular, the late 1960s was the high-water mark for a number of revolutionary movements that would be violently crushed by the region's armed forces in the 1970s, bringing about a dark period of military dictatorships. But for Stroessner, the late 1960s meant new impetus to expand his deadly formula for "paz y progreso (peace and progress)." There were challenges to Stroessner's rule, principally from a large organization of Catholic farmers and a small group of university students. Both attempts were dispatched by a well-oiled repression machine, which was prepared to take any measures to keep Stroessner in power. In addition, in the early 1970s the construction of the huge Itaipú hydroelectric dam began. It was a project that shook the Paraguayan economy out of its complacency, bringing in a wealth of direct and indirect jobs and investment, and (critically for Stroessner) a tangible symbol of state legitimacy.

As the construction of the Itaipú's benefits faded, the regime's decay stage began. It was within the Colorado Party where economic malaise's political ripples first appeared. The economic boom had created a new class of wealthy individuals, together with an inflated public employment roll[70] with direct links to the Colorado leadership. Once the economy regressed to low growth, the old Colorado factionalism that Stroessner had worked so hard to eliminate blossomed like a lapacho flower in September.[71] Furthermore, once the Itaipú boom receded, the Paraguayan government's real fiscal situation was revealed, and it was not pretty. The consequence of irresponsible spending submerged under the dam's economic tide reared its ugly head right at the moment when the global winds turned against the Paraguayan ship. The result was another painful economic contraction that would undermine Stroessner's legitimacy.

From an economic standpoint, the Stroessner dictatorship was neither a Robert Mugabe type of disaster nor an economic miracle. Compared to other contemporaneous dictators such as Pinochet or Lee Kuan Yew, the Stroessner administration did not build any foundations for long-term prosperity. Rather, it chugged along on mediocre economic growth but without triggering the type of economic crisis that brought down many Latin American despots. For instance, Stroessner neither engaged in costly import-substitution policies nor tried his hand at military-led development policies. A clear sign of the Stroessner government's unambitious economic agenda was that it went almost without taxation. Tax rates were low and largely unenforced, which gave Paraguay one of the world's lowest government revenues as a percent of GDP. As a result, there was almost no public investment in basic infrastructure, forcing Paraguay to rely on foreign aid and investment. His main accomplishments were the construction of two large dams in partnership with Brazil and Argentina, the Itaipú and the Yacyretá (started under his watch but finished after he was removed from the presidency), respectively.

In spite of the ups and downs, Stroessner managed to stay in power for a long time, specifically from 1954 to 1989. All in all, the Stroessner dictatorship was the longest ever in the history of South America, beating infamous South American leaders such as Augusto Pinochet, Juan Domingo Perón, and Getulio Vargas. The longevity also meant a horrific aftermath: the official 2008 report of the Comisión de Verdad y Justicia (Truth and Justice Commission) put Stroessner's regime criminal toll at 20,090 victims, including persons killed, tortured, and exiled, plus extrajudicial disappearances. The commission also estimated that 107,987 family members of victims were affected.[72]

Indeed, no theoretical definition of the Stroessner regime can define with precision its brutality and complete disregard for basic human rights. The case of Martín Almada, a Paraguayan educator and victim of the Stroessner regime's repression, is illustrative of the regime's nature. In spite of being a Colorado member, he was thrown in jail and tortured for writing a Ph.D. dissertation (in an Argentinian university) that simply criticized Paraguay's educational system. Once in jail, Almada was savagely tortured, and his wife died of a heart attack after the police called her and lied about her husband's death. His post-jail testament describes in tragic detail the standard violence employed:

> I felt terrified during the preparations. I was stripped naked, my hands and feet bound with electrical wire. My torturers, most of them potbellied, were dressed in black shorts. A man called Sapriza was the only one impeccably dressed; he wore dark glasses that he constantly took off and put back on. [...] The work was clearly divided: Tatá was in charge of the pileta, a bathtub filled with fetid water, excrement, and urine, into which someone threw me and put his foot on my chest to keep me down; Sapriza, the main inquisitor, kicked me and officiated as secretary; someone used karate on me, a man called Kururú Piré ("toad skin" for the warts covering his face), viciously attacked my back with the famous teyuruguái ("lizard tail," a whip with metal balls at the end) in one hand and a bottle of Aristócrata (brand of caña, cane liquor) in the other; and Laspina beat my head with a blackjack. Off to one side, a military sergeant around thirty years old, extremely pale and gaunt, urged the torturers to "make the subversive sing." A telephone rang incessantly, and after each call the

violence increased, sometimes with the receiver pointing toward me. Flashes of lightning unleashed by a storm reached the small room—sounds of rain and fierce winds from outside joined my cries of pain inside. Kururú Piré tore at my flesh with the teyuruguái while Sapriza shouted, "Talk, damn it, talk, son of a bitch, criminal, bandit." I felt like my body was on the verge of exploding. Not content with ripping my back to shreds, Kururú Piré beat the soles of my feet, and Sapriza kicked my legs with pointed shoes. Spurts of blood stained Sapriza's clothes, enraging him further. To appease Sapriza, Laspina battered my head with the blackjack. I didn't see people—I saw mad dogs. They were exasperated by my silence. They plunged me several more times into the pileta, demanding that I talk. Mercifully, I lost consciousness.[73]

Almada's courageous behavior continued after Stroessner fell, helping judicial authorities find the "archivos del terror" (archives of terror) on December 22, 1992. Almada was seeking restitution from the years spent under brutal torture and imprisonment common to the thousands of Paraguayans and foreigners who fell under the Stroessner regime for real or imagined hunt for communist plots. The "mountain of ignominy,"[74] as Almada called the archives of terror, revealed to the entire world the regime's true cold-blooded nature. They showed the paper trail of a machine that repressed, tortured, spied, exiled, and killed with methodical eagerness. Stroessner perfected in an evil way the method other Paraguayan leaders before him employed to deal with opponents: use of the state's coercive power to hound opponents. The first researchers[75] able to lay hands on the archives have documented how the regime arbitrarily repressed any person for as little as playing the wrong polka song at a family reunion, preaching the wrong sermon at Catholic mass or espousing minimally controversial views at a university gathering.

The archives also brought to light Plan Condor, a secret arrangement among South American military regimes to collaborate in spying on, abducting, torturing, and disposing of political opponents regardless of their location. Plan Condor members set an above-the-law cooperation mechanism to conduct secret operations, share all kinds of information, and exchange expertise, among other illegal ends. They also managed to convince the U.S. government they were the first line in the global fight against communism, and thus received corresponding diplomatic cover. By the early 1970s, U.S. government funds and advisors had already trained enough South American police and military officers on torture methods, counterintelligence, sabotage operations, and other such activities that their application had become prevalent. Not surprisingly, the Stroessner administration became an active player in Plan Condor; his government's widespread use of torture to gather information, arbitrary treatment of prisoners, and deep intelligence work reaching all corners of society was a perfect match for the plan's macabre ends. Condor operations first raised alarm among diplomatic allies of participating regimes with their coordinated assassinations of political opponents in third countries. Perhaps one of Plan Condor's most infamous operations was the murder of Chilean Orlando Letelier—a former minister of foreign affairs and ambassador to the United States during the Salvador Allende administration (1970–73)—on September 21, 1976, in Washington, D.C. The perpetrators were Chilean secret police agents who had previously tried to obtain visas to enter the United States using fraudulent Paraguayan passports.[76]

A more typical Condor operation involved Argentine plain-clothes police picking up a Paraguayan citizen in Argentina, inviting Paraguayan police to conduct joint torture sessions, and disposing of the victims either by way of assassination or by hauling the victim covertly back to Paraguay. If the victim made it alive to Paraguay, he or she was taken to one of the many Asunción-based detention centers, which unlike other countries in the region, were not secret or undercover. I visited one of those locations, currently the Museum of the Memories, and saw the building that used to house "La Técnica" (The Technical Office), one of Stroessner's most

One of the feared "Red Riding Hood" vehicles that during the Stroessner dictatorship (1954–1989) picked up citizens and drove them to torture chambers (author's photograph).

It's April 1986 and a group of citizens decided to confront the Stroessner regime's daily abuses of power. Less than three years later the dictator was gone (courtesy *Última Hora*).

February 3, 1989. A military faction rids Paraguay of Alfredo Stroessner (courtesy *Última Hora*).

infamous torture centers. Created in 1956, two years after Stroessner came
to power, with the support of a U.S. government advisor, it operated until
1992, three years after the dictator's fall. The house's 1960s office décor was
almost frozen in time, giving a chilling sense of tranquility. Walking to the
patio, one then sees the filthy prison cells with a pileta (bathtub) and metal
bed frames employed in torture sessions; they sent a shiver down my spine
when I thought about all the brutality that took place inside of it. I had similar dread when I saw Caperucita Roja (Little Red Riding Hood) parked in
La Técnica's garage. The old red Chevrolet C10 Suburban was employed by
the Paraguayan police to pick up the regime's victims; a ride inside it guar-
anteed its passengers countless torments on the way to a hell many Paraguayans never came back from. When I left La Técnica, it brought me back
the unnerving sense of futility in the face of human cruelty that I felt at
Hanoi's Hoa Lo Prison (aka the "Hanoi Hilton"), in Cambodia's Choeung
Ek ("Killing Fields"), and in Washington, D.C.'s Holocaust Museum. Just as
the Uruguayan Oscar winner Jorge Drexler says in one of his songs,[77] any
one of us could have been the pianist of the Warsaw ghetto.

A New Hope (1989–2020)

When Paraguayans woke up on the morning of February 3, 1989, to
the sight of armored vehicles and military patrols roaming the Asunción
streets, they could not believe their eyes. Paraguay was at last plunging into
the third wave of democratization[78] that splashed the world in the 1970s and
1980s. Few Paraguayans were old enough to remember the old days when
such scenes were almost routine; the majority of the population had grown
up knowing one and only one authority. Alfredo Stroessner grew used to
his omnipotence as well; when the tanks had hit the pavement during the
previous night of February 2, Don Alfredo was hanging out at the home
of one of his mistresses, unaware of any changes outside his daily bubble.
In his last years, Stroessner's management style became more hands-off
due to health and other reasons, and he probably missed the fierce plotting
that had been going on between the two regime factions trying to determine his successor. On one side were the supporters of one of his most
trusted generals and the father of his son Alfredo ("Freddy") Jr.'s wife, General Andrés Rodríguez. On the other side were those aligned with his other
son, Air Force Colonel Gustavo Stroessner. Unlike Leninist parties, sultans
are not good at successions, mostly because they do not want anybody to
succeed them. In one of his few post-coup interviews, Stroessner mused, "A
coup d'état is something that one doesn't expect. It's about lack of information."[79] And so, in true sultanist form, a member of Stroessner's inner circle

ousted him when General Rodríguez emerged on the winning side of the succession battle. Rodríguez unceremoniously showed Stroessner the door to exile in Brazil and became de facto president. Paraguay and the Stroessner family reunions have never been the same.

Hence, democracy in Paraguay did not come with a revolutionary bang but with a palace whimper. Rodríguez engineered a transition to democracy that resembled more a gentle regime change than a full institutional break.[80] After trying almost every political arrangement conceivable to humankind, Paraguayans were ready to give democracy a try. You say Maoist-style despotism? Caudillo rule? Hereditary autocracy? Traditional oligarchy? Corporatist authoritarianism? Hit-and-run civilian coalition? Ménage à trois? Military dictatorship? Check all the above for Paraguay. Not surprisingly, the post–Stroessner Paraguayan regime had the trappings of a democracy (elections, freedom of the press and assembly, etc.), but it was not a substantive democracy in the way political scientists understand it.[81] Its greatest accomplishment was ceasing to be the Stroessner regime. For instance, three months after the coup, Rodríguez won a presidential election considered largely free but barely fair.[82] Not only were the electoral institutions flawed but also the rotation in power and accountability of public figures for past misdeeds were almost non-existent. To be sure, there was never a sustained democratic period in Paraguayan history and thus no democratic roots or tradition existed to build a more consequential transition. Moreover, thirty-five years of military dictatorship had decimated the ranks of the opposition and its ability to bring the government to the negotiating table. The Acuerdo Nacional (National Accord) alliance of political organizations formed in 1979 to oppose the Stroessner regime was able to garner impressive international support, in spite of limitations, but it was dissolved in 1989 so its influence quickly faded away.

Still, the Rodríguez administration (1989–1993) lifted the state of siege and restrictions on the press, abolished the death penalty, and joined the American Convention on Human Rights. Rodríguez also oversaw the passing of the 1992 constitution, a considerable milestone in Paraguay's democratic life, which includes protection of universally recognized human rights, primary elections for political parties, direct elections of mayors, and once again, forbade presidential reelection. Municipal elections took place under his watch in 1991 (under Stroessner, mayors were appointed by decree), and the opposition won the biggest prize, the capital Asunción. At best, General Rodríguez must be remembered for what he did not do; as he had promised, once his term ended, he stepped down and handed the presidency to Juan Carlos Wasmosy, the first elected civilian president in forty-four years. Unquestionably, Rodríguez had profound moral shortcomings, as he should have in order to become a main beneficiary

Andrés Rodríguez, the military leader that brought down the Stroessner regime, assumed power following elections in May 1989 (courtesy *Última Hora*).

of the Stroessner regime's piratical system. His opulent residence, an eyesore inspired by the castles located in the Châteaux of the Loire Valley in France, still sits in Asunción's Las Carmelitas neighborhood, reminding visitors of Rodríguez's personal flaws. Nonetheless, Rodríguez had a positive impact equal to the problems he avoided. A *New York Times* article written five years before Stroessner's removal from office laid out the menu of political options following the old dictator's departure: "One is a war among the Colorado Party clans and the military factions; a new dictatorship, weaker, more brutal, more unstable; revenge, trouble, bloodshed."[83] Rodríguez avoided all of the above. It is clear his statesmanship was in line with Paraguayans' tradition of top-down political transitions under which the powerful set the political agenda. But remarkably, he broke decisively with Stroessner's thirty-five-year-long tradition of clinging to power and abusing it.

The transition "did not have a clear aim" as Diego Abente pointed out,[84] and once political and civil liberties were allowed, it acquired an unpredictable life of its own. General Rodríguez opened the democratic floodgates, unleashing old and new political forces jockeying for power like there was no tomorrow. New factions within the Colorado Party appeared, the Liberals came back from the cold, new personality-based parties stepped forward, and new alliances were formed to compete in elections and govern the country. However, legislators did not approve a new (and unadulterated) electoral registry until 1996, which meant electoral chicanery and outright fraud were still part of the game through the first seven years of democracy. A case in point was the 1992 Colorado Party's primary election that pitted old-style machine politician Luis María Argaña against Itaipú-baron Juan Carlos Wasmosy. Argaña seemingly won the election, but a later spurious recount based on the Stroessner electoral registry gave the victory to Wasmosy.

Meanwhile, the new constitution bestowed new rights and established new institutional dynamics to a citizenry not used to rule of law and democratic forms; in practice the old power structures were still in place and consequently Paraguay's democracy took shape as it went along. The aforementioned "Archives of Terror" discovery was one such instance where the old system collided with the new democratic order. A dialogue between a young judge leading the investigation and the police officer in charge of the building where the archives were located encapsulates the difference between rule of law and rule of force meeting head on.[85]

> *[Judge and* Martín Almada *walk toward the police station's gate surrounded by TV cameras and are confronted by a police officer].*
>
> **JUDGE:** We are here on a habeas data request brought by Dr. Almada. We have knowledge that there are documents located on this property and thus we will proceed to unearth them. By the powers vested in me I order you to facilitate our work.
>
> **POLICE:** Let me ask my superior.
>
> **JUDGE:** No need. The law gives me the power to compel you to act. We are simply enforcing the law. We are now in democracy, and in democracy, laws rule, okay?
>
> **POLICE:** Well, but I am an officer and need instructions from my direct superior.
>
> **JUDGE:** Now I instruct you, do you understand? I do not want to get nasty with you or use force.
>
> **POLICE:** [Mumbles]
>
> **JUDGE:** You are not going to get in trouble. We are here to enforce the law and that is the end of the story. I am the law and your legal guarantor.
>
> **POLICE:** [Nods in agreement.]

Andrés Rodríguez had supported Wasmosy and gladly handed over the presidency to him. The Wasmosy administration (1993–98) set the stage for what was to come in Paraguay's transition to democracy. In particular, it tested the new regime's institutional limits, stretching the boundaries of unstipulated civil-military relations and a weak rule of law. Although the key political conflicts and its resolutions still took place under the Colorado Party's tent, Wasmosy oversaw a "Governability Pact" in 1994 that

brought opposition parties to the governing table. The pact's key achievement was an agreement to broaden the political specter of judicial branch's
officers, including Supreme Court members. Yet, there were still birth
pangs to come for the Paraguayan democracy. Thankfully, Paraguay was
not internationally isolated anymore, so outright democratic violations
immediately elicited serious consequences from the international community. In 1995 and 1996, respectively, banks and an ambitious general would
test Paraguay's institutions and the patience of its democratic allies.

The massive 1995–98 banking crisis strained the country's economic
foundations. It started with bank runs and bankruptcies in Uruguay and
Argentina, and quickly spread to Paraguay's badly regulated banks. The crisis showed that Paraguay was no longer disconnected from global markets.
Two-time Minister of Finance Dionisio Borda estimated the banking crisis cost 10 percent of the national GDP.[86] When the financial dust settled,
only eighteen of thirty-four banks remained, and twenty-two of sixty-three
financial services companies survived.[87] The crisis also gave fodder to military officers and their civilian allies who were ready to hijack Paraguay's
democracy at their first chance.

The chance materialized in April 1996 when Wasmosy fired Army
Chief Lino Oviedo, an acolyte of General Andrés Rodríguez, who had
built a powerful political base in the shadows of the armed forces. Oviedo's
response was a reminder to the world that Paraguay's transition to democracy was still open-ended. The general refused the president's order and
launched a tense mutiny, which in the old days would have ended with
Oviedo usurping power. However, Paraguay's meager democratic defenses
responded in full force, and together with significant international pressure
to respect institutions, were able to thwart Oviedo's putsch. Still, Wasmosy
wobbled and offered Oviedo the Defense Ministry; the popular uproar
against the offer was swift and forced the president to withdraw it. Most
notably, the failed coup had the effect of finally taking the military out of
politics, prompting a clearer institutionalization of the armed forces based
on their complete subordination to civilian control.

While the attempted coup ended Oviedo's military career, it strength-
ened his political base, as he was seen as battling an unpopular government.[88] Such was the transition's unpredictability. The plot thickened the
following year when Oviedo beat Argaña to become the Colorado presidential candidate. Argaña once again claimed fraud, but it was a military tribunal who finally displaced Oviedo by jailing him for his failed coup. After
much horse-trading among Colorado power brokers, the party decided to
field a team of adversaries with Raúl Cubas, another Itaipú-baron and originally Oviedo's vice-presidential candidate, as presidential candidate, and
usual suspect Argaña as vice-president.

And so Cubas won the 1998 elections with Oviedo's support, and in return pardoned the retired general as soon as he took office. Cubas's unofficial campaign slogan, "Cubas al gobierno, Oviedo al poder (government to Cubas, power to Oviedo)" left no doubt about his intentions. The decision to free Oviedo triggered the violent events in March 1999 soon to be known as "El Marzo Paraguayo" (the Paraguayan March). It started with the cold-blooded assassination of Vice President Argaña at the hands of contract killers. Soon "radio so'o" (news and rumors spread by word of mouth) was proclaiming that the killing had been ordered by Oviedo and his allies in the Cubas government,[89] summoning up thousands of protesters to downtown Asunción. Oviedo's supporters showed their colors by shooting indiscriminately at the protesters, killing seven and injuring more

Paraguayan "ceaseless agitation" in action, here during the Marzo Paraguayo (Paraguayan March) crisis that followed Vice President Luis María Argaña's assassination on March 23, 1999 (courtesy *Última Hora*).

than 700 people. The bloodshed ended with Oviedo fleeing to Argentina and Cubas resigning his presidency and going to Brazilian exile. Oviedo was finally tracked down in Brazil in June 2000, but would only return voluntarily to face charges in Paraguay in February 2002.

The presidential succession tested the young Paraguayan democracy once again; it was finally passed along according to the constitutional mandate, a first and a significant milestone in Paraguay's political history. Accordingly, Senate president Luis Ángel González Macchi, next in line, was sworn in for the remaining of Cubas's term, bringing back normalcy with his dull incompetence and corrupt practices. The 1992 constitution awkwardly established an immediate presidential succession but mandated an election to select the new vice-president. New elections promoted the Liberal Party's candidate Julio César Franco to the office of vice-president, sharing power with an unelected and unpopular president. The peaceful sharing of political power was remarkable by Paraguay's historical standards, but brought with it an increase of political malpractice as well. Diego Abente described the country at the close of the President González Macchi's term as "a kind of no man's land" with the leading political and economic actors turned into "predators engaged in a rampant chase of privileges and sinecures."[90]

The subsequent presidential elections of 2003 brought another victory to the Colorado ticket, this time with Nicanor Duarte Frutos at the helm. Unlike other post–Stroessner Colorado Party candidates, Duarte was an apparatchik who rose from the party ranks instead of relying on personal wealth. He campaigned against "neo-liberalism," espoused causes associated with the Latin American left, and invited Fidel Castro to his inauguration ceremony. However, as soon as he was sworn in, he had to put aside his rhetoric and deal with a massive financial crisis; his administration's main recipe included signing a thoroughly neo-liberal package with the IMF. His finance minister, Dionisio Borda, declared that when he first started, he found only $2 million available in the treasury, amounting to 0.1 percent of the total annual budget.[91] More troubling, when the growth numbers came in for 2003, they showed Paraguay's GDP per capita was lower than it had been in 1983. Hopelessness was in the humid air; reflecting the mood, a young Paraguayan told the *New York Times* right after the election, "In truth, nothing will change because it will be all the same people."[92] What Paraguayans did not know was that a commodity boom was heating up and would more than double GDP per capita within ten years.

During his term (2003–08), Duarte for the first time attempted to reform the public administration's unruly and corrupt ways. Dionisio Borda described the Paraguayan office of the president at the start of

Duarte's term as an "institutional labyrinth," where responsibilities were diluted, practices were not transparent, and political power silos were created and used to reward benefactors.[93] Instead of the old distribution of spoils, Duarte constructed political coalitions based on programmatic consensus.[94] In connection to this reform he also moved to reform the judicial branch by forcing out Supreme Court members and bringing in new ones with congressional support, a move that proved to be wholly ineffective in improving the quality and probity of judges. The Duarte administration also passed the tax regime currently in force in Paraguay. Notably, it introduced an income tax for the first time in the country's history, reduced the corporate tax, and ramped up tax evasion controls with positive results in terms of higher tax revenue.[95]

El Marzo Paraguayo had also brought to politics an obscure yet outspoken priest from faraway San Pedro by the name of Fernando Lugo. His clerical work in rural areas and his liberation theology[96] inspired rhetoric touched a nerve with a wide constituency who were tired of the political business as usual. Lugo's commitment to celibacy, meanwhile, was similar to Paraguayans' casual approach to the rule of law; by the time he succeeded Duarte he was forced to recognize two children from different women, conceived when serving as a (seemingly underemployed) priest in rural Paraguay. Other women later came forward claiming Lugo as the father of their fatherless children. In a joke heard throughout the region, former Bolivian president Evo Morales (2006–2019) mocked Lugo as "the father of all Paraguayans."[97]

But it was President Duarte's political miscalculations that first catapulted Lugo to the national limelight and later to the presidency. First, Duarte attempted to change the constitution to allow for reelection. A popular uproar soon followed, with Lugo as the main figure, leading street marches and proclamations against the move. When Lugo declared his candidacy for the 2008 presidential elections, heading a coalition with the Liberal Party, Duarte tried to stymie his electoral strength by releasing the old troublemaker Lino Oviedo from prison. The move backfired because Oviedo ran as an independent and took away precious Colorado votes from the official candidate, Blanca Ovelar. The final tally for the 2008 elections showed an electorate divided in almost three equal parts, with Lugo's Patriotic Alliance for Change slightly ahead the Colorado Party's Ovelar, followed by Oviedo's National Union of Ethical Citizens. The fact that a unified Colorado ticket would have easily beaten Lugo revealed early on the structural weaknesses of his power. Likewise, Lugo's reliance on the Liberal Party's political machinery to pass legislation meant his political leadership was vulnerable. Indeed, these weaknesses would eventually serve as the political basis for his downfall.

Fernando Lugo, the Catholic priest turned political leader, assumes power August 15, 2008, bringing an end to the Colorado Party's 61-year hold on power (courtesy *Última Hora*).

Remarkably, when Lugo became president, Paraguay's democracy took a giant step towards institutional strength: for the first time in history political power was transferred from one party to another party peacefully and as a result of legitimate elections. The time-tested axiom of Paraguayan politics that "failing a miracle, the government's party always wins"[98] was finally proven wrong. Lugo was a member of the first generation of Paraguayans who grew up and entered adulthood knowing only Stronismo. His uncle Epifanio Méndez had helped bring Stroessner to power and was his Central Bank president for a time, but soon fell from grace and became, together with his supporters, a victim of Stroessner's repression machine. The 2008 regional political context could not have been more different than the 1955 context under which uncle Méndez went into exile in Argentina. His nephew Fernando Lugo's accession to the presidency came on the heels of a wave of leftist governments that included Argentina's Néstor and Cristina Kirchner, Brazil's Lula da Silva, Bolivia's Evo Morales, Ecuador's Rafael Correa, and Uruguay's Frente Amplio (Broad Front) governments. Lugo's rhetoric of economic transformation and fight against corruption was too optimistic in the face of nearly 300 years of Spanish colonial plunder followed by 200 of wealth-destroying Paraguayan governance. Nevertheless, Lugo did implement some momentous reforms. Principally, Lugo named Dionisio Borda, who had served under the previous Colorado government, as finance minister, to continue his agenda of sober public administration with a focus on the establishment of a professional non-partisan civil service.

Lugo's downfall four years into his mandate was swift. It started with a botched police intervention in the rural Curuguaty district on June 2012 to repress landless peasants occupying land claimed by a wealthy former Colorado senator. The confrontation's tragic outcome left eleven protesters and six police officers dead. Within a week, Congress impeached and removed Lugo from office with large majorities (the Chamber of Deputies voted seventy-six to one and the Senate thirty-nine to four). Paraguay's Supreme Court endorsed the impeachment's legality soon after. Marsteintredet et al. explained Lugo's fall as a "purely political, albeit parliamentary, logic: A weak president lost the confidence of most of his country's national legislators."[99] Alfredo Boccia, a full time medical doctor (hematologist), author of several books, columnist, and TV personality, described the Lugo years with a corresponding medical term: "historic arrhythmia."[100] That is, Lugo was an irregular beat of Paraguay's political heart, and came and went without changing its general condition.

With Lugo out, another transfer of power happened peacefully, and was handed to the next person in line according to the constitution. Vice-President Federico Franco succeeded Lugo in August 2012 and with him the Liberal Party was back at the top after a seventy-two-year hiatus. Franco's one-year tenure was a sort of déjà vu of the bad old days, with corruption and clientelism directing the Liberal Party's actions. For example, the Paraguayan newspaper *Última Hora* estimated Franco's net worth increased 748 percent during his time as vice-president (2008–12).[101] In 2012, Franco's government approved a 30.6 percent rise in government salaries, the largest increase in the democracy years.[102]

Back to political normalcy in Paraguay meant the Colorado Party in power with a wealthy president. Thus, Horacio Cartes, one of the country's richest individuals, won the 2013 presidential elections by almost 10 percent against the Liberal Party's Efraín Alegre, reaching more than one million votes for the first time in Paraguayan history. Unlike other Colorado presidents, Cartes spent time in prison *before* he reached the presidency (accused of currency fraud, though he was later acquitted). His rise to wealth is not without controversy either. He amassed a fortune in the shadow of the post–Stroessner years when little rule of law existed and all entrepreneurs had to walk a fine line between legality and illegality in order to succeed. For example, Cartes became the biggest Paraguayan producer of tobacco; his company produced a huge domestic-market surplus of cigarettes that ended up mostly in the Brazilian black market via third-party sellers. Still, when he became president, another democratic step was taken, as the ruling Liberal Party peacefully surrendered power to the Colorado Party for the second time in history.

The Cartes presidency (2013–18) brought a technocratic ethos, including the first ever female minister of finance, and carried out long-awaited transparency reforms in the public sector. It also continued Paraguay's cautious fiscal and monetary policies, in spite of several rounds of debt issuing to finance infrastructure investment. Overall, Cartes oversaw rapid economic growth, but his policies could not make a dent in the country's high poverty rate of more than 25 percent. His political reputation was not helped when in the final months of his term, one of the democratic period's biggest political scandals erupted with the release of phone conversations showing politicians exerting undue influence over judicial cases. Although the recordings left Cartes unscathed, they laid bare a system under which his political allies did his bidding in complete defiance of the law. Lastly, his government, like that of Nicanor Duarte Frutos, will be remembered for a reckless push to reform the constitution and allow presidential reelection. Only when the Congress was burning down and the whole country was paralyzed by it did Cartes relent and drop his reelection effort.

With the 2018 elections came another Colorado victory, albeit by the smallest margin ever (3.7 percent). Political apathy remained entrenched

Protesters set fire to Congress March 31, 2017, following an attempt to reform the constitution and allow presidential reelection (courtesy *Última Hora*).

with voter turnout reaching only 61 percent, the lowest of all elections in the post–1989 democratic period. The 2018 contest winner was Mario Abdo Benítez ("Marito"), who defeated the Liberal Party's Efraín Alegre in his second attempt at the presidency. If Cartes meant normalcy, Abdo Benítez meant the return of Colorado royalty. His father was not only Stroessner's private secretary and confidant but also a cousin. Abdo Benítez also ticked all the Colorado ugly must-haves: in addition to having a family relation to an important leader, he had family members involved in acts of corruption, and boasted a large personal wealth of unknown origin. Like all Colorado leaders he was unabashedly "pro-family" in spite of having divorced and remarried. Because his Colorado bona fides were so strong, he was able to downplay the fact that he spent many years living in the United States as a student and that he did not speak good Guaraní. His years attending college in the United States perhaps explain why in 2019 he came close to being impeached, however. He simply hadn't spent the years needed to build allegiances and a circle of loyalists. After a negotiation with Brazil over the Itaipú dam came to light, showing his administration's poor negotiating skills, the public backlash was swift. When members of his own Colorado Party jumped in to ask for his head, Abdo Benítez had to fire his foreign affairs minister and beg Brazil to annul the signed document. Throughout the crisis, Abdo Benítez looked out of his game, with one popular cartoonist depicting him as living inside a tereré thermos. His political credibility was further tested during the novel coronavirus crisis that started in March 2020. At first Abdo Benítez's government acted swiftly, with strict quarantine and social distancing measures that put Paraguay among the countries with the lowest rates of COVID-19. But as the pandemic advanced, the Abdo Benítez administration found itself unable to stop the virus from pounding the Paraguayan people. Although COVID-19 numbers remained low by international standards, the pandemic brought to light many of the problems we will explore in the pages ahead, including appalling health coverage and infrastructure, government corruption, and an insular diplomacy.

So, what exactly constitutes good political bona fides in Paraguay? We will find that out in the next chapter.

II

Politics
The Old and the New

When Alexis Tocqueville visited the young, imperfect democracy of the United States in the nineteenth century, he prized its "ceaseless agitation."[1] This "superabundant force" by which regular citizens discuss and are involved in politics was democracy's "greatest advantage" for Tocqueville. Paraguay's democracy is also young and imperfect, and it too shows the type of ceaseless agitation and energy that nurtures and sustains democracies in the long-term. Paraguayans show their agitation when they burn the national Congress to oppose a presidential reelection, or when they turn political party conventions into chair-throwing matches, or when they discuss any political issue with incredible passion via social media. Undoubtedly, Paraguayans do not take democracy for granted; they are willing to die in the public square to defend it. At a time when the world endures a democratic recession[2] and appears captivated by authoritarian leaders, in Paraguay the suggestion of a presidential reelection makes people run for the pitchforks. It has not always been so. When in 1984 a *New York Times* journalist came to Paraguay he reported a complete lack of agitation: "Most of Paraguay's people have learned to respond to rule-by-whim with the consistent reasonableness of silence."[3]

In my time there, Paraguayan agitation took the form of flying toilet papers and raw eggs. Out of the professional middle class that typically carries out revolutions in Latin America emerged a civil society organization that names and shames corrupt politicians and public officials. Led by two women, María Esther Roa and Aidé Vera, they regularly assemble a group of citizens via WhatsApp messages and march to the residence of a corrupt politician. With megaphones in hand, they denounce their misdeeds and shower the place with toilet paper rolls and eggs to illustrate the resident's filthy dealings. María Esther reminds me of Carrie A. Nation, the activist of the American temperance movement, who—hatchet in hand—terrorized taverns across the country to protest the evils of alcohol consumption. María Esther also instills fear in corrupt politicians and for the first time ever has made them think twice before engaging in illicit dealings. I went to one of their meetings and the energy, righteousness, and urgency of their cause was contagious.

There is a darker side to Paraguayans' Tocquevillian agitation too, in that Paraguay has also attempted coups d'état, seen a presidential resignation and an impeachment in less than thirty years of democratic rule. Moreover, one vice-president was killed in 1999 by sicarios (motorcycle hit men), and greater violence was averted only when General Lino Oviedo, the rebellious former general turned politician, died in a helicopter crash. Sometimes, it is as if Paraguayans want to treat their presidents as the local soccer teams treat their coaches, like circuit breakers that go off when the social current becomes unbearable. In a similar vein, Paraguayans' agitation is ceaseless but unsystematic. It has not translated into the type of civil society organizations that so impressed Tocqueville in the United States and that in mature democracies serve to channel citizens' grievances, without the need to torch public buildings.

In the United States, Tocqueville was interested in seeing with his own eyes whether democratic rule could work. In particular, Tocqueville was worried about the "tyranny of the majority" and the havoc it could wreak on political freedom. Tocqueville's qualms about majoritarian rule became largely true in Latin America, as powerful executives dispensed with constitutional constraints and violated rights one simple majority at a time. One only needs to look to Venezuela to see how current Tocqueville remains. However, unlike in most Latin American countries, Paraguay's Congress is powerful and thus it has impeded executive branch excesses. Notably, the 1992 Constitution gave Congress the power to override a presidential veto with a simple majority in both chambers, set budgetary levels with enormous discretion (to the point of setting salary levels for individual government employees), and most importantly, to impeach the president (and the vice-president, cabinet members, and Supreme Court judges) on the basis of an arbitrary "poor performance of duties" (mal desempeño de sus funciones) ruling. Indeed, Congress was not shy about using this last constitutional clause in June 2012, when its members swiftly removed President Fernando Lugo.

Paraguayans would wholeheartedly agree with Tocqueville's caveat that "democracy does not confer the most skillful kind of government upon the people."[4] Ask a Paraguayan at random, in any part of the country, about whether his or her representatives in government are doing a good job and the reply is likely to be a vigorous sneer. That might explain why Paraguayans seem to be dissatisfied with their democracy. Since 1995, the polling company Latinobarómetro has been asking Latin Americans about the value of democracy, economic outlook, and other variables of national progress. For Paraguay, the 1995–2015 trend is worrisome: Paraguayans support democracy less, value authoritarian governments more, and feel more negative about the country's overall progress.[5] In 2017, according to a Vanderbilt University study,[6] 48 percent of Paraguayans thought democracy was the best system of government, the second lowest number in the Americas. Another cause of discontent with democracy is political corruption; more than two thirds of Paraguayans think politicians are corrupt.[7] Even my Duolingo course for Jopará—the local mix of Guaraní sprinkled with Spanish words spoken by most Paraguayans—taught me "Heta senador ha diputádo oîva'erâ cárcelpe," which translates as, "Many senators and representatives should be in jail."

The discontent with Paraguay's democracy is a serious challenge to its legitimacy, unless Paraguayans embrace the aphorism, "Democracy is the worst form of government except for all those other forms that have been tried from time to time." Ultimately, democracy cannot survive if it does not fulfill the citizens' notion of a better life, including political freedoms, justice, and economic progress, compared to the alternatives or what citizens perceive existed before. The value of a democracy is to a great extent a matter of expectations. I work for the Center for International Private Enterprise, an institution whose motto is "democracy that delivers." There I learned that democratic and economic development should go hand-in-hand to be successful. Young democracies such as Paraguay come under pressure when popular demands for immediate results overwhelm political processes. The value of any democracy is undermined by the necessity to solve problems now without waiting for the long-term; no rational voter can emerge when basic nutrition, health, and education standards go unfulfilled. A mature democracy results from many years of building blocks—from separation of powers to rule of law—until reaching something close to Robert Dahl's "Polyarchy,"[8] or in Lant Pritchett and Michael Woolcock's more prosaic terms, becoming more like Denmark.[9] Moreover, the institutional zenith is reached incrementally once effective checks and balances are in place, preventing politically powerful groups from imposing their agenda on the rest of the population.

Unfortunately, the problem lies in reconciling the reality of multiple views about what constitutes progress with arbitrary perceptions of what constitute problems. While democracy experts can delineate basic standards to assess the quality of democracy, the public neither possesses these tools nor seems willing to acquire them, and there is little the government can do about it. Famously, between 2000 and 2015, Venezuelans had one of the region's highest satisfaction rates with their democracy, while at the same time their elected government was steadily eroding the foundations of democratic institutions.[10] Paraguayans' displeasure with their democracy might as well be because the current democratic institutions have not lived up to previously high expectations. Paraguayans have never experienced the type of democracy that gets high grades in international rankings, and all indications are they remain uninterested in learning more about such democracies. Rather, Paraguayans seem to dislike democracy because they are either unhappy about the economy or disagree with current political leaders. Based on surveys alone, Paraguayans have never been too enamored with democracy; their current discontentment did not follow a trajectory starting with massive support followed by disbelief after failure to produce results. The clear pattern post–Stroessner is one of mild support for democracy: While in 2017 more Paraguayans agreed with the claim "democracy is preferable" than in 1995 (55 percent versus 52 percent, respectively), the average for the period was 46 percent.[11] Moreover, the many improvements and some backtracking observed in Paraguay's democracy for the past decades have not impinged on their quality assessment. When Latinobarómetro asked Paraguayans to assess their country's political regime on a range where 1 is "not democratic" and 10 is "fully democratic," they have responded "5" consistently in almost every year of the twenty-first century.[12]

Likewise, the tools policy makers and analysts have at their disposal are seriously limited by a lack of empirical work. Indeed, Paraguay's status as Latin America's least-studied country is evident in the lack of systematic and rigorous social science research. Political science in particular is an area where the supply of academic research is sorely lacking. Almost two decades into the twenty-first century, there is still no PhD program in political science in Paraguay. When I attended the Paraguayan Association of Political Scientists' second congress ever, I learned the Universidad Nacional de Asunción—the largest institution of higher education—buried its political science department under the law school. Notably, the largest center of Paraguayan studies is located in Argentina.[13] Granted, a lower-income country like Paraguay has significant opportunity costs to engage in political science research, but it is remarkable how little Paraguayans have theorized about their political ailments. Political scientist Liliana Duarte-Recalde attributes the problem to the historical parochialism of Paraguayan thinkers, positing that an incorrect attribution of exceptional features to Paraguay's case (one Paraguayan author called it, "the cemetery of theories") coupled with a nationalist view of history has hindered the application of political science tools and theories to the study of Paraguayan politics.[14] Helio Vera probably exaggerated, but was not far from the truth when he said that in Paraguay, "historians are almost always former politicians trying to justify themselves."[15] In spite of its insularity, political ideas never had a problem reaching Paraguay. No jungle, desert, muddy road, or unfavorable weather stopped the Paraguayans who wrote the 1870 constitution from learning about the ideas expressed in the U.S. constitution or prevented Paraguayans in the early twentieth century from embracing the world's worst political fads (Nazism, Fascism, Communism, etc.). Some of the country's top intellectuals—Fernando Masi, Diego Abente, and Eduardo Bogado Tabacman—were members of a Marxist-Leninist underground revolutionary group bent on bringing down the Stroessner regime and imposing the dictatorship of the proletariat. And large-scale emigration meant Paraguayans absorbed foreign ideas that eventually circled back to Paraguay. I once heard somebody say the reason Paraguay does not have more intellectuals is due to a shortage of political exiles.

Paraguay must also contend with a state capacity unable to meet voters' demands. Andrews, Pritchett, and Woolcock call this challenge the "capability trap"[16]; as the authors put it "schools get built but children don't learn, IT systems are introduced but not used, plans are written but not implemented." As a result, countries "get stuck"[17] implementing failed policies or figuring out how to implement otherwise sensible policies. For instance, according to an Inter-American Development Bank (IADB) index, Paraguay has the worst efficiency of public spending in all Latin America, with bad scores in strategic planning and evaluation and project selection. The IADB also found that it takes two years on average for an infrastructure project to go from approval to commencement, the third worst in the region (Bahamas was the fastest with an average four months).[18] Unlike the Asian economic miracles, where patronage and clientelism existed but were disciplined by a technocratic elite, Paraguay's bureaucracy for many years was fully staffed with Colorado Party cronies who lacked technical expertise. In Paraguay there were no "Chicago Boys" like in Pinochet's Chile, or a "Berkeley Mafia" like in Suharto's Indonesia to infuse economic oomph through Econ 101 principles. Only the Central Bank has served as an island of technical expertise, albeit limited to monetary policy. So as Paraguayan academic Gustavo Setrini put it, "Accustomed to trading favors up and down the clientelistic chains that link resources from the political center to the demands made by groups outside the state, the public ministries lacked the expertise to generate broad public policies and the stream of public goods aimed at improving economic competitiveness of Paraguayan industry and agriculture."[19]

The Paraguayan state is particularly burdened with an overabundance of public employees that constrain its financial capabilities to improve productivity and deliver quality services. Traditionally, victorious political parties have dispensed government jobs in return for political favors.

Additionally, years of lackluster private sector growth have also increased the lure of a government job, further bloating the public sector. Seen through the prism of GDP, the recent economic picture does not look too bad: in the period 2006 to 2016, eight out of every hundred guaraníes produced in the country went to pay government salaries.[20] However, according to 2016 data, government wages comprised more than three quarters of public income derived from taxes.[21] The trend from 2007 to 2016 is not encouraging: tax income grew on average 12.2 percent annually, while public wages grew 13.6 percent.[22] As a consequence, the government has little flexibility to engage in more productive investments. And what little remains left for investment is not utilized effectively. For example, according to the IMF, Paraguay ranks below the regional average in public investment efficiency.[23] To top it all off, state-owned enterprises, stacked with politicians' family members and cronies, underperform and depress growth in the rest of the economy.[24]

For a long time, state capability in Paraguay meant "faculty to deliver public treasury to political friends." Basic tasks historically associated with government, such as paving roads, picking up the trash, or delivering mail, have been an afterthought in Paraguay. And it shows. The typical answer of a Paraguayan public employee to any request is, "No me complique (Don't make my life difficult)," largely because he or she was not hired to serve a public function but to fill a pre-determined quota based on political spoils. For example, I once tried to mail a letter in Asunción, but I soon realized the task was not as simple as it looked. To begin with, post offices are hard to find, and when I asked Paraguayans for a post office location, they acted as if I had inquired about an obscure physics theory. Just as frustrating, if you ever do uncover a post office, your letter may or may not reach its intended recipient. In 2014, a group of researchers studying state capabilities investigated 159 countries (Paraguay included) to determine the average number of days it takes for countries to get a letter back, mailing letters to non-existent addresses and measuring how many made it back to an address in the United States and how long it took. Paraguay scored among the worst with a total of 232.5 days; 50 percent of the time the letter wasn't returned at all![25]

In this context of public service for political spoils arose the Paraguayan phenomenon of "planilleros," ghost workers who earn a monthly paycheck but either rarely or never show up to work. Planillero cases include unrealized consulting work, holding fake second jobs while working at real (public or private) primary jobs, holding jobs but not spending time at the workplace, and in some cases earning the salary of a deceased employee. Planilleros are equivalent to what mob bosses in the TV show *The Sopranos* call "no-work jobs."[26] Many Paraguayans still recall the so-called "VIP Secretary" case, an administrative worker at the Comptroller General's office who logged twenty-seven-hour workdays in her time sheet. The planilleros situation is so bad that is common for every new cabinet member or senior government official to "rake" the office's employee list to get rid of planilleros, often with the goal of substituting old planilleros with a new cohort. Government and press investigations have frequently revealed cases where 5 to 10 percent of employees at a particular ministry or secretariat are planilleros. Supreme Court judges and members of Congress constantly complain privately and in public that they do not know how many employees are in their institutions. The planilleros' presence constitutes a twofold cost to Paraguayan taxpayers: there is the financial cost of paying a salary and the capability cost of having an actual government function go unfulfilled.

Notwithstanding their many shortcomings, Paraguay's democratic governments have overseen tangible socio-economic benefits, albeit to an underwhelming degree. A clear example is the country's compliance with the 1990–2015 Millennium Development Goals. Paraguay improved in almost all areas, but its average progress fell below that of Latin America as a whole. Remarkably, in June 2018, the World Health Organization (WHO) announced that Paraguay had officially eliminated malaria, becoming the first country in Latin America in over forty-five years to beat the disease. Paraguay also improved in the United Nations' Human Development Index (HDI) from 0.58 to 0.69 (one is the highest score) between 1990 and 2015, an increase of 19.5 percent.[27] Yet again, the country's HDI 2015 score remained below the Latin American and the Caribbean average. The Paraguayan government has formalized a system of social insurance with a conditional cash transfer program (Tekoporã, or "good life" in Guaraní) that eliminates the political middle man. Most notably, the Tekoporã Program—a fairly straightforward welfare program implemented with success in other Latin American countries—helps those most in need (children, youth, pregnant women, Indigenous people, persons with disabilities, etc.) without major overhead, hidden or otherwise political transaction costs. What in the past forced an individual or family in need to engage with a local party boss in order to access social services is today a bureaucratic process like any other developed-world welfare program. Even with its potential shortfalls, it constitutes a significant improvement over the previous system.

Political Parties Are Colorful

Two political parties have historically dominated Paraguayan politics, the Colorado Party (Asociación Nacional Republicana) and the

Liberal Party (Partido Liberal Radical Auténtico). As we have seen, both are nineteenth-century creatures, founded in the same year—1887. In the beginning, as political scientist Paul Lewis put it, they were "nothing more than a cluster of personalist factions."[28] I find plausible U.S. political scientist Byron Nichols's explanation of the way political parties in Paraguay emerged[29]; when I look at everything that has been written about Paraguayan politics, his view remains both relevant and current. Nichols traced back the two parties' founding to an agglomeration of "carais,"[30] a number of regional leaders whose wealth and power originated in the encomienda system. According to Nichols, the encomienda system put the carais on top of the pecking order and evolved an all-encompassing leadership style that shaped whole communities. Specifically, "The carai was an absolute ruler on his ranch, not only in a political sense but also socially and economically as well. He allocated goods and provided for medical assistance, housing, and clothing among his subjects, and in return he was revered and honored."[31] As a result, in Paraguay political parties not only became intermediaries between the people and the state, but more fundamentally actual providers of public goods and services; party membership was in practice served as insurance against adversity and the key to access public services. Parties were what anthropologist Frederic Hicks described as "mutual aid societies and channels of social mobility."[32] To this day, Paraguayans will tell you "tojearreglá la ipartidoŷva" (you are on your own if you do not belong to a party). Consequently, the dispensation of favors became the main tool for political leaders to recruit followers, implement policies, and stay in power. One Paraguayan bureaucrat quipped that he wanted to mount a nipple in his office's door to serve all the suckers looking for jobs, deals, and favors.[33] By the same token, the political arena turned into a zero-sum game of vengeful fights. In this arena political parties became, as anthropologists Elman and Helen Service put it, "loose aggregations of small bodies or factions of would-be officer-holders, professing personal allegiance to their leaders but continually jockeying for greater power by forming new alliances and destroying old ones."[34]

At the same time, political parties' multi-functional attributes crowded out society, pushing out other social organizations, such as labor unions or rural and civil-society organizations, from playing any representative or intermediary role. Notably, to this day, the Federación Nacional Campesina (National Farmers Federation) manages to disrupt Asunción traffic once a year while remaining on the fringes of the political spectrum, with few achievements in terms of land reform or farmers' rights, its principal objectives. Meanwhile, public sector unions act more like jobs rackets than advocates of labor rights. Although both political parties later developed a structure and a set of binding sentiments, they never produced any ideological foundations or core principles other than pliable loyalties to leaders or factions. Rather, they became tools for what Eligio Ayala, one of Paraguay's most distinguished political figures and thinkers, called "political utility," the country's "national god."[35] Without political power, non-government organizations or civil society institutions have either not emerged or struggled to have an impact. Only the Catholic Church has been able to shape the policy-making process operating from outside the political system, mostly because 90 percent of Paraguayans are Catholic—the largest percentage in Latin America.

Key to understanding the parties' permanence across the years is grasping their ability to adapt to changing times. While the current spectrum of congressional representation includes nine parties, Paraguay remains, in practical terms, a two-party system because only the Colorado and Liberal parties have real chances of winning an election. One important reason why they have endured across three centuries is because they have been effectively devoid of ideology. They are the very definition of "catch-all parties," a term coined by the German political scientist Otto Kirchheimer to explain a political arena without substantive disagreement and lacking a principled opposition.[36] When I visited the Colorado Party website[37] and clicked on "ideology," I got a blank page. In practice the party usually adopts center-right positions by Latin American standards—a general openness to private enterprise coupled with conservative social values (candidates typically express opposition to legal abortion or gay marriage). However, reading its official declaration of principles from 2007 one can get confused with their support for a "humane socialism," tirades against neoliberalism, and a blank check for the state to intervene to improve the social welfare condition of Paraguayans. The party also remains unrepentant about its past; Alfredo Stroessner is still an honorary member of the Colorado governing body.

On the other hand, the Liberal Party's website[38] does not even bother with presenting its principles or ideology. The party's history of internal divisions, encapsulated in its current mouthful name (Partido Liberal Radical Auténtico or Authentic Liberal Radical Party), certainly mimics a catch-all status. Thus, in modern Paraguay's politics, principles and practice all point to the same bipartisan all-encompassing direction, resembling the old quip, "Them feller citizens are my principles, but if they don't suit yer exactly, they ken be altered."[39] Paraguayan rock and roll godfather Chester Swann had politicians in mind when he intoned, "Big mouths, short hair, morals up for sale or rent."[40] For instance, the 2017 campaign to amend the constitution and allow for presidential reelection triggered a number of political alliances that illustrate the political system's ideological elasticity. Within each of the two major political parties there were factions for and against the amendment. The "Yes to reelection" menagerie included a Colorado Party faction representing the country's sitting president, a group supporting the only former president from an opposition party, and random members of the Liberal Party. In opposition were Colorado Party members associated with the Stroessner regime, far-left parties, and random members of the Liberal Party.

This catch-all nature allows for a dynamic amalgam of policy positions, which at times seems inconsistent and frankly puzzling. For example, some of the political system's strongest disagreements happen within parties and not between parties. But as political analyst José Tomás Sánchez argues,[41] this "internal incoherence" is not a problem but an asset, particularly in the case of the Colorados. By embracing political differences, the two parties can reach out to the whole political spectrum of voters with tailored policy proposals.

Moreover, the only sustained difference between the parties across time has been the color of their banners: the Colorado identifies with red and the Liberal with blue, and people's alliances to one party or the other often begin at birth. Political platforms and leaders' views across time have consistently shown that little else distinguishes them. Like an unidentified source told the legendary American journalist Hunter S. Thompson during his visit to Asunción in 1963, "You have to realize that political philosophy is not a major factor in politics here—the main things are leaders, personalities, and power."[42] As economist Fernando Masi told me, "Paraguayans vote but don't choose."[43] What seems to stir voters is what Paul Lewis called "inherited resentments accumulated over generations."[44] Therefore, policy proposals take a back seat to the ballot's color. Luis María Argaña, a Colorado leader who thrived equally under both the Stroessner dictatorship and the subsequent democratic system, famously quipped, "A Colorado always votes for the Colorado Party, even if the candidate is Donald Duck."[45] Or as another Colorado politician explained in 2018, their party "is not an association of free thinkers."[46] That is, vote the party line, and leave the thinking to the opposition.

Given the political parties' lax ideological stances, Paraguayan voters are amenable to candidates considered "outsiders." At least three of the seven formally elected presidents can be considered political outsiders, but with one important caveat: they did not come from the political world, yet they embraced the traditional political parties in order to run their campaigns. Political parties are also amenable to using wealthy individuals' largesse and have no qualms about granting expedited membership in return. Similarly, a lack of class-based grievances among political parties has allowed wealthy individuals to successfully run for office. It also helps that money flows freely and with little transparency. Paraguayan legislation mandates political parties to report their financial statements and disclose all financial donations to the Electoral Tribunal. Yet there are neither limits to how much individuals can spend nor constraints on how funds are channeled. When the Electoral Tribunal published the list of the parties' biggest donors for the 2018 elections, President Cartes' name did not turn up in spite of being the Colorado's top donor, as Cartes himself or any Colorado would have told you. In this context, seven of the past presidents were either wealthy or super rich.

In this way, a typical corollary of catch all–based political systems is voter apathy. In numerous surveys, voters in general, and young voters in particular, express little interest in politics.[47] Most worryingly, despite compulsory voting, a great many Paraguayans choose to stay at home on Election Day. In the past five presidential elections (1998–2018),[48] the average voter turnout was 66.8 percent of the electorate, a relatively low rate by mandatory-voting standards. Young voters especially have shown low propensity to vote.[49] Granted, voting in Paraguay suffers from the same lack of effective sanctions and enforcement that affect other laws. But all things considered, without a carrot or a stick, many Paraguayans do not rush to the polls.

Meanwhile, so-called "listas sábanas" (closed lists) allow individuals with access to financial resources to effectively dictate who can participate in politics. In this process, political parties choose and rank candidates, and then voters vote on the entire ballot block. This allows party bosses to select a group of people to stand for election while voters can select ballots with the party-established order. On election day most voters vote for their party, often by identifying the top candidate. All the other candidates buried underneath the headers surface after the election like a cucumelo[50] following a rain shower. A 2019 law amended the Electoral Code to allow voters to determine the candidates' ranking and thus alter the party-imposed order; yet, parties still determine the list of names in the ballot. While listas sábanas can theoretically play a constructive role in a democracy by forcing individuals to follow party mechanisms and values, in practice they have created a system of pay-to-play party politics and allowed all kinds of disreputable characters to stand and win political office. A great many of the ghost candidates found in listas sábanas are indeed shady and they include individuals accused or convicted of fraud and illicit enrichment. Corrupt candidates literally buy their spots on a party list by funding campaign expenses or otherwise donating money to party leaders. Furthermore, listas sábanas promote the political status quo, thus prolonging the type of "structural and cultural inequalities with historical roots," which, according to political scientist Liliana Duarte, "stand as barriers to the equitable participation of various social sectors in the electoral process."[51]

Women's political participation is particularly hampered by structural and cultural inequalities. The case of Serafina Dávalos, the first woman to graduate from a Paraguayan university, exemplifies some of these historical roots. Dávalos was brought up in the post–Triple Alliance War period, when the female population outnumbered males four to one.[52] However, unlike other countries where an increased female participation in the labor force brought permanent changes to women's political rights, in Paraguay little changed. Traditionally, Guaraní women were the homemakers, so it can be argued that after the war Paraguayan women's role in society was restored to the antebellum situation. U.S. economist Benjamin Friedman argues that steady economic growth is a prerequisite in all societies for political and social liberalization reforms, such as women's suffrage and economic empowerment.[53] In this sense, Paraguay's historically lethargic economic growth did not help women's rights. Paraguayan women would step up again during the Chaco War, but the wave of post-war authoritarian governments thwarted any hope for greater political rights. Still, a more dynamic economy after the Chaco War helped women enter professions outside the household and to improve educational levels. No matter, as Paraguay was the last country in Latin America to grant women the right to vote; women in Paraguay had to wait until 1961 to cast a ballot, and until the 1990s for their votes to count, following the arrival of democracy and electoral reforms.

Although the 1996 Electoral Code established a 20 percent quota of female candidates in primary party lists, the number of women elected to political office has remained low. The problem's historical roots are evident in the lack of impact from legislation; hundreds of years of unequal treatment continue to prevent more women from running for office while encouraging men's participation. For example, it is common for parties to set a higher than 20 percent quota for women in electoral lists, but the actual placement of women tends to be in the bottom. Thus, a lower percentage is elected. And this phenomenon is not explained by a higher electoral turnout rate for men, since it is similar for both sexes.[54] According to an investigation by expert and political activist Lilian Soto, female participation is lower than men's within parties' membership rosters, amounting to 47 percent on average.[55] Moreover, party membership does not translate into a corresponding participation in the parties' decision-making bodies. Around a third of all political parties' leadership positions are filled with women and less than a quarter in the two leading parties.[56] Similarly, women hold few leadership positions at the national level. In Paraguay the percentage of female political leaders in Congress, the national cabinet, and provincial and municipal governments is typically below 20 percent. There has never been a female president, vice president, or head of the Central Bank; in 2017, Lea Giménez made history when she became the first finance minister in Paraguay's history. For the 2018–2023 period, not a single woman was elected governor in the seventeen departments.

Nonetheless, Paraguayan political parties fit some valid preconceptions about their role in society. Founded almost 150 years ago, they have been the main conduits of politics, selecting leaders, mobilizing followers, and developing policies. Alas, when compared to more mature democracies, Paraguayan political parties are lacking in terms of democratic credentials. Consider the following: the United States, Uruguay, and Paraguay all feature political parties founded in the nineteenth century that remain relevant in the twenty-first century; however, their historical roles could not be more different. In the case of the United States and Uruguay, parties have traditionally played a key role as arbitrators of political currents and thus as the foundation for democratic regimes by competing in elections, expanding the participation to all citizens, and respecting democratic governance rules. And those are precisely the basic functions political science ascribes to political parties. But evidently the way Paraguayan parties have operated in reality has deviated from these standards. Political parties, more often than not, have obstructed the democratic institutional development in Paraguay.

While human agency is certainly complex and thus political motivations are not easy to pinpoint with complete accuracy, Paraguayan political parties have consistently pursued two goals: (1) gain absolute power; and (2) divide spoils exclusively among followers. As crucially, the active forces pursuing these goals have been elites detached from mass political following and armed with shifting power sources (the military, economic resources, foreign backing, etc.). The historical vicissitudes related in Chapter I show that domestic and international trends at many times overwhelmed the parties' particular agendas. However, another key to understanding Paraguayan politics is the parties' tendency to exclude other parties from power and to treat government assets and resources as patronage fodder. Although democratic rules and institutions have tamed these century-old tendencies, they continue to guide political action. As a 2009 USAID report described it, "the principal democratic governance problem in Paraguay … [is that] the major political parties seek to capture the state and use their power over public resources for their benefit and that of their allies."[57]

Similarly, political parties continue to engage, even if less overtly, in the same old practices of giving gifts to voters before elections or chauffeuring voters to the polls. The local NGO Semillas para la Democracia carried out a survey during the 2018 elections and found that political operators transported 17 percent of voters to the polls.[58] When I visited the little town of Jesús de Tavarangué in late 2017, the local Colorado Party seccional (party office) was draped in bright red, with polkas blasting out from speakers, and pictures of the preferred candidates smiling from the walls. A steady flow of potential voters walked out the premises loaded with strong incentives to vote for the Colorado candidates, in the form of bags of enriched soil and pesticides. Any interested voter can stop by during any holiday or weekend at one of the local Colorado seccionales or Liberal comités and obtain these benefits in exchange a casual partisan pledge. While sometimes patronage translated into social or economic improvements, most of the time it did not. At other rare times, it brings in groups historically cut off from the public sphere, like the Colorado's inclusion of the Pynandi ("the barefooted" in Guaraní) during the 1947 civil war. But the inclusion never lasted long once political power is captured. During electoral campaigns political currents generally are a side show to the main event featuring promises to distribute the booty.

From the founding of Asunción to the culmination of modern Paraguay, the rent-seeking behavior associated with government mandates, regulations, and public monopolies has been the norm in the country's polity. Paradoxically, the Paraguayan historical standard of milking the state and excluding the opposition developed in a homogenous society without ethnic, regional or social cleavages and united by a bilingual national identity. Why a country with a small homogenous population took so long to develop a more collegial politics remains a puzzle. Lacking more concrete empirical evidence, the old adage "Pueblo chico, infierno grande" (small town, big hell) remains a valid explanation.

What has changed in modern Paraguay is that the two main parties are less prone to excluding opponents, but rather show a tendency to integrate those willing to join the gravy train regardless of political color. In the old days, Colorado Party candidates would leave behind their differences, seal their unity, and move on together to set the party machinery in full throttle with an "abrazo republicano" (republican embrace). Once victory was achieved, party members would divide up the spoils among themselves. In present times, the abrazo republicano still signals party unity and carries weight during electoral times, but in post-election negotiations it gives way to a more flexible approach for political negotiations. The republican embrace does not exclude other parties anymore. As Argentine political scientist Magui López explained to me, the parties' current political behavior does not follow a traditional "government–opposition" dynamic, but a "ruler–second in command" one, where governance involves the two parties' active participation.

Following the Abrazo Republicano (republican embrace) Colorado Party members agree on every motion (courtesy _Última Hora_).

An Ongoing Transition to Democracy

As the story goes, shortly after General Stroessner went into exile in Brazil, he picked up a newspaper, glanced at the new government's inauguration coverage and said, "Allí sólo falto yo (I'm the only one missing over there)." Regardless of its veracity,[59] the phrase illustrates a key element at the center of Paraguay's modern political regime: many of the Stroessner-era apparatchiks held on to power and shaped a long transition to democracy that is still ongoing. A useful way to understand this transition in broad terms is to look at it through political sociologist Larry Diamond's distinction between "electoral" and "liberal" democracies.[60] In electoral democracies, free and fair elections are held regularly; in liberal democracies, in addition to elections, political rights and civil liberties are well established. Paraguay is secure in the "electoral democracy" category, but only inching towards "liberal democracy" territory.

International indexes measuring relevant democratic indicators reveal a picture of gradual improvements for Paraguayan democracy in the past decade. The trend is nonetheless positive compared to the rest of the region and the world, where such values have either stagnated or declined. For example, in Freedom House's 2018 report[61] Paraguay holds a "Partly Free" status, with a score of 64 (Most Free = 100); the status has remained the same since 1999, though there have been improvements in the "political rights" score. Paraguay's "freedom" rating is lower than all the South

American countries, except for Venezuela and Ecuador, whose values deteriorated significantly in the last ten years. Freedom House titled the 2018 report "Democracy in Crisis," a condition that does not fully apply to Paraguay. More accurately, Paraguay's democracy can be described as a "Flawed Democracy," as the Economist Intelligence Unit's[62] Democracy Index 2017 categorized it. Paraguay shares this category with the United States and all the Latin American countries except for Uruguay. And Paraguay's overall score ranks in the lower half of Latin America and the Caribbean's region. Indeed, if there is one country in the "Flawed Democracies" category that fits the bill it is Paraguay. Yet, the country has been making steady improvements, going against the regional and global tide. According to the same index, between 2006 and 2017 Paraguay's score improved, unlike the world's and Latin America and the Caribbean's regressions.

Paraguayan analysts describe a democracy without depth. Diego Abente describes its quality as "a purgatory"[63] between the Stroessner dictatorship and a high-grade democracy. Meanwhile, Alfredo Boccia calls it a "decaffeinated democracy."[64] This state of affairs has something to do with flawed rules. For instance, the constitution does not allow individuals to run for president or vice-president at the same time they run for Congress. Up-and-coming political leaders normally opt out of running for president or vice-president unless their chances of winning the election are high. Otherwise, when parties do not have a strong chance at winning the presidential election, they choose weak candidates or symbolic candidates without any interest in or apparent knowledge of politics.[65]

However, in general the democratic shortcomings are not due to a lack of proper legislation; rather the 1992 constitution borrowed heavily from the U.S. and European constitutions and the country's legislation is largely in line with international legal practices and human rights standards. No, there is something about the way Paraguayan politicians carry out their democratic business that is immune to written mandates. It is reminiscent of F.A. Hayek's distinction between laws and legislation: the former being largely spontaneous, unwritten, and something to be discovered, as opposed to legislation's top-down, deliberate, and planned nature.[66] For example, the Paraguayans who wrote the 1992 constitution wanted to avoid power centralization above anything else, leading them to structure the election of congressional seats according to the D'Hondt proportional system, which in simple terms allocates seats based on the proportion of votes earned. For example, if Party X wins 40 percent of the votes, then it would gain about 40 percent of the seats. Likewise, if Party Y receives 2 percent of the votes, they earn 2 percent of seats. The system is intended to favor the parties that earn the most votes to the detriment of those with small constituencies, with the goal of strengthening majority formation, and thus governability. Yet, in Paraguay the system coexists with a high degree of political fragmentation among and within parties. Political gridlocks are common and typically unlocked by wheeling and dealing that is both short-term oriented and narrowly circumscribed. Add the listas-sábanas to the mix, with their roster of unwholesome political characters, and few incentives are left to deliver legislation aligned with the electoral majority's demands.

Critics[67] rightly argue the system disincentives the type of policy consensus necessary to tackle the country's political and economic challenges. However, it is hard to see how a parliamentary system or a more presidentialist one could overcome the Paraguayan way of doing politics. Political parties and their agents have demonstrated across history they can work the system (probably any system for that matter). Paraguayans have met their political enemy and the enemy is themselves, not the rules. In this sense, there seems to be a high degree of factionalism within the political spectrum that predates the current proportional system and will probably outlive a regime change. For example, political analyst Fernando Martínez-Escobar described the immediate post–Stroessner but pre–1992 Constitution Colorado Party as comprising four factions: autonomous/orthodox, renovator, intermediate generation, and democratic traditionalism.[68] For modern Paraguay, political strategist Victor Benítez González lists five electoral-block "archetypes" that transcend specific parties and voters and can overlap within each party: progressive humanism, anti-imperialism, moderate anti-liberalism, traditional conservatism, and efficiency-oriented management.[69]

Its unreformed clannish political culture is a case in point. Although kin-based politics is not unique to Paraguay, it defines the Paraguayan polity and explains many of its dynamics. Traditionally, Paraguay's small population (and even smaller concentration of elites, due to high inequality) has meant a few well-connected families sit at the political table. In 1967, U.S. political scientist Byron Nichols calculated that around 50 percent of the Colorado Party's executive committee was related either by blood or marriage to at least one other member of the committee.[70] From my own interactions with modern Paraguay's political elite I reckon there are at most two degrees of separation between any two of its members. Similarly, the Paraguayan state's failure to provide impersonal legal or otherwise civilian protection to its citizens meant clans were the only channel available to benefit from public services. Or perhaps it was the other way around and clans prevented the emergence of impersonal public services. Regardless, kin-based politics have dominated Paraguay for a long time, at least since Francisco Solano López inherited the throne from his father in 1862. That trend is palpable in modern Paraguayan politics, where fewer than ten political clans possess disproportionate political sway. For example, the so-called Zacarías Clan wielded heavy influence over Ciudad del Este (CDE)'s politics. This clan featured at the top the power couple Javier Zacarías Irún (former CDE mayor, congressperson, and current senator) and his wife Sandra McLeod (CDE mayor 2007–2019). Additionally, there is Javier's brother, Justo, a former Alto Paraná (departamento where CDE is located) governor and current congressperson, and his son Alejandro, a CDE council member. And that is only the first layer of relatives. A second layer includes more siblings and relatives together with their spouses and children working at the Itaipú Dam Corporation, Supreme Court, and Electoral Tribunal.[71] The country's transition to democracy has not altered kinship dynamics; instead it has opened the spectrum of channels available to influence. In turn, the old system of patronage and clientelism has given way to a more "democratic" distribution of spoils[72] among the different parties. Although there is a law against nepotism, all the political parties continue to engage in nepotist practices. It remains customary for politicians of all stripes, regardless of their seniority or closeness to power, to have members of their families either directly employed by the state or working under a government contract. The local newspaper *Última Hora* uncovered a typical case: a legislator had thirty-two family members working in the public sector.[73]

Social identity-based politics is another central component of Paraguay's democracy. Its long-standing nature was first analyzed by Byron Nichols in 1969 and continues to shape they way voters ultimately decide. Fundamentally, social identities trigger a cognitive dissonance on the part of the electorate. On the one hand, polls show Paraguayan voters are not enamored with political parties, exude cynicism about their inner workings, and show a consistent pessimism about their prospects for improvement. On the other hand, membership in political parties is high compared to countries in the region, amounting on average to more than three quarters of registered voters. Moreover, affiliation numbers have grown consistently since 1989.[74]

In Paraguay, partisan identity seems to be formed early in life, passed down from family members, like soccer team fandom. Those Paraguayans with political science expertise and those with less interest in politics alike largely agree that the family and the narrow social circles explain why a Colorado does not vote for a Liberal and vice versa. For political scientist José Nicolás Morínigo, partisan membership is an integral element of a person's identity. Further, Morínigo argues, "belonging to a party is a fundamental necessity just like having a religion or almost like having a last name."[75] In this sense, political scientists Lachi and Rojas note the most common term used in Paraguay for a fellow party member—"correligionario"—is telling: the word in Spanish denotes someone who shares a religion.[76] Helio Vera observes Paraguayan political identity is "transmitted biologically, like hemophilia."[77] The key caveat is that the heritability of political beliefs is a scientifically uncertain domain; it is intuitive and some findings confirm a genetic component, but it all remains controversial, to say the least. Still, Paraguayan history does indicate party affiliation has been based more on personal loyalties than political ideals. In this sense, elections reveal party loyalties to be rather stable. For example, the Colorado Party has typically captured a percentage of the vote close to its post–Rodríguez (1989–1993) average of 42.3 percent, while the Liberal Party (in alliance with other parties) has hovered around a third of the electorate. Close to a quarter of voters can be considered independents. The Colorado Party has only twice reached 50 percent of the vote in presidential elections since 1989. This means that opposition parties could have won the presidency a number of times if Paraguay had established a run-off system, where the two candidates with the most votes in the first round run against each other in a second round.

Strong partisan identities logically lead voters to disregard relevant information and knowledge necessary to cast a ballot. If I already know that my ballot is red/blue, why bother learning about political platforms? This phenomenon is informed by common knowledge at the national level

Liberal Party members disagree vehemently during a political convention (courtesy *Última Hora*).

and supported by a few empirical studies. Political scientist Carlos Miranda surveyed the four largest of these studies and found Paraguayans have a meager interest in political activities and a low knowledge of political information and facts.[78] Likewise, the only study available at the departamento level—by political scientist Marcello Lachi—confirmed Paraguayan voters' ignorance of basic political information.[79] For example, 91 percent of Ñeembucú department voters did not know how many Congress members there are, and only 16 percent knew their governor's name.[80] This phenomenon is not unique to Paraguay. Voters in democracies around the world either do not have the incentives or the time to research politics and policy adequately enough to make informed decisions during elections, and if they do, they refuse to do so. U.S. political scientists Christopher Achen and Larry Bartels could have been describing Paraguayan voters when they assessed American voters' behavior as follows: "At election time, they are swayed by how they feel about 'the nature of the times,' especially the current state of the economy, and by political loyalties typically acquired in childhood.... Those loyalties, not the facts of political life and government policy, are the primary drivers of political behavior."[81] Furthermore, they concluded, "voters, even the most informed voters, typically make choices not on the basis of policy preferences or ideology, but on the basis of who they are—their social identities."[82] Equally worrisome, in all democracies there is a good deal of cognitive dissonance among the population. In spite of survey after survey showing that voters are ignorant of basic political and economic facts,[83] they still demand policies that could cause great political and economic damage. It is no different in Paraguay. For instance, only seven years after reinstallation of democracy, Paraguayans held Stroessner and his regime policies in a highly favorable light.[84]

The Colorado Party's biologically-transmitted loyalties are mostly due to the party's long-held power. For much of Paraguay's history as an independent nation, it not only served as a traditional party but also functioned as an arm of the state. As we saw in Chapter I, the Stroessner dictatorship forced the military, government officials, and entrepreneurs seeking to contract with the state to become party members. Additionally, the minister of the interior used to appoint both the mayor and sheriff of each city. Not surprisingly, membership in the Colorado Party went from around 140,000 members in 1947 to around 1 million members in 1989.[85] During the Stroessner years the party held tremendous sway via 236 offices spread around the country.[86] Visit any small town in modern Paraguay and you will find one of the most prominent buildings is the party's seccional, a multipurpose, socially-inclusive civic center where the young can play soccer, the old can play cards, and birthdays and weddings can be celebrated. These party offices gave significant power to party bosses in times of authoritarian Colorado dominance due to their key role as vote-gatherers. After the introduction of primary elections in the 1992 constitution, seccional-affiliated bosses lost preeminence to professional political operatives, known as "seccionaleros," who in turn became more involved with national politics.[87] Former Minister of Finance Ernst Bergen (2005–07) recalls his time in office when one angry party boss left threatening voice messages after he refused to meet her. Bergen eventually abided and met with the party boss.[88] The Colorado political machine is also ingrained within the state in the form of public employee associations. These associations lobby Colorado candidates to hire only Colorado people for election day get-out-the-vote efforts.

However, the Liberal Party survived the Stroessner era, and it boasts the only national structure capable of competing on equal terms with the Colorado political might. Only these two parties can bring to the negotiating table a national political machine equally adept at contending elections and dispensing political favors. Even in those areas of the country where the state has limited reach, parties have set up shop and provided citizens with a political voice.

Absent a national political structure, name recognition is key to successfully running for elective office. Two comedians, an entrepreneur who was kidnapped by a rural guerrilla group, and an anti-corruption agitator famous for defecating in a court were some of the new legislators elected for the 2018–2023 congress. A 2018 Electoral Tribunal–run mock presidential election for children returned a significant advantage for the Colorados vis-à-vis the opposition (65.5 percent to 21.6 percent), presumably based on the party's intense and widespread political advertising.

By and large, Paraguayan politicians are shameless political operators ready to hire family members, help cronies, and engage in the most grotesque types of skullduggery. When a former embassy colleague called traditional Paraguayan politicians "hustlers," I nodded in agreement; politicians stop at little when it comes to pursuing their goals. They are as likely to launch a program to buy brand new cars right before presidential elections[89] as to justify including deceased individuals in petitions because "that is part of the Paraguayan culture."[90] And they are open to changing political allegiances as soon as the political winds change. On average, they resemble "public choice theory's"[91] most dismal examples of political behavior. A public choice theorist would look at Paraguay's political system, assess the incentives available to its agents, and probably conclude, "skullduggery makes sense." In practical terms, politicians get away with most of their misdeeds by holding sway over the judicial system and preventing it from punishing wrongdoers. As we will see in Chapter IV, the judiciary grants politicians almost universal impunity, which in turn serves as a major incentive for political corruption, while potentially decent politicians face a significant competitive disadvantage. Until 2019, thirty years after the establishment of democracy, no member of Congress had ever been convicted for corruption and only four executive branch members were sent to prison.

Indeed, how do you compete against an Oscar González Daher (OGD)? This long-time politician from Luque, a suburb of Asunción, is a symbol of the political system's incentives for mischief. Starting off as an obscure lawyer, he gained enormous political power and economic wealth after a steady climb of almost three decades. A prosecutor's investigation revealed OGD and his family managed more than $1.4 billion in ill-gotten assets. He accumulated power by gaming the political system and squeezing every drop of patronage out of it. OGD built a large constituency by appointing political hangers-on to lucrative jobs and by delivering employment, government contracts, and legal protection to his supporters. His political pinnacle came when he became the president of the Jury for the Prosecution of Magistrates (Jurado de Enjuiciamiento de Magistrados, JEM). From the JEM he was able to apply undue influence over those individuals investigating him and his allies' dealings. A simple call threatening a judge with a reprimand or a dismissal would end all investigations or start new ones against his enemies. His downfall eventually came when unknown sources released audio conversations documenting OGD's modus operandi; the calls included a nauseating roll of threats, bribes, and blackmail. The exposé was too much even for the Congress, who voted to expel OGD and strip his congressional immunity, the first time ever for a legislator.

Yet, the parties' responsiveness to social identities means voters have a high tolerance for political mischief. Voters rarely punish wrongdoers; instead they normally bless their behavior, or at least turn a blind eye, by reelecting them or electing one of their family members. OGD was reelected to the senate for the 2018–2023 period. And why not? As Estela Ruíz Díaz, one of Paraguay's top political columnists told me, to the average Paraguayan voter, "A poor politician is a vyro (fool)." Politicians win the majority of political offices in Paraguay through micro-politics, the formal and informal contest at the local level, where filial bonds, comradeship, and social identities determine electoral success. In turn, a politician's performance is assessed based on whether he or she returns favors. These favors are tangible as they come: a government job for a daughter, a public work contract for the uncle's company, a consulting gig at a state-owned company for a brother-in-law, and so on. Equally problematic and intuitive is the fact that Congresspersons' salaries are outrageously high, averaging more than $90,000 annually including benefits (GDP per capita in

Paraguay was $9,000 in 2016 purchasing power parity),[92] constituting one of the highest ratios of salary to per capita GDP.

As Eligio Ayala described it in 1915, "in Paraguay there is no religious, industrial, agricultural or military pursuit other than politics and only politics."[93] Modern Paraguay's bigger economic pie has opened up new opportunities to climb the economic ladder and has made political office less lucrative. Yet, the political virus continues to permeate private economic initiative. Although a government job does not always means quick enrichment or financial salvation, entrepreneurs still rely on regulatory capture and rent-seeking mechanisms in order to prosper. In 2007, Diego Abente saw that "while the strength of the state remains low, its centrality has reached a high."[94] In other words, while the Paraguayan state was not able to effectively enforce laws and reach all corners of the country with public services, it was still the 800-pound gorilla that could make or break economic fortunes. In modern Paraguay, the gorilla has slimmed down; it is not always obvious which way causality runs, whether through wealth-because-politics or politics-because-wealth. The state, though, remains captured in some areas by powerful constituencies. I was disappointed when I first arrived in Asunción to learn Uber (or any other peer-to-peer ridesharing service) was not available. My disappointment turned into irritation when I had no choice but to ride in local taxis; their stink of sweat, general lack of air conditioning, shoddy quality of vehicles that seem to disintegrate into a yellow dust every time they hit a pothole, and rip-off pricing schemes were a metaphor for the many state-protected services. Licenses to operate taxis are owned by politically connected individuals who wield significant power in the Asunción legislature. Taxi unions are also a powerful lobby, and they have the operational capacity to bring the city to a halt with their "yellow swarming" protests, blocking major intersections and making life miserable for commuters.

In spite of all this, and notwithstanding the Colorado dominance, the fact is incumbent candidates have been beaten in recent elections. By any measure, modern Paraguay is akin to U.S. political scientist Adam Przeworski's definition of democracy as "a system in which incumbents lose elections and leave office when the rules so dictate."[95] In the 2013 elections alone six out of sixteen candidates for departamento defeated the incumbent.[96] And within parties, incumbents have been beaten even more often. In the Colorado primaries of 2017, for example, the incumbent was a former finance minister of the sitting president, Horacio Cartes, who was riding a wave of sustained economic growth. In addition to the usual incumbent's prerogatives of being in power and abuse of the position during an election period (campaigning at government ribbon cutting ceremonies, etc.), Cartes's personal wealth meant he could have outspent any candidate. The contender was the son of Stroessner's private secretary and himself an avowed defender of Stroessner, whose main message was, "I am a true Colorado." After the contender's victory, political commentators were quick to proclaim the demise of "big money politics," but it could have been voters were nostalgic for the Stroessner years or perhaps they really wanted a "true Colorado" to run for office and not a technocratic carpetbagger. Regardless, another incumbent lost.

However, democracy also brought greater political stability. Although incumbents are transient, presidential tenure has been more stable since before or during the Stroessner dictatorship. According to a calculation by Amílcar Ferreira, from independence (1811) to Stroessner (1954), Paraguayan presidents lasted on average twenty-four months.[97] The numbers for the democracy period through the end of the Horacio Cartes term (2018) yield an average of forty-four months in office, almost double the historical average. While the average conceals the rocky years post–1989, it does reflect a more mature democracy. If in 1989 Paraguay's democracy was "in its diapers" as political satirist P.J. O'Rourke put it when he visited the country,[98] the modern version is akin to a teenager entering adulthood. As we will see next, the country's economy is quickly growing up.

III

An Emerging
Emerging Market?

I know an emerging market when I see it. To me this technical term, which I will define below, consists of bustling commercial streets where car repair shops exist side by side with produce stands, street food stalls, mom and pop groceries, semi-dilapidated stores, and shiny new commercial offices. If I close my eyes, I hear white industrial noise intercepted by honking. The traffic is thick with cars, mopeds, and pedestrians shuffling to find a clearance in the road. The air smells at times smoky, with breezes of decay and fried food. My three previous places of residence—Hanoi, Quito, and Asunción—are emerging. Less visible yet more significant for the economic emergence process are the quiet fields of soybeans and the methane-emanating cattle ranches. Together with the buzzing of barges moving goods down rivers to export markets, these elements are what make Paraguay an emerging market on the rise, even if the historical macro numbers tell a less dynamic story.

To celebrate Paraguay's bicentenary (1810–2010), two of the country's leading economists, Dionisio Borda and Fernando Masi, edited an economic history of Paraguay. In it they summarized 200 years of history with brilliant concision: Paraguay is "an economy based on the exploitation and export of natural resources, with unstable economic growth but stable macroeconomic indicators. It is an open economy with low productivity that features low government intervention and high poverty and inequality levels."[1] Likewise, Paraguay's economy has shown a number of structural continuities since colonial times. For example, economic historian José Cantero notes that there have always been two exports dominating Paraguay's history: yerba mate and cotton from Independence to the Triple Alliance War (1810–1870), wood and meat from the end of the War until the Federico Chaves administration (1870–1954), and cotton and soybeans during the Stroessner years (1954–1989).[2] Since the dawn of democracy, electricity has joined soybeans in dominating Paraguay's foreign sales.

Remarkably, Paraguay has been an island of macroeconomic stability, surrounded by spendthrift neighbors with a tendency to debase their currencies in order to cure financial hangovers. In more than seventy years Paraguay has not experienced the type of hyperinflation or financial debacles with sovereign debt defaults that characterized most of Latin America. Since adopting the Guaraní as the national currency in 1944, Paraguay has never changed the name or chopped-off zeros as other countries have done to hide past monetary misadventures. Cantero asserts the country's macroeconomic steadiness has to do with U.S. technical assistance in the early 1940s. In particular, Cantero attributes the success to renowned Belgian-American economist Robert Triffin, who helped Paraguay create its own currency, found the Central Bank, and implement legislation to create a modern banking system.[3] Triffin was at that time working for the U.S. Federal Reserve, and with other advisers (famed Argentine economist Raúl Prebisch also worked for two years as an advisor to the Central Bank) helped Paraguay design legislation that was in many ways ahead of its time, including flexible, non-arbitrary currency conversion, and a general harmonization with international financial standards.[4] Triffin's biggest triumph was to design a system that made it more difficult for politicians to be fiscally irresponsible by establishing a technical process to draft the budget and account for public spending. The reforms also brought a permanent IMF office ascribed to the Paraguayan Central Bank that served as a shadow monetary advisor.

More than seventy years after Triffin's reforms, the Central Bank and the Ministry of Finance are by far the most competent public offices, with the most qualified staff in the government. These two institutions have solidified what IMF researchers call "the Twin Anchors" of inflation targeting and fiscal responsibility.[5] Since 2011, the Paraguayan Central Bank has engaged in "inflation targeting" aimed at a 4 percent annual rate and has for the most part hit the target; the average for 2011–17 was 4.4 percent. Meanwhile, in 2015 the government approved a fiscal law that imposed a budget deficit ceiling of 1.5 percent of GDP. Like many laws in Paraguay the fiscal target is not set in stone, but it has been well enforced; the average budget for 2011–18 had a 0.9 percent deficit. As a result, Paraguay boasts one of the region's lowest debt-to-GDP burdens, amounting to an average of 12.8 percent for the 2007–2017 period. To top it all off, Paraguay has a safe cushion of international reserves, typically averaging 6–8 months of imports and enough to cover short-term debt payments.

Yet, look beyond the macro economy and the picture looks less fixed. Inside the Paraguayan economy there are major changes taking place, with new and innovative ways of trading, behavioral adaptations to new technologies, and industries leapfrogging from the nineteenth to the twenty-first century. Like the Paraguayan consulting firm MF Economía described it, Paraguay's population is transitioning from being "few, poor, rural and market-isolated" to "numerous, rich, urban and market-integrated."[6] Ask trade association members, corporate executives, Central Bank analysts, or workers in the service sector about the modern economy and what they describe sounds more like a foreign country than Borda and Masi's still accurate summary. In this context, researchers at the IADB believe that Paraguay "has the potential to be one of the emerging economies with the highest dynamism, within and outside of Latin America."[7]

In broad terms the modern Paraguayan economy does bring to mind the old French saying, plus ça change, plus c'est la même chose (the more things change, the more they stay the same). To a great extent, this seemingly stable picture is due not to stagnation but to a slow rate of change. Costa Rican economic advisor Roberto Artavia once likened Paraguay to a dinghy because it neither drowns nor picks up speed.[8] More technically, Paraguay resembles what *The Economist* magazine defined as an "emerging market," those that become so because, "they have grown quickly" but remain so, "because they have not managed to grow steadily."[9] Furthermore, the magazine added, an emerging market is "an economy that is not too rich, not too poor and not too closed to foreign capital."[10]

While all of the above suits Paraguay to a tee, the country still lacks deep and liquid financial markets. The country's stock market capitalization as percentage of GDP has been consistently under 4.5 percent in the two decades before 2019 (compared to Brazil's average of 48.6 percent in 2000–2016 or Argentina's 15.2 percent).[11] Still, the amount of funds the Asunción stock exchange manages has seen a steady growing trajectory. In 2019, the exchange was expected to reach a historic record of $1 billion, climbing from $50 million in 2006.[12] The planned opening of a new, bigger, and more modern stock exchange building illustrates the bullish mood among local stockbrokers.

But Paraguay's clearest sign of "emergingness" is its lack of an investment grade rating, which means investing in the country is considered to be speculative and subject to high risk. The rating agency Moody's gives Paraguay a Ba1 grade and Fitch a BB+, both one notch below "investment grade" rating, while Standard & Poor's is BB, two steps below "investment grade." The upside is a substantial potential for improvement and rapid growth as long as the government remains committed to fiscal responsibility. Bond markets so far believe the Paraguayan government has both the ability and willingness to pay its debts and can withstand external and domestic economic shocks. In 2013, Paraguay entered the global bond markets with a splash, earning the lowest rate ever recorded for a sovereign bond debut. The Paraguayan government has since continued to issue bonds with demand and interest rates similar to an investment-grade country; it has already issued sovereign external bonds with ten- to thirty-year maturities at rates below 6 percent. Likewise, rating agencies give Paraguay a positive outlook, fueling rumors among investors that an upgrade to "investment grade" is around the corner.

Dynamic, Above Average, and Volatile

From the end of the Stroessner dictatorship in 1989 to 2018, Paraguay's economy grew at an annual average rate of 3.5 percent. The rate is higher than the averages for Latin America and the Caribbean as well as emerging markets for the same period, albeit relatively low for the country's developmental needs. Indeed, the rate is not even close to the 6 to 9 percent average growth experienced by the "Asian Tigers" during their boom times. A good rule of thumb to calculate how long it will take output per person to double is to divide seventy by the growth rate. This "rule of seventy" lays bare the urgency of growth. For Paraguay, the 3.5 percent average growth rate that prevailed in 1989–2018 would double output per person every twenty years. This means by 2057 Paraguay's per capita income will reach Greece's circa 2016. Now if we apply the 5 percent average rate of the 2013–2018 period—as to reflect the more recent economy—output per Paraguayan would double every fourteen years. That is, Greece by 2045. Disturbingly, if Paraguay were to grow at Latin America and the Caribbean's puny 1.1 percent average rate of 2013–2018, output would only double in sixty-three years! Keeping in mind the witticism that predictions are hard, especially about the future, the IMF expects the Paraguayan economy to grow at a 4 percent average rate in 2019–2023 (slightly below the 1989–2018 rate).

As encouraging as the Paraguayan average growth looks, it hides a high volatility. Paraguay had one of Latin America's most volatile economic growth rates of this century's first two decades. For instance, the Paraguayan economic growth's graph in 2009–13 shows a rollercoaster worthy of Disneyworld. It sank -5.2 percent in 2009, bounced back to 11.5 percent in 2010, coasted at 2.9 percent in 2011, and shrank -2.5 percent in 2012 before another dizzying climb to 12.5 percent in 2013.[13] The period's average was a vibrant 3.8 percent, but it took courage and a barf bag to ride the coaster. In this way, Paraguay has behaved like a traditional emerging market, offering investors potentially higher returns but subject to higher volatility.

One significant source of volatility is also one of Paraguay's advantages: the economy is wide open to international trade, as measured by the "openess ratio" (the sum of exports and imports of goods and services as a share of GDP). According to 2016 data, 81 percent of Paraguayan GDP consists of exports and imports, a lot higher than the world's average of 56 percent and the Latin America and the Caribbean's 44 percent.[14] It means global conditions determine, for better or for worse, the fate of the Paraguayan economy. Indeed, Paraguay's high volatility makes sense given its reliance on two fickle sources of growth: commodity prices and weather. Specifically, soybeans and cattle plus electricity have powered Paraguay's exports recently, albeit with strong fluctuations. And these exports are not well diversified, with four countries (Brazil, Argentina, Chile, and Russia) dominating its export markets and also four countries dominating imports (China, Brazil, Argentina, and the United States). The IMF's Export Diversification Index shows Paraguayan exports in 1994–2014 became less diversified.[15]

However, Paraguay's economic growth does show positive signs of autonomy from its two large (and volatile) neighboring economies. Paraguayan economists call the latter "decoupling," which sounds slightly impious, but describes accurately Paraguay's recent economic trajectory. For obvious reasons, Brazil and Argentina's economic cycles have historically affected Paraguay's economic growth. Since the end of World War II in particular, Paraguay has danced to the Brazilian economy's tune, with its samba-like unpredictable swings. However, in 2012–18, Paraguay's economy has achieved a feat that would have been impossible by historical standards: it posted high growth rates in spite of Brazil and Argentina's recessions and meager growth rates. The good news does not stop there; the decoupling has what looks like sustainable foundations. According to Central Bank economist Humberto Colmán,[16] the decoupling is largely anchored by two domestic trends: (1) higher public and private investment in infrastructure and (2) higher foreign direct investment.

The country's vast and relatively new maritime infrastructure is another area where things remain the same (agricultural exports) but the means (modern ports and fluvial transport) are different. Paraguay's estimated 3,000 barges comprise the world's third largest fleet of barges behind the United States and China. Three-quarters of all the Paraguayan exports and imports move via rivers.[17] Along the country's two large rivers, the Paraguay and the Paraná, there are thirty-five grain terminals with many more under construction.[18] Many of these ports feature the type of infrastructure, technology, and machinery found in the top maritime exporting countries.

At the same time, economic agents behave differently than a decade ago thanks to new technologies and increased mobility. Start with internet use: in 2006, only 8 percent of Paraguayans used the internet, but by 2016 that number increased to 64 percent. However, the current number probably underestimates internet usage as 97 percent of Paraguayans own a cellphone.[19] I was surprised to see how many daily transactions take place via WhatsApp, the instant messaging mobile application owned by Facebook. Even though WhatsApp was only released in January 2009, Paraguayans use it with more dexterity and readiness than they drink tereré. WhatsApp usage is facilitated by extensive use of cellphones; they are ubiquitous, in the hands of everyone from the housekeeper to the taxi driver to the CEO, to the point where there are more cellular subscriptions than people.[20] Paraguayans use social media more than any other Latin American country, with over 80 percent of the population connected to social networks.[21] And yet, WhatsApp (or any other application) does not provide the type of payment services and multifunctionality available in other countries, such as for example, China's WeChat.[22] Moreover, Paraguayan companies are the second worst in the region when it comes to utilizing internet for business-to-business (B2B) transactions and among the bottom third for business-to-consumers (B2C).[23] In terms of mobility, Paraguayans own more motor vehicles than ever before. In 2006, only 39 percent of Paraguayans owned either a car or a motorcycle. In 2016, that number nearly doubled to 72.5 percent.[24] As someone who has dealt with Asunción's traffic on a daily basis, I can attest that higher vehicle ownership is not an absolute benefit. Even worse, the combination of cellphone use with vehicle steering so common in the streets of Asunción creates a whole range of extra challenges.

Solow Growth

To understand the Paraguayan economy and its prospects, it is useful to employ the "Solow" model, a theoretical tool named after the Economics Nobel Prize–winner Robert Solow. The model at its most basic level explains short-term economic growth based on three variables: labor, capital, and technology/ideas. For underdeveloped economies, the model counsels adding more inputs of these variables; the more the merrier, up to a point. The growth ceiling is reached due to capital's diminishing returns, which in basic terms means that a country might need one or two steel factories to grow, but not five. At some level, investing more capital becomes unproductive; no country grows by piling up capital on top of capital, and other variables eventually become necessary. A drive around Asunción or a longer exploration of the interior's infrastructure indicate an undersupply of capital goods, mainly in the form of roads, bridges, and industrial machinery. As a matter of fact, 6.3 percent of Paraguayan roads are paved.[25]

Floods are a common occurrence and mild rains are a socially-accepted excuse to miss a meeting or for students to skip school. According to the 2017 Global Competitiveness Report, Paraguay's road quality is more than lacking, ranking 136th out of 138 countries.[26] I cannot wait to drive from Asunción to Ciudad del Este once the ongoing expansion of the two-lane road becomes a four-lane highway. I bet exporters are excited too. Paraguay has South America's highest transportation costs, burdening exporters with almost 10 percent extra cost to the final value.[27] Coincidentally, during the pyrotechnic events of March 31, 2017, President Horacio Cartes inaugurated Asunción's first road-connector, a ceremony that in developed economies is led by the city's mayor or a junior officer in the Transportation Ministry. When I first arrived in Asunción, it used to take me forty-five minutes to drive to the airport from my house; now thanks to the road-connector the trip takes thirty minutes or less depending on traffic. Multiply those extra fifteen minutes by the thousands of daily users and the high rate of return becomes clear.

The good news is that under this scenario Paraguay's economic growth potential is significant. That is because, in Solow Model's terms, Paraguay is in the "catching up growth" stage, which predicts a faster rate than the "cutting edge growth" of developed economies. The "catching up growth's" oomph is provided by a higher rate of return to investments. Likewise, low-income countries do not need to reinvent the wheel—they can imitate, instead of innovate. In the case of the road connector, the rate of return would have been lower if Paraguayans had not been able to imitate this innovation and instead had to come up with a new way of solving the problem.

In the Solow Model's three-pronged growth formula, a country like Paraguay needs to increase: (1) the workforce and its skill level; (2) the amount of physical capital invested per worker; and (3) ideas/new technologies, also known as the "Solow residual." The increase in these variables does not need to happen simultaneously; sometimes one variable can do the growth heavy lifting. In this sense, a 2015 Ministry of Finance study[28] confirmed that capital has been the key variable explaining Paraguay's economic growth in the previous decade, while the other variables showed lackluster growth. For example, a joint Organization for Economic Co-operation and Development (OECD)–IADB report[29] revealed that Paraguayan labor productivity remains below the Latin American average.

The same OECD–IADB report had a silver lining for Paraguay. From 2000 to 2015, labor productivity in Paraguay grew at an average 3.7 percent rate, "mainly driven by total factor productivity (TFP)."[30] While it may sound like an obscure economic statistic, TFP is key to economic growth and overall prosperity. It is the indicator that can make the difference between slow-burning growth and booming Asian-tiger type of growth. TFP also equals the "Solow residual" because it is the variable unexplained by increased capital and labor. In simple terms, TFP is the effective use of labor and capital to get more output out of equal inputs. In simpler terms, it means more bang for the same buck. It also means economies can grow on the heels of TFP, even if capital and labor are stagnant; TFP can make or break a country's long-term growth prospects as labor and capital have distinctive ceilings to their expansions. Notably, TFP growth is technically unlimited, it does not have capital or labor's innate characteristics, such as decreasing returns or declining fertility rates, which can constrain growth rates. The TFP residual is also linked to intangible factors such as institutions or cultural factors such as how much we esteem bourgeois values.[31]

In the Paraguayan context, economic agents have strong incentives to invest in capital and neglect labor and TFP-boosting innovations. From the Solow Model, we can see how more and better machinery and infrastructure can go a long way in Paraguay's current development level. Sure enough, according to a 2017 World Bank survey, the percentage of firms buying fixed assets (e.g., machinery, equipment, land, buildings) in Paraguay (48.2 percent) is above the world's (41.3 percent) and Latin America and the Caribbean's (44.5 percent) levels.[32] In addition, a young and growing labor force coupled with a large informal sector pushes employers to invest in capital. It does not help that employers have to pay one of the region's highest minimum wages, calculated as a percentage of per capita income. So if it becomes profitable for an employer to hire a worker "under the table" his/her incentives to invest in education/training are lower than if he/she had a formal labor contract. As of 2017, only one out of ten Paraguayan formal firms considered poorly educated workers as a constraint to their operations, according to the same World Bank survey.[33] As low productivity-workers in rural areas are substituted by machines, they are pushed to urban areas, where they pull down the productivity average for other industries.[34] This generous flow of new workers further decreases the employers' incentives to invest in existing labor. And without contract or otherwise expected labor stability, employees have a similar incentive to move on to better paying jobs as soon as they open up.

Still, the benefits of capital investment do have a limit. Although an IADB report claimed 64 percent of Paraguayan workers are in occupations with high risk of automation, the Artificial Intelligence (AI) revolution is not anywhere close.[35] At least in Paraguay, hiring humans with all the administrative and financial costs involved remains cost-effective compared to substituting with robots. Nonetheless, in a preview of a future AI transition, the agriculture sector has shown Paraguay is unprepared to deal with anything close to a major disruption of its labor market. In spite of more than thirty years of steady mechanization of agricultural production, rural workers continue struggling to reinsert themselves in the labor market. Most of those workers substituted for machines are left with few options but to move to urban areas and find employment in the informal sector.

Paraguay's capital dependency does not bode well for the economy's long-term prospects because of capital's decreasing returns. Paraguayans should know this as they already experienced a capital-fueled boom and bust period not long ago in the 1970s and early 1980s. Under the Solow Model's "catching up" phase, it is common for countries to go through a short-lived economic miracle—or high-growth spurt—before they settle on a more stable trajectory; normally the miracle's economic foundations are transient either due to unique international circumstances or a domestic one-time demand shock. Alas, the problem is the miracle does not last long and countries go back to low growth. In the case of Paraguay, the miracle already happened once thanks to the construction of the huge Itaipú hydroelectric dam (1971–84), which poured billions in hard currency into an economy estimated at $3.3 billion in 1971.[36] The dam-triggered economic boom was a reflection of Paraguay's undeveloped economy. The economy was so pastoral that the simple demand shock of dam construction fueled seven years of high economic growth and employment. Before the construction there were twenty-two family-owned construction companies and by the time it finished the number expanded to 250 companies, including large corporations.[37] Although the Itaipú growth was widespread, it was particularly beneficial to politically connected construction companies. The boom created a new caste of millionaires called "Itaipú Barons" that would later deliver two of Paraguay's presidents. As expected, once the construction ended, the Paraguayan economy regressed to low economic growth.

Paraguay's less than stellar economic performance in the past fifty years is clearly visible when seen through the prism of economic convergence. Not only the Solow Model but also the dismal science at large predict economic convergence[38]; poor countries' incomes tend to converge towards rich countries, albeit slowly. Paraguay in particular has been slowly but steadily converging only in the past decade; the years before 2006 were lost convergence time. If we measure convergence as a percentage of U.S. per capita income,[39] we see that Paraguay's was stuck at 6 percent between 1960 and 2006. When measured for 1960–2016, we see a familiar macro trend: stagnation through 2006, some progress afterwards, with the rate increasing from 6 to 8 percent. However, the picture looks better if we compare Paraguay with the average income of Argentina, Brazil, and Uruguay taken together: in the 1960–2016 period, Paraguay's per capita income jumped from 21 to 34 percent.

Freedom's Just Another Word for Nothing Else to Measure

There is no shortage of indexes measuring how hard it is for an individual to engage in commerce within and outside any national border; the breadth of measurements include economic freedom, ease of doing business, and overall openness to investment and entrepreneurship. They all stem from Peruvian economist Hernando de Soto's brilliant idea from the early 1980s to calculate how long it took to legally open a business in Perú's capital Lima (it took 289 days). Later on, World Bank economists increased the number of indicators and added some technical sophistication to create the "Doing Business Report." Soon, the World Economic Forum's brought its "Global Competitiveness Report," which includes more than one hundred variables organized under twelve pillars of macro and microeconomic competitiveness. These indexes joined two other existing indexes focused on economic freedom, the Canadian Fraser Institute's "Economic Freedom of the World" and the joint Heritage Foundation–*Wall Street Journal*'s "Index of Economic Freedom." The basic premise is that law-abiding entrepreneurship is an unalloyed positive good that governments should promote instead of constrain. Economists can get technically fussy when trying to draw too many conclusions about whether more economic freedom or constraints to businesses are the sure shot to economic prosperity. Still, by and large those countries that have the most economic freedom are the richest and those that put a lot of barriers are the poorest.

Overall, Paraguay does not do well in these reports, typically scoring in the lower third of global rankings and either close to or slightly above the Latin America and the Caribbean (poor) average. Paraguay gets good grades for its macroeconomic stability, tax burden, and labor market flexibility. On the other hand, what all the indexes and surveys criticize about Paraguay's economic legal regime are the lack of strong institutions, its fundamentally flawed judicial system, lack of transparency in transactions involving land, and the labor force's limited skillset. These obstacles add hard to quantify transaction costs to all businesses operating in the country; they can prevent business formation, daily operations, and the smooth cessation of activities.

The problem in Paraguay is that around half of all businesses operate with complete freedom because they do not pay taxes or follow regulations. Paraguay is notable for being both a low tax-rate and high tax-evasion country. For example, Paraguay's Value Added Tax (VAT) is 10 percent, one of the lowest rates in the region. Yet, around a third of Paraguayans evade the VAT.[40] Two exasperated academics noted, "[Paraguayans] famously avoid taxes wherever and whenever possible."[41] As a former employer of a housekeeper I was surprised to find the onus for paying taxes is on the employer, who must go through the bureaucratic hoops in order to comply with the law. In most countries, the state by default takes its share from taxpayers, who must then appeal if they believe their tax burden should be lower. Similarly, when the country introduced an income tax, it did so with the goal of formalizing businesses, instead of using it as a tool to raise more funds. Companies can basically claim almost any expense and deduct its income tax expenses. Moreover, it created a cottage industry for accountants and a backwards incentive system that favors spending over saving. The Ministry of Finance estimated that only half of those registered to pay income tax actually did so and that bigger companies paid less than smaller companies.[42]

Economics models largely predict countries with low tax rates will feature high compliance rates. Conversely, if tax rates are set so high it becomes unprofitable for companies to operate, economic agents will either go underground or adopt idiosyncratic legal structures to pay less in taxes. There are two types of countries that are an exception to the taxation level–compliance relation: countries with competent and frugal governments and Paraguay. In fact, that is the average taxpayer's most common complaint—the government is neither frugal nor provides quality public services. And worse of all, tax monies tend to end up being fodder for graft or misuse.

As a result, Paraguay is a dual economy, with highly productive sectors competing in global markets and low productivity sectors confined to the local informal economy. It resembles the national flag, with its different reverse and obverse designs. As we will explore in the next chapter, there is a mismatch between legal and regulatory mandates and the ways businesses operate in reality. This mismatch adds extra obstacles to formal businesses that are not obvious to a casual reader of economic reports. For Paraguayan formal sector firms, the informal sector is one of their two biggest operation constraints (the other one is corruption).[43]

To formal firms, Paraguay offers a number of important legal incentives. The country's triple 10 tax rate (VAT, Personal Income, and Corporate are all set at 10 percent) lures foreign investors, particularly overtaxed Brazilians, Argentinians, and Uruguayans (where tax rates can be double or triple that amount). It also guarantees full repatriation of capital and profits, offers zero tax on machinery imports, and gives companies investing more than $100 million a stable tax rate for twenty years. In this vein, an undeclared yet relevant benefit for local and foreign investors alike is the weakness of the country's labor unions. For many reasons that have to do with the country's historical political structure and economic foundations, unions have not been able to acquire enough leverage to impose better working conditions. As a result, companies do not think twice when hiring and firing employees; neither do they have a heavy fiscal burden to comply with union demands. In Paraguay, collective bargaining remains a foreign practice equivalent to playing cricket.

Another significant incentive is the maquila regime that started taking shape in 1997. Maquilas are private businesses that can import duty-free products to be assembled into manufactured goods for re-exportation. Developing countries like Paraguay promote maquilas as a source of labor-intensive industries and foreign technology transfer. While these maquila operations can be located in any part of the country or industry, they have mostly settled in eastern Paraguay to serve the Brazilian market. Nonetheless, many companies still settle for locations close to Asunción where they have a bigger pool of qualified labor. In 2017, Reuters estimated that of the 126 foreign manufacturers with operations in Paraguay, four-fifths were Brazilian.[44] Maquila operations are champion exporters; according to an IADB report, between 2012 and 2016 they doubled from $150 to $300 million. Almost half of maquila sales are auto parts, with the other half divided between apparel and plastics.[45]

In spite of the maquila success story, foreign direct investment (FDI) in Paraguay has been underwhelming. Paraguay's FDI annual average for the twenty years between 1997 and 2017 only reached 1.5 percent of GDP, less than half the Latin American average for the same period. Even the amount of remittances Paraguayans sent back every year for the same period was larger at 2 percent of GDP. Also, Paraguay's FDI number is low compared to the Asian Tigers during their boom years; Singapore, a country many Paraguayan policy makers wish to emulate, averaged 9.1 percent of GDP for the 1976–1996 period. As the case of Singapore illustrates, a small domestic market like Paraguay's does not need to be a constraint for FDI. Instead what prevents greater FDI in Paraguay is its weak linkages to the global economy as well as a poor road and river infrastructure to move goods in and out of the country. Paraguay has been stuck for a long time with Argentina's and Brazil's protectionist policies through the Mercosur agreement; because countries cannot negotiate bilateral trade agreements without the consent of the other members, Paraguay has not been able to open new markets and attract greater FDI. The Mercosur–European Union trade agreement, key for Paraguay's economic and commercial needs, has gone on for more than twenty years of negotiations without reaching a final agreement. In addition, Brazil and Argentina put numerous trade and non-trade barriers on Paraguayan goods and services within Mercosur so foreign investors struggle to reach those big markets from Paraguay. And based on what international organizations, rating agencies, and local economic analysts repeat over and over again, foreign investors are discouraged by Paraguay's judicial system. There is truth in it, except for the immeasurable caveat that many economic development success stories featured high FDI hand-in-hand with questionable judicial practices.

The lack of stronger FDI prevents Paraguayans from accessing products and services of higher quality and at lower prices. First, it prevents the transfer of knowledge on best practices and corporate knowhow. Secondly, it allows local firms to operate with reduced competition pressures and thus reduced incentives to innovate. In turn, the Paraguayan non-tradable sector—the industries and businesses that are not in competition with foreign trade—employ inefficient practices and technologies for far too long, burdening the rest of the economy as a result. Ernst Bergen, the former finance minister quoted in Chapter II, pointed to an inefficient non-tradable sector when he explained, "We have no foreign investors in our country, so our domestic businesses can get away with being mediocre, sluggish, and lazy."[46]

Another hard to measure feature of the Paraguayan economy is that the government does not try its luck at industrial policies. Unlike most Latin American countries, Paraguay has a long history of unambitious government when it comes to economic development. There are few state-owned enterprises[47] and little export/import controls or trade regulations aimed at steering resources to specific industries. And what little industrial policy exists rarely goes well. For example, Paraguay's infrastructure development is hindered by one of the country's few active industrial policies. The cement industry's main player is the state-owned enterprise National Industry of Cement (Industria Nacional de Cemento, INC), which suffers from inefficiencies and overemployment due to the political constraints to its operations. In addition, Paraguayan law does not allow companies that produce cement locally to import clinker—cement's main input. As a result, there are constant cement shortages with their corresponding price hikes. Many construction companies are forced to suspend operations for extended periods of time before the supply and its price level are able to meet the local demand. Per capita cement consumption in Paraguay at under 440 pounds a year is low by regional levels, at par with Guatemala, El Salvador, and Honduras per capita use.[48] And there is also ANDE, the National Electricity Administration, featuring similar problems of political mismanagement, as we will discuss in Chapter VII.

The Emerging Reality

American researchers visiting Asunción around the middle of the twentieth century described the city as "rustic, run down, and poor"[49] and "[filled with] cockroaches, heat, and incredible amounts of dust."[50] Hunter S. Thompson described the city in the early 1960s as "boiling hot, painfully dull, twice as expensive as Rio de Janeiro."[51] Modern Asunción could not be more different than its 1960s self. Furthermore, it has changed significantly compared to its state in the 1990s and early 2000s. When Paraguayans or foreigners alike who visited or lived in Asunción some years ago and came back recently were asked their impressions, they all agree the capital is a different place. The amount of construction, new buildings, shopping malls, hotels, and road traffic shocks all returnees. Longtime residents of Asunción find the city's skyline unrecognizable from the low rise view they grew up with. Keep in mind that the skyline has remained largely unchanged for the previous hundred years. Last time I checked there were over twenty tall buildings overlooking la Costanera, the city's waterfront, with several construction cranes dotting the fast-changing landscape. According to developers, the skyline will continue to evolve as the demand for office towers and condos aimed at "young professionals" and the emerging middle class will remain robust for at least a decade. Some of the new towers, with English names like "Jade Park" or "Eminent," resemble buildings with Miamiesque appeal seen in other Latin American capitals. Corporate real estate is also growing. In addition to its existing Asunción location, the World Trade Centers (WTC) Association is building a second Paraguayan WTC complex in Ciudad del Este and plans a third one in the southern city of Encarnación. The real estate giant Century 21 is currently expanding operations to Ciudad del Este as well.

The steady expansion of Asunción is creating a whole range of problems too. One does not have to be an urban planning expert to see the city is not fully prepared to cope with rapid growth. Having lived and traveled widely in Asia I found Asunción's demographic density to be ridiculously low. There are no high-density areas to speak of, except for the shanty town abutting the city's waterfront. The city feels like a big suburb overrun with people and cars; cobblestones still blanket many streets and you can hit the random lapacho tree standing in the middle of a road. According to an IADB report, the larger metropolitan area of Asunción covers 312 square miles and houses three million residents, which based on their calculations is less than half the minimum required to be sustainable.[52] The main trouble with low density is connectivity and provision of services. During rush hour, traffic comes to a halt when the few city arteries originally designed for horse carriages burst with Paraguay's favorite automobiles: pick-up

Bay of Asunción with skyline in the back, circa 2019 (courtesy Oscar Rivet).

trucks and SUVs. Whenever I drove my car and heard on National Public Radio (NPR) that the U.S. infrastructure was "crumbling" I had to contain my laughter in order to avoid one of Asunción's numerous lunar craters locals call potholes. The metropolitan area fails at providing services due mostly to a political problem of borders; the city proper and its surrounding suburbs are independent entities and have a hard time coordinating efforts to improve and build public services. With half a million inhabitants and around 150,000 taxpayers, Asunción is overpowered from Monday to Friday with 2 million people from the suburbs. Furthermore, as separate entities, Asunción and its suburbs do not raise the necessary funding for large-scale public infrastructure. For instance, 94 percent of the city's sewage is not treated and heads straight to rivers and waterbeds.[53] This lack of basic public infrastructure is most evident when the Paraguay river surges following sustained rains and Asunción's "flood refugees" migrate from their dwellings in the low-lying areas near the river to improvised shacks on sidewalks and squares around downtown. During a particularly bad rainy season in late 2018, around 6,000 people had to flee their residences in Asunción alone; because school buildings were affected, the sight of children and dogs swimming in water teeming with sewage and garbage became a daily occurrence.

These "flood refugees" point to another challenge that Paraguay struggles with. In spite of robust economic growth, around a quarter of

The two faces of modern Asunción (courtesy *Última Hora*).

population lives in poverty, based on official estimates.[54] According to the international poverty line, which measures the share of individuals living on less than $5.50 per day (using 2011 purchasing power parity dollars), the number for Paraguay was slightly below 2 percent.[55] At any rate, two trends are clearly visible when it comes to poverty: a steady reduction since the dawn of the twenty-first century and a reduction slow-down starting around 2016. Because Paraguay still has a large rural population (around 40 percent), the large slums characteristic of some Latin American, African or Asian metropoles are not widespread in Asunción. Nonetheless, many challenges remain, even though they seem buried in rural poverty. For example, in the Paraguayan rural areas almost half the population living in extreme poverty are children under fourteen years of age.[56]

Something I heard repeatedly among those that study Paraguayan poverty is that when it comes to the economic and social data, Paraguay is a Central American country. Indeed, it has a young population (around 60 percent is under thirty years of age), a large rural population, low income from taxation, persistent poverty rates, low rates of educational attainment, and high frequency and duration of public service disruptions. Furthermore, Paraguay's key Central American feature is high economic and social inequality. Although the rising economic tide has lifted all Paraguayan boats, the lifting has been uneven; that is, the economy as a whole has grown more than its people's average per capita income. Measured by the

Gini coefficient, which ranges from 0 (full equality) to 100 (full inequality), Paraguay is one of Latin America's most unequal countries, with a score of 47.9. According to the United Nation Development Program (UNDP)'s inequality-adjusted Human Development Index for 2017, which combines the Gini coefficient with other health, education, and income data (where 1 is full equality and 0 full inequality), Paraguay scores 0.522. And what is the average for Central America not including Costa Rica (a long-standing outlier in terms of social indicators)? It, too, is 0.522.

Economic inequality is reflected in a domestic market dominated by a few corporate groups with operations in the main industries and ownership of the leading media companies (newspapers, web portals, radio and TV stations). Three groups in particular—Cartes, Vierci, and Zucolillo—vie for the title of commercial *mburuvicha* (leader). Based on the cacophonous editorials in their newspapers, it seems they truly dislike each other and compete amongst themselves without engaging in anti-competitive practices or otherwise setting up oligopolic schemes to benefit at the expense of consumers. These groups are also some of the country's main taxpayers. Except for former president Cartes's group, the other two do not engage in party politics, despite their strong opinions about the government's actions.

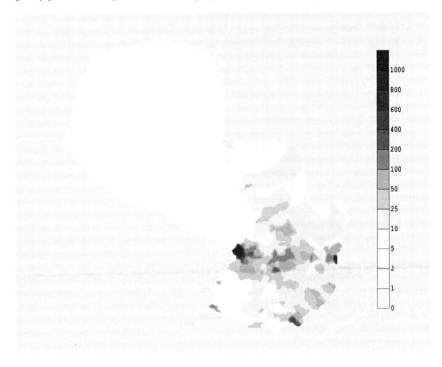

Paraguay's population density (Giorgiogp2, Wikimedia Commons).

These economic groups all had their start during the Stroessner years, when familial links or cozy relationships with apparatchiks were crucial to career ambitions. Likewise, as we will see in the next chapter, either due to legal loopholes or lack of law enforcement, these entrepreneurs thrived on trade arbitrage operations with Brazil and Argentina that would not be considered acceptable under modern trade rules. Interestingly, these conditions and the general regulatory regime existed in equal terms for other members of Asunción's small economic elite. However, unlike other entrepreneurs with fleeting success, none of the groups' founders held senior government jobs during the Stronismo. One of them, Aldo Zucolillo, founded a newspaper that was critical of Stroessner and was subsequently shut down by the regime. These economic groups also benefited from their parents' and immigrant families' economic success and access to capital. Notably, the groups' dominant position emerged after the end of the Stroessner regime with the general liberalization process brought about by democracy.[57] More than anything, they were able to navigate the changing political and economic circumstances for a sustained period of three decades during which many other economic groups failed. Thanks to their knowledge of local conditions they were also able to beat large foreign conglomerates that came to dominate in other Latin American countries. The result is that those looking to invest in the industries they control must either deal with them or compete against them. It also means there is plenty of room for disruptive innovations.

Not surprisingly, according to a Latinobarómetro report from 2018,[58] just 16 percent of Paraguayans agreed with the statement "income distribution is fair." Similarly, when asked about their economic wellbeing Paraguayans were unimpressed with the state of the economy. The same report showed less than half of Paraguayans expected their economic situation will improve in the following year and listed unemployment as the country's biggest problem, notwithstanding the country's macroeconomic dynamism. In a different 2016 survey, almost two thirds of Paraguayans thought the economy had worsened in the previous twelve months[59] in spite of a brisk 4.3 percent economic growth rate. These views are reflected at the ground-level too, where my anecdotal data based on conversations with regular Paraguayans reveal a pessimistic view of the economy, typically stemming from living paycheck to paycheck.

Whatever economic problems Paraguayans may have or gloomy assessment of their economic welfare, their emotional wellbeing seems to be unaffected. Paraguay has led the world in Gallup's Global Emotions report (a.k.a. "Happiest Country in the World") from 2015 to 2018, with a score of positive emotions well above the global average.[60] Although happiness surveys should be taken with more than a grain of salt, Paraguay's consistency atop Gallup's survey indicates a certain resilience to a bad economic situation, perceived or real. I saw this emotional disposition every day when the most common answer I got when I asked Paraguayans "mba'eteko pio" (how are you doing?) was "tranquilopa" (everything is chill). The Israeli historian and best-selling author Yuval Harari could have been describing Paraguay when he noted that "People with strong families who live in tight-knit and supportive communities are significantly happier than people whose families are dysfunctional and who have never found (or never sought) a community to be part of."[61] Maybe Paraguayans' sunny dispositions are a cultural coping mechanism that gives a positive spin to a negative reality. Regardless, the result is not despair or resignation to reality.

A Tale of Three Tobatís

The town of Tobatí holds a special place for social scientists interested in Paraguay. It was in Tobatí where American researchers Elman and Helen Service carried out the first rigorous study of Paraguay for an academic audience; their study was published in 1954 in book form as *Tobatí: Paraguayan Town*. The Services chose Tobatí as a quintessential Paraguayan town, a sort of Springfield, U.S.A., where they could draw conclusions relevant to the country at large. They came in 1948 to a country still reeling from a bloody civil war but that had nonetheless remained intact in terms of economic and social structures. Indeed, the civil war, like previous political revolts, was largely restricted to Asunción and surroundings; the great majority of rural towns like Tobatí were politically and economically isolated from the capital's dramas.

Following in the Services' footsteps came another American academic, James Eston Hay, who in 1988 carried out another rigorous study in Tobatí that in 1993 became his Ph.D. dissertation, "Tobatí: Tradition and Change in a Paraguayan Town." Hay was a Paraguay veteran who had spent seven years working for Peace Corps in Asunción before he moved to Tobatí to work on his dissertation. Taken together, these two studies depict a different Paraguay, one that was living in the Middle Ages when the Services were there and barely entering the twentieth century when Hay visited. Yet there are still some important characteristics that help understand modern Paraguay.

Seventy years after the Services and thirty after Hay, I decided to head to Tobatí and see with my own eyes what they so thoroughly described. The purpose of my trip was not to match their research agenda and carry out a similar deep dive into the town's anthropological profile, but to understand the broad economic changes that have shaped modern Tobatí and shed light on the country's general progress. Unlike the Services and Hay, there was no need to dwell in Tobatí for an extended period of time as almost all the economic, social, and demographic data[62] that they had to unearth going door to door are available in digital form.

Tobatí is located forty-four miles east of Asunción and nestled in a scenic region of rolling hills and ancient rock formations. The city was founded in 1539 upon a hill also named Tobatí as a shield against Indigenous groups trying to attack Asunción. Tobatí reminds me in many ways of the place where I grew up in rural Uruguay, with its slow pace of life (including the sacred siesta time) small-town cordiality, and general feeling that the world's problems are far, far away. These traits have not changed at all since the Services' trip. When I first visited, I walked in unannounced to the city government's building and was welcomed by the cultural affairs director, who spent a generous amount of time describing the town's history, politics, and economy. Likewise, Tobatí remains safe in a way most Latin American cities are not; houses are not guarded with walls and window bars, bicycles are left unlocked, children walk around unaccompanied by adults, and police presence is barely noticeable. The church at the center of town was open for any visitor to explore, with three men working on the scaffolding as the only informal sentinels.

However, changes are all around. To begin with, it only took me two hours by car to get to Tobatí from Asunción. When the Services and Hay traveled to Tobatí, the main road connecting the town to the outside world was not paved and required a significantly longer journey. In 1948, the Services hopped on a truck and described a "terrain so difficult that the inexperienced passenger hangs on with both hands, watching the route ahead, hoping to anticipate the next jolt."[63] That same road was paved in 2000. Local residents still remember when a heavy rain would flood the road and people had to roll up their pants and walk in the water to get into and out of town.

In terms of telecommunications, the changes could not be starker. There were no telephones in Tobatí in the time of the Services, only a telegraph they described as "unreliable." When Hay was there, he characterized landline telephones as "a privilege reserved for the well-to-do."[64] International calls required a half-hour wait. In contrast, in modern Tobatí cellphones are everywhere, and every little service is offered and can be accessed through WhatsApp. In a random walk down Tobatí, I saw all kinds of locals clutching at their phones: teenagers texting and checking social networks, men tracking soccer news, and older ladies catching up with their (typically large) extended families. While in Tobatí I was even able to have a video call with my mother-in-law who lives in Oregon without a glitch. Granted, Tobateño men may still prefer a half-hour wait before their suegra calls.

The population has grown significantly since the Services counted each one of the 1,368 Tobateños, even though it still has the feel of a small town. Forty years later, during Hay's stay there were over 9,000 residents and currently there are around 30,000 people. At current rates there will be another 5,000 residents by 2023. The larger population together with better access to regional markets deepened the town's division of labor, which as Adam Smith explained is limited by the extent of the market. In 1948 Tobatí resembled Smith-era's highlands of Scotland, where "every farmer must be butcher, baker, and brewer, for his own family."[65] According to the Services' household census, there were twenty-six different occupations practiced by men and seventeen by women.[66] In general terms, the labor force consisted of "store owners, a few cattlemen, purveyors of various services, politicians, petty manufacturers, and wageworkers."[67] Subsistence agriculture dominated, with few links to price-based markets, local or regional. Farmers did not use fertilizer, insecticides, or rotate crops based on yield productivity; oxcart was the most indispensable kind of farm transport. In other words, the division of labor was not deep. By 1989 Hay found 104 occupations, including traditional occupations such as cowboys, prostitutes, or herbal healers, but also communications workers and architects. Hay observed how the bricks and ceramics industry had become the main industry, supporting a growing service-sector and wage-earning population. In particular, Hay identified a larger manufacturing base that originated in the Itaipú dam's demand for value-added products and services. For example, the need to build houses for the dam's workers was a boon for Tobatí's ceramic industry. And though the industry was hurt by the post-dam economic slowdown, it did not disappear and rather was able to resume operations once the economy returned to a growth path. Indeed, the bricks and ceramics industry is the main economic force in modern Tobatí, employing nearly 7,000 workers in 1,600 brick and 260 ceramic enterprises.[68] The city government estimates the industry employs around 80 percent of the local labor force. Although highly mechanized, manual brick making is still practiced, typically involving whole families and their children. Upon entering Tobatí, a visitor can observe brick making factories everywhere, surrounding the downtown area with mostly small-sized operations. The industry not only provides material for the national economy but also exports to Brazil and Argentina.

Greater economic dynamism has brought improved services. While in 1948 Tobateños drank and utilized water from nearby rivers and creeks that women carried in large ceramic jars on top of their heads, by the time Hay lived in Tobatí, water flowed directly to every house via internal plumbing.

At present, almost no house in the town lacks water. There was no electricity in 1948, and though locals had to wait until 1973 for the first connection to the grid, in 1988 electricity reached only one in four rural households. Modern Tobatí households have an almost universal coverage of electricity. Still, the greater coverage has not translated into better provision; as we will see in Chapter VI, electricity provision remains a national challenge. Similarly, in 1948 Tobatí there were no trained doctors[69] and only one hospital of unknown capabilities served the whole town. The Services noted a prevalence of goiter due to a diet low on iodine that was seemingly under treated. The most common death causes were gunshot and knife wounds, pulmonary diseases (tuberculosis, pneumonia, bronchitis), and syphilis.[70] Most of these diseases were treated with herbs. Hay reported there was a "health center" where one medical doctor worked during weekday afternoons and a couple of private clinics where the same doctor served better-off Tobateños. Modern Tobatí is served by two medical clinics offering the full gamut of services, though most people go to the large, public, and neglected hospital in nearby Caacupé. Just like in Asunción, in Tobatí the supply of pharmacies seemed to be larger than the market's needs, a fact that may be explained by the rise of local pharmacy chains with better logistics and capacity to achieve economies of scale.

When the Services landed in Tobatí there were "two small hotels."[71] The house where the Services lived "had plenty of windows, though no glass." They called it an "upper class style of living."[72] Like a good Peace Corps volunteer, Hay did not put much thought into his abode's features or the available lodgings in town, but it would be safe to assume other homes were not that different from what the Services found, except for the lack of glass in windows. American political scientist Paul Lewis in his book *Paraguay Under Stroessner* described the average Paraguayan house circa 1972 as follows: "[It] had only two rooms, mud floors, no running water or electricity, no inside toilet, and no system of sewage disposal."[73] Nowadays, almost every house in town has brick walls and roof tiles. Until it recently shut down, the main hotel in town was not different from a mid-priced hotel in California, with a large pool, manicured lawn, and professional staff and modern yet quaint facilities. When I visited the hotel, uniform-clad waiters served a pretty good lunch with a menu offering as many options as in Asunción. Although I did not stay the night, TripAdvisor's 3.5 score (out of 5) seemed accurate.

On the whole, Tobatí, like the country at large, has changed for the better when seen from a long-term perspective. The type of changes in economic structure, services available, and overall well-being of its people are remarkable, even if they have come along too gradually. The Services were not bullish on Paraguay, for good reasons indeed; they concluded, "We view the immediate future of Paraguay with profound pessimism."[74] Hay's forecast was sunnier; to him, "There are opportunities for each individual, which were undreamed of fifty years ago, and there are undoubtedly unsuspected opportunities which will be revealed as the country changes even further."[75] I second Hay's prognosis, notwithstanding his fondness for the prefix "un." Modern Tobatí faces diverse challenges, but their urgency are several degrees below what the isolated Services' Tobatí faced, trapped in subsistence agriculture with little prospects of change. Even under a scenario of less than stellar economic growth, the town's links to regional markets and capacity to absorb new technologies ensure at least a steady path to middle-class status for most of its citizens. Whatever the circumstances, Tobateños will adapt. After all, they are like the rest of Paraguayans and know how to master the country's way of doing business.

IV

Paraguay's Way
of Doing Business

One of my first visits in Asunción was to Mercado Cuatro, a chaotic market located in the heart of the city. At Mercado Cuatro, a customer can find anything under the Paraguayan sun: fruits and vegetables, counterfeit products of all stripes, and food stalls with tasty sopa paraguaya.[1] Every time I asked a Paraguayan about buying a random item (a traditional dress for my daughter, a battery for my 110–220 v transformer, a hammock, etc.) the answer was always the same, "Have you tried Mercado Cuatro?" They remind me of Walter Sobchak—the endearing psychopath of the Coen brothers' movie *The Big Lebowski* (1998)—when he dismisses a grisly proof-of-life from a kidnapper as easily faked by saying, "I can get you a toe by 3 o'clock this afternoon, with nail polish." Similarly, the sprawling hurly-burly of the market is a symbol of Paraguay's way of doing business: half legal, half informal, with lots of ingenuity channeled both to good and to shady purposes. It is also a sort of protest against the insufficiencies of life after too many bad governments. Paraguayans seem to be saying to the world that, in spite of the distances between themselves and the rest of the world, they can get whatever they want from global markets by 3 o'clock this afternoon.

With similar haste but at a steady pace, the Paraguayan state has been reformed since the end of the Alfredo Stroessner dictatorship. To use academic terms, it started as a traditional "predatory state"[2] built upon "extractive institutions"[3] where a small minority connected to Stroessner controlled state resources. It then moved to the post–Stroessner "rent-seeking"[4] state where a larger group of people gave away favors and access to businesses. In plain language, these terms describe economic manipulation by a few at the expense of the majority in various degrees. Finally, it arrived at the current state where those vices of economic manipulation are tamed but still ingrained in the way Paraguayans do business.

Asunción's Mercado Cuatro, where world trade meets Paraguayan ingenuity (courtesy Oscar Rivet).

The resulting institutional reality features a mix of traditional market-based transactions under national and international laws coupled with three native mechanisms: trade arbitrage, corruption, and informality. These three mechanisms are supported by a judicial system that applies the rule of law unevenly, generally favoring politically connected individuals, grants unequal access to justice based on socio-economic circumstances, and fosters impunity. The Paraguayan way of doing business has side effects; as we will see below, they involve mostly guns and drugs.

Trade Arbitrator

Paraguayans have a propensity, as Adam Smith might have said of them, "to truck, barter, and exchange one thing for another."[5] Nowhere is this propensity more evident than in Ciudad del Este (CDE), Paraguay's second largest city. It benefits from a strategic location on top of where Argentina's leg kicks Brazil's underbelly. CDE bloomed after the construction of the first road connecting Asunción to Brazil in over 400 years since the Paraguayan capital's founding. First paved in the 1960s with U.S. government funding, this road is now expanding to four lanes and will more efficiently connect the two largest urban areas in the country. CDE is a roaring city of almost 300,000 inhabitants and a melting pot of nationalities, as some of the consulates indicate: France, Germany, Mexico, Peru, Slovakia, Syria, Taiwan, and Turkey. Asuncenos look down on the scrappy CDE, like Quiteños disparage Guayaquil or Hanoians condescend to Ho Chi Minh City. Old capitals are traditional, conservative, and less open to innovation than trade-oriented, unplanned urban agglomerations such as CDE.

CDE's previous name—"Puerto Presidente Stroessner" (President Stroessner's Port)—is telling; the city was supposed to be an orderly trading center, a signal to locals and visitors about who was in charge. It was so disconnected from the country's economic routes that a subtropical Berlin airlift had to be implemented to bring food and other basic supplies when it was first inaugurated. Obviously, things turned out differently, as entrepreneurs from near and far disembarked in CDE lured by the sweet smell of profits. The new CDE residents were mostly Israel Kirzner–type[6] entrepreneurs. These species—let's call them Kirznerios—have a special sensitivity to unexploited opportunities and thrive under conditions of economic uncertainty. In simple terms, Kirznerios' profits derive from good old trade arbitrage: buy low on this side of the river, sell high on the other side of the river.

So what are Kirznerios exactly arbitrating in CDE? Argentine and

The Friendship Bridge, linking Paraguay and Brazil, was inaugurated in 1965 and spurred Ciudad del Este's growth from sleepy hamlet to Paraguay's second biggest city (Ekem, Wikimedia Commons).

Ciudad del Este means (shopping) business (courtesy Alfonso Velázquez).

A Kirznerio in his natural habitat of Ciudad del Este.

Brazilian consumers are avid shoppers but do not like paying high prices. Paraguay steps in and offers them a way out: we will import cheap consumer goods from the global bazaar free of your high taxes and byzantine regulations and will make them available to you where the Iguazú and Paraná rivers converge. I call this the Tri Deal. Kirznerios take the Tri Deal and make a splash like the Iguazú Falls after a rainy month.

Although the Tri Deal originated with Brazil and Argentina's misguided import substitution policies during the 1960s–70s, it currently consists of two regulatory components. The first legal component is Paraguay's exemptions to the Mercosur Common External Tariff (CET). Although the CET averages 11.5 percent, some items are taxed at a 35 percent rate. Circa 2019, Paraguay was exempting 649 items from the CET, which means in practice the average import tariff was 3.4 percent,[7] with many items entering Paraguay at a 0 percent rate. Legal component number two is the high value-added taxes (VAT) in Brazil and Argentina. It is simple math: Paraguay's VAT is 10 percent, Argentina's 21 percent, and Brazil's average is 17 to 20 percent (Brazil boasts one of world's most byzantine tax systems; only Kirznerios know the real rates). Consider the iPhone 7's price differential: circa 2017 it cost on average over $1,100 in Brazil whereas you could get one for less than $800 in CDE.

In the case of Paraguay–Brazil trade, the system works *legally* as follows: Brazilians are allowed to import from Paraguay $300 of duty-free purchases plus $200 extra at a lower tariff. At the same time, Paraguay allows imports either tariff-free or at low rates intended for "re-exportation" through a law called "régimen de turismo" (tourism pass). Multiply a daily $300 by thousands of traders every week and you are talking about real money. And real goods too. Several major cities in Brazil have their own street markets packed with CDE-imported goods and widely known as "Paraguayan markets." In addition, there is a large *illegal* trade that reaches the far corners of Argentina and Uruguay through the same process but without the pesky legal hoops of the Brazilian trade. Informal economy expert Robert Neuwirth estimated in 2011 that the informal trade in CDE alone was worth $2.5 billion a year, amounting to more than 15 percent of Paraguay's total economic activity.[8] CDE is one of the key reasons why close to a third of Paraguay's exports are re-exports.[9]

It is highly probable that without the Tri Deal, CDE's economic fortunes would take a big hit. The only way the Tri Deal would stop making economic sense is if Argentina and Brazil ever get serious about Mercosur integration. Seriousness in this case would take three basic reforms: (1) implementing a Schengen-type agreement under which internal border checks are abolished; (2) establishing a low and truly "common" external tariff; and (3) harmonizing VATs at a low rate. Under this scenario, some

CDE entrepreneurs might move to the border with Bolivia and found "Ciudad del Oeste" (West City) to keep their business model. In any case, both formal trade and contraband would be a whole lot less profitable without the Tri Deal. And needless to say, none of the above reforms will happen anytime soon. Neither Brazil's nor Argentina's government have the political will and domestic support to make Mercosur more like the European Union.

But do not get the wrong impression. The Tri Deal's economic dynamism has made CDE the center of an expanding maquila industry and the country's soybean boom. Brazilian businesses are increasingly lured to the city's location and its lower labor and production costs. A headline from the British newspaper *Financial Times* summed up CDE's evolution, stating, "Former 'contraband capital' gets down to business."[10] Both national and local governments are taking steps to formalize and bring the city's underground economy into the bright light of taxes and regulation. For example, the World Bank's 2017 Doing Business Report praised Paraguay for introducing a single window for exporting and thus reducing the time for border and documentary compliance.[11]

Paraguayans of course love a deal every bit as much as their Brazilian and Argentinian neighbors. There is a counterpart to CDE on the Argentine border with Paraguay called Clorinda, a city of less than 50,000 inhabitants located in the province of Formosa. Just a short drive from Asunción, Clorinda serves as a small scale CDE for Paraguayans looking to buy gas, shampoo, sugar, and other random products that happen to be significantly cheaper on the Argentine side. Although the estimated bilateral trade is small compared to the Tri Deal, Kirznerios also thrive in Clorinda as trade arbitrators. Called "ants" for their micro-trade operations, Kirznerios in Clorinda closely monitor the Argentine peso–Paraguayan guaraní exchange rate and seek profits accordingly on either side of the border.

In addition, throughout the country a few shipping companies have made shopping in the United States (via online retailers such as Amazon, eBay, etc.) available to all Paraguayans. If you live in Paraguay you can shop online like any other U.S. resident, ship your purchases to a U.S.-based postal box, and then have the company (for a small fee) bring them to the country. Since the government does not limit these purchases, Paraguayans are now free to buy low and sell high anywhere they can find a gap to fill with their homegrown arbitrage.

Corruption Rules

Year after year, Paraguay reaches the Latin American naughty summit in Transparency International's (TI) annual Corruption Perceptions

Index and sits in the global bottom third. According to a Paraguay-specific TI survey,[12] between a third and half of Paraguayans pay bribes. The situation has gotten so bad that even the watchdogs themselves are pulling up stakes. In a bit of head-spinning irony, TI couldn't adapt its local operation to the Paraguayan way of doing business and closed its country office in 2009.

To be sure, corruption isn't Paraguay's problem alone. According to the most up-to-date research, more than half of the world's population is located in countries facing corruption.[13] Corruption, in many cases, illustrates the "tragedy of the commons," a situation where a bad collective outcome is reached through the aggregation of individual decisions, any one of which is neither good nor bad. In the original story, as conceived by the nineteenth century British economist William Forster Lloyd, the problem arises when cattle herders decide to bring more and more cows to land shared among the larger community. Although the decision makes economic sense for each herder, it creates a problem of over-use at the general level if they all make the same choice. Corruption, in Paraguay and everywhere else, also starts with an individual making a rational decision to pay a bribe and results in a larger problem when thousands of individuals engage in the same practice. Once these actions become the norm, they metastasize to the whole body politic.

However, the individual bribe does not take place in a vacuum. Corruption is also a problem of macro incentives, which create what anti-corruption guru Ray Fisman calls a "[bad] social equilibrium."[14] Or as the Nobel laureate in economics Douglass North put it, "[I]f the institutional framework rewards piracy then piratical organizations will come into existence; and if the institutional framework rewards productive activities then organizations—firms—will come into existence to engage in productive activities."[15] We can see this framework in action when looking at Venezuela and Chile, two countries which had similar per-capita incomes and economies dominated by a single commodity (oil in the case of Venezuela, copper in the case of Chile) yet extremely different corruption levels. Since the advent of the late Hugo Chávez, the Venezuelan government pushed the private sector out of a number of activities (running hotels, distributing toilet paper, etc.), the state-owned oil company Petróleos de Venezuela (PDVSA) became an arm of the presidency, and massive regulations were implemented to control the private sector. Meanwhile, Chile's public sector remained both smaller and more constrained than Venezuela's. Just as important, public institutions such as the judicial branch kept their independence in Chile, while they lost it in Venezuela. In sum, institutions became a whole lot more piratical in Venezuela. Predictably, TI shows Venezuela's corruption perception ranking sinking from 77 in 1998 to 166 in

2016, and Chile dropping four spots in the upper reaches from 20 in 1998 to 24 in 2016.

Likewise, corruption in Paraguay became a destructive social equilibrium through many years of building piratical organizations. For most of its history, Paraguay's political regimes served as government "of the elites, for the elites, and by the elites." Paraguayan politicians saw the state as booty to be taken and divided among supporters. Worse, under President Alfredo Stroessner, it became a government "of the faction, for the faction, and by the faction." Increased rent-seeking opportunities stemming from a growing economy found the perfect match in Stroessner's Colorado Party and entrenched corruption practices to the present day. His piratical ways had the sorry consequence of imbuing all public sector interactions with a culture of corruption. As we have seen, the transition to democracy in Paraguay did not constitute a full break with the past but rather an adjustment to democratic rules. As a result, the majority of the people grew accustomed to disregarding the law and conducting business according to the established (corrupt) norms. Ernst Bergen, the first and only Mennonite to serve as the country's finance minister (2005–07), recalled how he found a double accounting system within the ministry, a practice that Bergen noted "was very common in Paraguay then."[16]

In modern Paraguay, the usual incentives for large-scale corruption, such as multiple exchange rates, price controls, trade licenses, import quotas, and government discretionary power to expropriate private property are not prevalent anymore. Big-money corruption in Paraguay thrives via favoritism in government contracts and public procurement processes and in a myriad of micro-transactions involving politicians, public employees, and the court system. For example, according to a 2015 academic investigation, a common corruption practice is the "exceptional" purchase mechanism for government procurement. By labeling it "exceptional," parties can bypass legally required minimum standards of transparency and competition. The authors found the practice "is used much more frequently than what should be expected from international best practices."[17] Additionally, companies can avoid transparency and competition clauses by engaging in transactions below the amount that triggers them.

Corruption afflicts traders and bureaucrats, of course, but it turns up in non-traditional settings as well. For example, a famous study analyzed the data on parking violations by diplomats accredited in New York City.[18] These individuals face the same temptation to skip out on fines, since they all operate under the same diplomatic immunity when their cars were parked illegally. All that set them apart from one another was their specific social norms. The paper's finding was as convincing as it was intuitive: "Diplomats from high corruption countries […] have significantly more parking violations, and these differences persist over time."[19] In other words, there is a strong positive correlation between a diplomat's behavior in New York City and her country's ranking in TI's corruption index. As expected, Paraguay came in at number 49 out of 146 countries, with number 1 being the worst offender and 146 the most conscientious.

But why did Singapore, another expanding economy ruled by a small faction, during Stroessner's reign, not experience similar levels of corruption? Although Singapore's founding father Lee Kuan Yew had the same incentives as Stroessner to create piratical institutions, he did not. It is hard to tell why institutions diverged at certain times. Take a few development economists to happy hour and ask about the "Asian Tigers" and you will quickly ascertain that there's no consensus; maybe the best we can say is Singapore got lucky in the leadership lottery. Nonetheless, it is clear that once a certain social equilibrium is established (good or bad), changing it becomes difficult. Consider U.S. president Gerald Ford's efforts to switch the American customary units to a metric-based system. For seven years after its passage in 1975 until its abolition in 1982, the Metric Conversion Act was completely disregarded by the American people. In spite of the United States' strong attachment to the rule of law, the social equilibrium born of centuries of inches, yards, and miles proved immune to change. Likewise, Paraguay's current social equilibrium allowing corruption to take place will not simply disappear with the passage of sound legislation.

Yet, social norms change and bad equilibriums can be reversed. Take the small town of Atyrá, located twenty-seven miles from Asunción. When I first visited and saw its squeaky-clean colonial-era buildings and cobblestone streets, I was impressed. I had come on the recommendation of my Guaraní teacher, who described Atyrá as "a sight to behold." For a long time, the town was known as a source of manure-tainted grass.[20] But starting in the 1990s a new mayor implemented an active campaign to clean up the city and, most importantly, to keep it clean. The mayor's efforts touched a nerve and Atyrá's 20,000 inhabitants are proud to call it "Paraguay's cleanest city." Remarkably, the city has earned international prizes and is considered a culture within a culture. Just as crucial, even though the mayor did not come from a traditional party and went on to lose his reelection, the traditional politicians that came next embraced the new reality.

Similarly, Paraguayans are able to embrace developed-world cultural norms just as well. Nothing in the culinary history of Paraguay or legacy of social inequality would have predicted a behavior I witnessed in both Asunción and in the small town of Coronel Oviedo. In a country where the economic rules are messy, roads are a free-for-all, and regulations are mostly honored in the breach, fast-food customers stand in orderly line, clear their tables, and take their trays to the trash can after eating at McDonald's. How did Paraguayans seamlessly adopt a social norm originated in the American Midwest? Hard to tell; there lies the difficulty and the hope for positive social change. The McDonald's example shows culture is not forever fixed and people everywhere discard pernicious beliefs when faced with the right incentives, normally in the form of direct costs.

Unfortunately, when pressed about the country's corruption, Paraguayans of all stripes fall back to a metaphysical cultural concept, expressed in Guaraní as "peicha nte" (anyway works/that's the way it is and there's nothing we can do about it). This cultural fatalism fills the gap when explanations fall outside the realm of empirical evidence. The peicha nte factor is also a sign the social equilibrium is set in place in its most problematic phase, when incentives are aligned in such a way individuals are indifferent to what the rules denote as right and wrong.

Paradoxically, Paraguayan corruption does not slap you in the face. A 2017 TI survey[21] found that 23 percent of Paraguayans paid a bribe in the previous year, a relatively low number compared to Latin America's worst offenders Mexico (51 percent) and Dominican Republic (46 percent). Unlike in other high-corruption countries, Paraguayans neither have to bribe doctors to get medical attention, nor pay schoolteachers extra to educate their kids, nor swat away the upturned hand of traffic police. It is hard to notice the extent of Paraguay's corruption in everyday life. In general, Paraguayans regularly engage in a subtle form of influence peddling; it usually involves somebody calling her buddy from school, who now works in a government office, to speed up a bureaucratic process. Frederic Hicks, a U.S. anthropologist, painted a picture in 1971 that remains spot-on today: "[In Paraguay] it is considered a friendly gesture, if not actually an obligation of friendship, to grant to friends, and of course to relatives also, what favors one can by virtue of one's position, knowledge, or skills. It is assumed that the favor will be returned should an appropriate occasion present itself."[22] A leading Paraguayan intellectual and vocal campaigner against corruption told me a typical story: when he found out a police report had mistaken his identity (the document included an armed robbery at age one) he too fell in the trap. In order to amend the document, his three options consisted of (1) pay a $100 bribe on the spot; (2) sue the government and endure around a decade-long wait for the judicial system to resolve the matter; or (3) contact his high-school friend who was at the time a Supreme Court judge. Option 3 carried the day and so his paperwork was fixed in no time. All corruption practices considered; it is hard to gauge to what extent the public's perception correlates with actual corruption. And here lies the Paraguayan paradox: corruption is at once central and almost imperceptible.

The good news is that increased scrutiny over corrupt practices is having the hoped-for effects. In the recent past, there has been a rush toward transparency legislation unseen in the country's history, with laws providing for access to public information, disclosure of public sector salaries, and channels to whistle-blow corruption practices. Also, the government has instituted several reforms to make all state procurement and public administration processes more fair and transparent. These laws are so momentous and so unlike previous administrations that President Horacio Cartes hailed them as his government's main accomplishment during his participation at the 2017 World Economic Forum in Davos, Switzerland.

Looking forward, Paraguay has two advantages: (1) as countries pass middle-income levels, corruption tends to decrease; and (2) countries with a free press are more effective at bringing corruption practices down. In addition, the social and international pressure to keep reform momentum remains high. As the "Lava Jato"[23] (Car Wash) corruption trials in Brazil show, sometimes anti-corruption efforts come out of nowhere and can quickly snowball. Paraguay has already instituted basic legislation and public institutions, though it needs to move ahead with second-generation reforms and follow through with prosecutions. For example, the new legislation established transparency and anti-corruption offices as administrative units under the President's Office, which consequently lack the necessary autonomy.

Informal Is Normal

"¿Con o sin factura?" (With or without receipt?) is the usual question at Paraguayan businesses, one that prompts customers to participate in a potential tax avoidance scheme. If the customer declines the receipt, the business may or may not keep the sale off the books. Because the practice is so common and so many other transactions go undisclosed, measuring informality with accuracy is difficult. It would be far easier if it were all formalized data. Still, different research institutions have developed neat formulas to gauge informality, and they all reach sizeable proportions. The non-governmental organization (NGO) Pro Desarrollo Paraguay estimated that since 2010 the informal economy has hovered around 40 percent of GDP, meaning nearly half of the Paraguayan economic pie consists of under-the-table transactions. Based on their 2018 report, the informal economy amounted to $16.5 billion.[24] Researchers Michael Pisani and Fernando Ovandoy, working for the local think tank CADEP, took various measures of informality and constructed a weighted average, which yielded a 65.4 percent of informality.[25] An IMF report by Leandro Medina and Friedrich Schneider calculated that the Paraguayan "shadow" economy

averaged 34.4 percent of GDP in 1991–2015.[26] In terms of employment,
the picture is equally worrisome. According to the government's statistics office, in 2017, 65.2 percent of the non-agricultural workers toiled in
the informal sector.[27] A World Bank report calculated that labor employed
in the informal economy constituted 60 to 71 percent of national employment.[28] As a result, many millions of dollars go untaxed and a few million
workers are employed without full legal protections. The majority of informal workers are low-income and have few options available to join the formal sector. According to an IMF paper, "[In Paraguay] the average salary of
an informal worker is still around 40 percent below that of a formal worker,
after controlling for individual characteristics including education, age,
experience, and gender."[29]

Although Paraguayans are not unique by developing-world standards
in testing legal boundaries when doing business, their habit is both customary and far-reaching. A normal routine for personal or business matters
involves one legal transaction, the next one not so much, and the following
goes under the table. Let me illustrate: one day I needed a haircut and so I
went to a barbershop a friend had recommended. Alas, it took me a long
time to find the place, as it did not have a sign, barber's pole, or any familiar marker. Once I found the unassuming house, I saw its inside had most
of the trappings of a haircutting business: a waiting area, a barber's chair,
gossipy magazines, etc. Chatting with the barber I learned he had legal per-
mission to operate the business, but lacked another one to put the sign up.
Apparently, the man got tired of going to City Hall and having to submit
to one window after another. "No tengo plata para perder tiempo (I cannot afford to waste time)," he declared and proceeded to trim my sideburns.
Later that day I drove home and stopped at a red light; informal vendors
offered me juicy tangerines for a low price, so I got a bunch. Once at home,
I ordered pizza online from a U.S.-based corporation and thirty minutes
later the delivery guy arrived; I paid him, got my receipt, and ended the day
on a satisfying note of legal compliance.

The data reflect this modus operandi. According to the World Bank's
2020 Doing Business Report, Paraguay ranked 125 (out of 190) in the Ease
of Doing Business table.[30] Specifically, the report calculated it costs 121 days
and 14 procedures for entrepreneurs such as my barber to deal with construction permits.

Informality is also a solution to the problem of the state's failure to
put in place sound regulations. The same World Bank report shows it takes
378 hours a year and 20 different payments to comply with Paraguay's tax
regime. The 2017 numbers are not much different than the 2006 numbers;
back then it took 328 hours and 33 payments to comply. In turn, Paraguayans have not paid much in taxes and do not currently pay much tax. A line

attributed to Benjamin Franklin proclaims, "In this world nothing can be said to be certain, except death and taxes." Old Ben can be forgiven for not knowing about Paraguay, where only death is certain. The old cri de cœur from the American Revolution, "taxation without representation" has been reversed in Paraguay to "representation without taxation."

And why would Paraguayans not pay their fair share of taxes? This question brings us to government spending. Looking back in history, the Paraguayan government has not made much progress in terms of public services and infrastructure. Instead, public largesse has been employed at best to buy or return political favors and to promote partisan loyalty. Taxpayers in Paraguay face a conundrum: they can pay existing rates and receive low quality public services in return, hoping eventually government's effectiveness will improve, or they can avoid paying taxes and expect no improvement in services. For a long time, the Paraguayan government was not even able to collect taxes. However, it has started to do a better job of securing more funds with the same rates; tax income has grown considerably, going from 6 percent of GDP in 1990 to 18 percent in 2015.[31] Although Congress passed a law in 2013 that limits government annual spending to 1.5 percent of GDP, the problem remains mostly one of quality spending, not quantity.

Likewise, public policies have supported the type of crony capitalism that defined Paraguay for much of its history. Nowhere is this behavior clearer than at the customs agency, which for most of the past sixty years has served as a prize for individuals with political connections.[32] Paraguayan customs bears most of the burden for keeping contraband out, and, as expected, it fails miserably. Certainly, as the 1920s Prohibition Era in the United States and Paraguay's own Mercado Cuatro demonstrate, no matter the institutions or state capabilities, the law of supply and demand always wins. And so Paraguayan customs officials have played the trade arbitrage + corruption + informality game like no one else. They have facilitated the emergence and continue to grease the wheels of Paraguay's vibrant informal economy. The Washington, D.C.–based organization Global Financial Integrity estimates that more than a fifth of all imports in Paraguay are under-invoiced.[33] A typical trick involves importing high-tariff women's perfume and registering it as a lower tariff good, say, industrial paint. Once again, buy low, sell high. Some customs officers even managed to create import companies, register them with family members, and operate for years with large profits and few legal hurdles. Customs officials' behavior is conspicuous wherever you look. For example, when you browse the local newspaper *ABC Digital's* section "¿De dónde sacó la plata? (How did he/she make his/her money?)"[34] you find it is full of newly rich customs officers who managed to acquire properties worth several times their modest annual incomes. Many of them are active in social media, posting pictures of new cars, houses, or golf classes on Facebook.

Informality also responds to unwarranted legal burdens. Paraguay—like most countries with civil law regimes—must bear the additional cost of dealing with public notaries. In the World Bank's 2019 "Doing Business Report" on Paraguay there were twenty-two entries when I searched "notary" in the list of requirements to start a business.[35] Unlike in common law countries, in Paraguay public notaries must stamp or sign most legal transactions, working as an unnecessary tax and extracting undue rents from economic agents without adding any actual value. Public notaries not only have incentives to be rent-seekers but are also at the center of most corruption cases involving economic transactions both in the public and private sectors. In Paraguay they give a legalistic patina to what in practice it is called "la patria contratista," networks of favoritism intended to exploit personal connections and insider knowledge in business operations. Thus, an informal transaction in Paraguay has the considerable blessing of avoiding public notaries.

The Paraguayan state also fosters informality every time it neglects to regulate or formalize existing markets. Take for example parking in Asunción. All drivers in the city want a "free" parking space readily available whenever they hit the streets. When the parking space does not materialize, Asuncenos get mad, but they fail to see the real problem. If you listen to the drivers complaining on the radio, read their Facebook venting, or watch their viral videos, the enemy is usually the "cuidacoches," the informal workers who pop up everywhere to help drivers find a space and "watch" over their cars whenever the supply of parking does not meet demand. The economic disconnect normally happens when there is a sporting event, a concert, or in most areas of downtown Asunción. To be sure, cuidacoches tend to offer lousy customer care and many times are in cahoots with car thieves. However, they respond to a basic government failure to allow the market to allocate limited resources. The way countries with low informality have tackled the cuidacoches problem is by putting a monetary price to parking, usually via the introduction of parking meters.

As a basic rule, trade takes place when people engage in a mutually beneficial exchange. Unless both parties benefit, no exchange takes place. Sometimes the mutual benefits are so compelling that people are willing to engage in illegal trades. To what extent this willingness stems from an acquired behavior based on economic incentives or a general failure to abide by the rule of law remains less clear. For instance, trade arbitration at the borders would be smaller if the economic incentives were significantly lower and Paraguayans had a less casual approach to formal rules. The widespread informal trade in Paraguay is also explained by the state's failure to formalize informal practices. Government officials, usually under pressure from (formal) business corporations, go after informal traders instead of creating a level playing field where everybody can supply the products and services Paraguayans demand. But then, why should Paraguayans abide by misguided rules that benefit a few and prevent the least favored from bettering their condition?

Unruly Law

Paraguay's trade arbitrage, corruption, and informality are enabled by the country's weak rule of law. Judges, public prosecutors, and administrative staff operate a legal system that is unable to provide equal protection, bends to favor political forces, and suffers from low credibility. Informal rules also permeate the system and hamper the country's judicial independence.[36] Auspiciously, the rule of law has made progress in the last decade; from access to information to case assignments, the current judicial apparatus appears to be fairer, if less efficient when compared with the past. What positive elements exist in the Paraguayan rule of law come from recent reform efforts, though the reality remains highly problematic.

The González Macchi case illustrates many of Paraguay's rule-of-law pitfalls. During the Stroessner years and the early democracy period, around 50 percent of cars in Paraguay entered illegally from Brazil. Thieves would pick cars up in Brazil, bring them to Paraguay, and re-register them as legally traded vehicles. Needless to say, people with solid political connections were actively taking part in this business. It got so bad it reached President Luis González Macchi (1999–2003), who oversaw the purchase of an armor-plated BMW stolen in Brazil. In 2002, Congress voted to begin an impeachment process against President Macchi and the stolen BMW was one of the accusations. Many legislators who raised their hands to impeach the president either owned stolen cars or facilitated their registration for family members. As had been the case throughout Paraguayan history, justice was applied arbitrarily with the aim of punishing political foes. It did not matter that there were solid legal grounds for prosecuting González Macchi; in this case the judicial system served as a tool for political forces.

Indeed, there is a great disconnect between the legal framework (as laid out in the laws) and how it operates in practice that is central to understanding Paraguay's rule of law problems. Judicial experts refer to it as the gap between de jure and de facto judicial independence.[37] In simple terms, the proof of the Paraguayan legal pudding is entirely in the eating. While the 1992 Constitution and the current legislation are in line with international standards of justice and human rights, Paraguay's actual application of laws lags behind the times. With almost perfect consistency, every time I asked a Paraguayan about a specific law, the answer came back, "But that is not how it actually works." There is a deep cultural trait that makes Paraguayans engage in legal deception, regardless of political regime or circumstances. It reminds me of former prime minister of Russia Viktor Chernomyrdin's definition of a similar trait: "Whatever organization we try to create, it always ends up looking like the Communist Party."[38]

There are many legal clauses that illustrate the wide gap between the spirit and the letter of the laws afflicting Paraguay, and how Paraguayans end up recreating their own Communist Party. For instance, the rule of law too often fails in Paraguay under the rubric "justice delayed is justice denied." To start off, there is on average a two-and-a-half-year delay between investigation initiation and trial. And once a trial gets started it can go on and on until it is dropped. According to Paraguayan law, if a legal case does not have a sentence after four years the judge must drop the charges against the accused under the so-called "prescription clause." Once the four-year clock starts to tick, lawyers and defendants set in motion all manner of legal chicanery in order to delay procedures and eventually reach prescription (statute of limitations). The prescription clause is there to resolve a case within a reasonable length of time, but in reality serves to deny justice. A reasonable fix would be to pass a law to limit legal chicaneries, but that law already exists.[39] In case you are wondering what happened to the case against former President González Macchi, it expired in 2003 and the charges were dropped.

This case illustrates another key negative feature of Paraguayan rule of law: impunity for politicians and senior government officers. As the 2016 U.S. Department of State Human Rights Report put it, "Although indictments and convictions for corruption of low- and mid-level public officials occur with regularity, high-ranking public officials enjoy a high degree of impunity. Sometimes such officials are forced to resign or are indicted, but formal complaints rarely lead to convictions."[40] Despite the Paraguayan press's daily denunciations of corrupt politicians and government officials, few make it to court. It seems as though corruption cases enter a judicial Bermuda Triangle of legal chicaneries and either get lost under the radar or are mishandled. Like people living in cold-weather areas have many expressions for "snow," Paraguayans have many expressions for legal chicaneries. For example, *cajonear* (hold it up in the back of a drawer), *poner en el freezer* (put on ice), *embarrar la cancha* (throw in a red herring), *recurso dilatorio* (dilatory action), *ñembotavy* (to play dumb to avoid responsibility), or *oparei* (to let a judicial case fizzle out with no legal consequences for those involved).

The data on Paraguay's judicial sector is generally scant[41]; data on convictions, judge turnovers or legal rulings are hard to access. In 2018, USAID hired a veteran Paraguayan lawyer to look into high-profile corruption cases between 2009 and 2017 and what he found out was disturbing. Even with the Supreme Court's institutional support, the team of investigators was only able to find 56 of the 127 cases targeted for review. And "find" here means locating the actual physical files as the court has no electronic case management system or digital storage system for court records and cases. The USAID report confirmed what every high-powered suspect knows: unless you have a lawyer who can pull the right strings or has direct access to the judge responsible for the case, your litigation strategy will be severely constrained. The available data paints a straightforward picture: rule of law in Paraguay has significant problems, both in terms of the provision of and access to justice. For example, the Heritage Foundation's Index of Economic Freedom places Paraguay in the middle, with a ranking out of 80/180 countries and a designation as a "moderately free" economy. Once you disaggregate the data, you see Paraguay's lowest score comes from the "Judicial Effectiveness" category. The report warns that "cases languish for years in the court system without resolution, and offenses often go unpunished due to political influence."[42] Similarly, the World Bank's Worldwide Governance Indicators[43] give Paraguay a percentile ranking of twenty-eight (out of one hundred) in the rule of law category, based on 2015 data.[44] Although the ranking underscores Paraguay's weak rule of law, it is an improvement over the 2005 rank, which was fifteen. Nonetheless, both rankings put Paraguay well below the Latin American and Caribbean average.

At its most basic, the rule of law should follow Lady Justice's key attributes: blindness and balance. Paraguayans frequently catch her peeking out of her blindfold or putting her thumb in the scale. These problems start from the outset, when Paraguayan politicians sometimes meddle in, sometimes outright dictate, who becomes a judge and who is allowed to remain on the bench. The current selection framework stems from the 1994 "Governability Pact" among the major political parties, which was supposed to be a "democratization" of the judicial branch. The reform made sense at the time; the goal was to clean house by getting rid of Stroessner appointees at the Supreme Court and other key positions. Political parties agreed to institute a political quota system for the Council of Magistrates and the Jury for the Prosecution of Magistrates, two eight-member organs responsible for selecting Supreme Court members, judges, prosecutors, and public defenders, and for reviewing judges and prosecutors' performances, and dismissing them if necessary. The Pact did democratize the process, but unfortunately only served to spread old power dynamics under which politically connected individuals exercise veto power. Although only three of the eight members in each organ are strictly "political" (one for the executive branch and two for the legislative), political loyalty trumps merit in the selection and punishment of magistrates. In turn, judicial appointments become a matter of political loyalty instead of skills and experience, and political calculus carries down to judicial verdicts. As a result, the system does not punish bad behavior whenever the accused holds political leverage. Judges skew legal cases and their verdicts in favor of prevailing political power structures and away from any reasonable application of the law. For example, political influence makes prosecutors and judges employ legal chicanery to pursue legal cases, both to favor insiders and to protect their own job stability. As a Paraguayan lawyer told me, "Prosecutors have more threats to lose their jobs than their lives." Although current law has clear punishments for chicaneros, undue political influence prevents their application. What's more, political influence over the judicial system results in a lack of a legitimate arbiter of last resort. Given that both the arbiters and the legal processes are tainted by political shenanigans, there is great legal uncertainty about what is right and what is wrong.

There is nothing intrinsically bad with having politicians have a say about judicial appointments. In countries that score well on governance rankings, the political filter is a critical part of the judicial branch's selection of personnel. Ultimately, however, this filter is either removed or constrained enough to allow judges, once installed on the bench, to interpret the law and not follow party orders. In Paraguay, the political filter never disappears, even if at times it seems to be in hibernation.

There is a slight technical distinction that explains the Paraguayan situation: the difference between rule *of* law and rule *by* law. The former prescribes essentially that no person is above the law of the land. Instead, for most of the country's history, Paraguayan political leaders at all levels (from the president down to the district chief), applied a type of rule *by* law, "la ley del mbareté" (law of the powerful). In other words, laws emanated out of the barrel of a gun. Although different governments had constitutions and legal frameworks in place, de facto legal authority came from holding exclusive political power. As a result, there were no legal loopholes because someone in possession of authority could interpret ad-hoc the law of the land. As the sharp-witted Paraguayan author Helio Vera put it, "The law [in Paraguay] is a rule that only applies to foreigners, the inattentive, and the enemy."[45] The laws were also arbitrary; who bore the legal brunt depended on obscure calculations based on standing in the political hierarchy.

By some measures, Paraguay is currently in the midst of a transition from rule *by* law to rule *of* law. While the trajectory is still open-ended, it has been bending slightly towards justice. For example, the 2017 Index of Digital Access to Judicial Information[46] placed Paraguay among the region's top three countries, with a score higher than thirty-one Latin American and Caribbean countries. Even better, Paraguay advanced thirteen positions in relation to the first index published in 2004.[47] Without a doubt, the rule of law consists of more than a user-friendly website, but the index shows Paraguayan justice is making some progress. Significantly, there is now a white-collar crimes unit in the attorney general's office; legal payments (fees, compensation, bail, etc.) are processed through an electronic payment system (instead of handing cash to judicial staff, as was done in the past); trial cases are assigned to judges randomly via an electronic system to prevent "judge shopping"; and there are audits in place to assess judicial administrative management and improve productivity.

Most importantly, the political tectonic plates seem to be shifting towards less corruption, at least the idiosyncratic type. The 2017 release of secretly taped audio recordings laid bare the corruption in the judiciary; in the recordings, politicians apply undue influence over judges and prosecutors to gain both political and economic favors. The resulting public outrage triggered what might become an overhaul of the judiciary. The exposure of public corruption and its corresponding impact on politicians' electoral calculus is exactly what normally pushes governments to change their ways. As locals say, "jahechata (we will see)."

For the moment, impunity, cronyism, and inefficiency remain and have bred a cynicism about the legal process that undermines its sanctity and further limits access to justice. The oft repeated phrase among Paraguayans, "Las leyes se acatan pero no se cumplen (laws are acknowledged but not followed)," reflects this cynicism. More importantly, if justice is not delivered equally, independently, and in a timely fashion, why would anybody go to court at all? A 2017 Latinobarómetro poll reflected this mood: 75 percent of Paraguayan respondents distrusted the judicial system.[48]

Alas, there are probably disappointments ahead for the trusting 25 percent if they decide to pursue justice through formal channels. The 2017 Global Impunity Index, which measures impunity across three dimensions—security, justice, and human rights—ranked Paraguay as the eleventh worst country in the whole world.[49] The index analyzed Paraguay's security and justice systems and their capacity to protect human rights and found them lacking in their structural and existing capacity. For all its problems, the Paraguayan judicial system does not fail to send people to prison. Quite the opposite; when it comes to minor crimes and suspects of limited economic means, the Paraguayan legal system implacably sends people to jail. In the 2008–2018 period, the inmate population grew from 5,867 to 14,630.[50] In general, for a low-income woman who speaks mostly Guaraní, lives in a rural area, and is not a member of a political party, the chances of a fair hearing and eventual trial are the lowest.[51] To begin with, those who cannot afford a lawyer face significant challenges, as the Ministry of Public Defense does not always provide competent defense attorneys, and when it does they are overworked with some managing 500 cases per year. Depending on the person's place of residence, there might or might not be a court nearby; there might not even be a state presence at all in the vicinity. Finally, the court official might not speak Guaraní or might otherwise lack the expertise to handle the case (e.g., ensuring that seeking recourse in cases of domestic violence does not endanger the victim). To further complicate matters, once an individual has been detained and accused of a crime, there is little certainty about the trial's length, unless the accused can produce a skilled lawyer to hold back the process for four years. Civil cases on child support or alimony payments last over a year for those without access to legal services. Thankfully, Paraguay is a relatively low-crime country, with 8.3 homicides per 100,000 inhabitants, which is nearly a third of the Latin American average (granted, a savage average compared to other regions).[52]

There are problems in the commercial realm too, especially for foreign corporations. Often their expensive lawyers are not enough to deal with the judicial system's lack of expertise in cases of intellectual property rights (IPR) or matters involving companies' intangible assets. Almost no one is convicted for IPR violations and nobody goes to jail for them. The Paraguayan government is known to use pirated Microsoft software in its computers. When a large U.S. credit card company litigated an outlandish case for more than eight years and spent millions, it accomplished little. The company had been sued for $120 million plus interest by an Argentine publicist with operations in Paraguay who claimed the company's advertising agency McCann plagiarized the slogan, "There are some things money can't buy. For everything else, there's…."

And on top of everything, the quality of Paraguayan lawyers is lacking, to say the least. To start with, there is no official bar examination; the only requirement to become a lawyer is to have a "legal degree." Alas, there is not even strict control of how the legal degree is attained. So-called "garage universities" dole out legal degrees with few requirements at best, and for a fee at worst. Not surprisingly, there are an estimated 722 lawyers per 100,000 people in Paraguay, the largest ratio in Latin America (far behind in second is Costa Rica with 389 per 100,000; in over-lawyered United States there are around 300 per 100,000 people). This oversupply of lawyers without common professional standards fits particularly well the small-town chumminess that generates corruption and hinders the full enforcement of laws and the pursuit of justice. Every small-town judge and his neighbors are willing to look away or help a friend in need even if the act is not in full accordance with the law. The oversupply of lawyers also responds to rent-seeking opportunities. A group of American economists found that countries with large rent-seeking opportunities will feature a high relative share of lawyers vis-à-vis engineers; these economists also found a high proportion of lawyers has a negative effect on economic growth.[53]

The judicial sector's troubles not only contribute to citizens' distrust but also undermine its crucial role as a check on the powers of the legislative and executive branches. Under Paraguayan law, judicial review is supposed to play a critical role in upholding the rule of law. Disappointingly, the organ responsible for assessing the constitutionality of laws and legal procedures—the Constitutional Court[54]—lives up to Paraguayan legal standards. To begin with, as Paraguayan attorneys will tell you, the court does not seem to follow any legal precedent or rely on any settled legal doctrine; the judges' legal reasoning normally follows an ad hoc logic. Because rulings on the constitutionality of laws apply only to the specific cases and parties, and not to future cases, as in the U.S. system, the whole process is infused with ongoing legal uncertainty. As a result, every time a high-profile case reaches the court judges are forced to consider the prevailing political forces, instead of simply interpreting the laws.

Perhaps the most emblematic judicial review case is "El Caso Oviedo" (Oviedo's Case). General Lino Oviedo was a military man who attempted a badly timed coup d'état in 1996 and was, as a consequence, ousted from the military. Unfazed, Oviedo hit the campaign trail and won the Colorado Party's presidential primary. Polls indicated he was headed to the presidency (the Colorado ticket did ultimately win the election), until Paraguayan rule *by* law intervened. Then-President Juan Carlos Wasmosy ordered the creation of a legally suspicious military tribunal that promptly condemned Oviedo to ten years in prison. Called in to review the case, the Constitutional Court confirmed the tribunal's validity and upheld the sentence, automatically ending Oviedo's political run. "El Caso Oviedo" is, like many of Paraguay's legal procedures, exasperating. On one hand, the end result was positive: as a result of a previously established legal process, a person who assaulted democratic institutions went to jail and was prevented from participating in elections. On the other hand, that end result came through a legally fraught process that was dictated by political circumstances. When the next high-profile case comes around, the court will probably not look back to the Oviedo case in search of legal precedent, but rather search for a political exit.

There is a chance, however, that the Supreme Court will act with less political attachment in future cases. The basis for greater judicial independence is the re-interpretation of the Supreme Court members' tenure. The initial interpretation of the 1992 Constitution held that the same rules applied to all the judges, regardless of rank. After their initial appointment,

Supreme Court members needed to be "reconfirmed" twice by the Council of Magistrates in order to obtain life tenure (with a limit of seventy-five years of age): one confirmation after the first five years of service and another one after ten years. In turn, before their tenure was up for reconfirmation, judges ruled with an eye to the council's political forces. But in a move resembling *Marbury v. Madison*[55] in the United States, some members of the Supreme Court have declared themselves life-tenured based on their cabinet-level rank. They did so by appealing and winning the case with the Constitutional Court, and so Supreme Court ministers can now only be removed by political trial. However, legislators and members of the executive branch have not fully endorsed the new interpretation and some have condemned it. The new jurisprudence will be tested next time there is a vacancy, when the president and Congress will have a chance to express their views. If rendered permanent, the change constitutes a significant step towards judicial independence, and yet two snags remain. First, the current Supreme Court members were selected recently enough to retain firm political loyalties. Second, Congress still has the power to initiate a political trial against judges based on "poor performance." Overall, the switch to lifetime tenure for judges illustrates the intrinsic untidy nature of judicial reforms in Paraguay. While it is possible to sympathize with the Supreme Court's greater independence, the current members' less-than-exemplary judicial pedigree and their worrying political connections must throw tereré-cold water[56] on rule of law optimism.

Side-Effects: Narcopolítica, Guerrilla, and Hezbollah

If you are the type of person inclined to engage in contraband, drug-trafficking, or otherwise disreputable activities, modern Paraguay does offer a welcoming business platform. Its trade arbitrage, corruption, and informality together with its problematic judicial system offer ideal conditions for crooks, thugs, and everything in between. In particular, these conditions have facilitated three worrisome developments: (1) they have brought money derived from the illegal drug trade into politics and government activities (narcopolítica); (2) they have fueled the rise of a rural guerrilla group; and (3) they have made it easy for terrorist organizations to move money around.

The narcopolítica is an expected phenomenon once the trade in illegal substances becomes large in any specific area. From the infamous Al Capone to the classier Joe Kennedy during Prohibition in the United States to Pablo Escobar's bloody Medellín Cartel, local politicians everywhere have been overpowered by the violence and free-flowing cash these activities entail. Paraguayan politicians are not different, particularly in the towns spanning the 848-mile border with Brazil—called "terra de ninguen" ("no man's land" in Portuguese)—where drugs and contraband flow freely. A lack of asset control before or after politicians leave office certainly does not help. But even if the Paraguayan way of doing business consisted instead of an immaculate political system with an operational rule of law, it is hard to imagine how the country would not have become a narco-center given the territory's advantages for the drug trade. Paraguay has ideal weather conditions to produce marijuana and holds a strategic location in the heart of South America to transport cocaine originating in the Andean region (Colombia, Peru, and Bolivia) onwards to Brazil, Argentina, and global markets. Add the Chaco's flat emptiness offering suitable terrain for clandestine landing strips and—presto—you have the perfect conditions for large-scale drug distribution. It also helps that the Paraguayan government does not have complete radar coverage, and what little it has requires airplanes to signal their approach, something narcotraffickers are not inclined to do. And Paraguay does not have legislation authorizing the military to shoot down suspected drug planes, unlike other countries in the region like Colombia, Peru, or Argentina.

Because of the existing global prohibition drugs fetch high profits, earning huge fortunes to those willing to pay the cost in violence and legal troubles. An estimated 200 metric tons of cocaine go through Paraguay each year, an amount comparable to 200 Liberty Bells. Still the emphasis should be on the "estimated" as the actual number is probably higher. Local authorities estimate four airplanes carrying nearly 800 pounds each land in Paraguayan territory on a daily basis. A 2016 report by investigator Guillermo Garat estimated that in Paraguay there are around 20,000 farmers involved in farming nearly 17,300 acres of marijuana, with an annual profit amounting to $700 million.[57] Those numbers have only increased in the years following the report's publication. Paraguay-based producers used to harvest marijuana twice a year, but genetically modified strains now allow for three harvests per year.

Drug money trickles down to obscure small-town narco-bosses, who run day-to-day operations, including the drug trade, but it also supports operations bribing politicians, judges, police and military, murdering nosy journalists, laundering proceeds, and offering knowledge of local conditions to foreign outlaws. When in 2018 the Paraguayan government snatched local drug-lord Reinaldo "Cucho" Cabaña, they found him in possession of several properties, including mansions with portraits of Pablo Escobar and a fleet of luxury cars featuring a yellow Lamborghini. Wiretaps of Cucho's phone conversations later revealed he had police officers, judges, and politicians on his payroll, including at least one lower house member who ended up in jail. A Brazilian drug kingpin jailed in Paraguay revealed to the *New York Times* that he paid $100,000 to a senior Paraguayan police official "to establish trust" plus a monthly $5,000 stipend to alert him when the police came chasing after him.[58]

While the Paraguayan police and prosecutors keep breaking drug-busting records, with operations intercepting bigger and bigger amounts of drugs and money, the fight remains unwinnable. According to the United Nations Office on Drugs and Crime's (UNODC) 2018 World Drug Report, "the [world's] range of drugs and drug markets are expanding and diversifying as never before."[59] The same report noted that "Global cocaine manufacture in 2016 reached its highest level ever: an estimated 1,410 tons."[60] These global trends overwhelm Paraguay's weak institutions, which lack the human and financial resources to cope with the narcos' trade innovations and capacity to reproduce. A 2018 U.S. government report admitted that efforts to reduce money flowing from the drug trade into the Paraguayan financial system "have not yet produced substantial results."[61] In fact, the UNODC branch in Paraguay shut down in 2019 following lack of international interest and frustration about limited accomplishments.

Paraguay's losing battle against narcos is evident in the border town of Pedro Juan Caballero (PJC), a city of 110,000 people located 280 miles northeast from the capital Asunción. PJC is the unofficial capital of the "terra de ninguen" and a major operation center for two big Brazilian crime syndicates, the First Command of the Capital (Primeiro Comando da Capital, PCC) and the Red Command (Comando Vermelho). PJC's streets and usually the scenes of violent clashes between these two groups reminiscent of the fighting between the Medellín and Cali cartels in the 1980s. As a police criminal investigator confided to me, almost a third of all murders in Paraguay happen in Amambay, the department where PJC is located; and almost all of those Amambay murders are sicario-style killings. For instance, in June 2016 PCC members murdered drug boss Jorge Rafaat in downtown PJC. The PCC gunners used a M2 heavy machine gun mounted inside a Toyota Fortuner that completely obliterated Rafaat's armored Hummer vehicle; the ensuing street battle lasted for four hours. Moreover, the turf battles continue unabated, with regular tit-for-tat murders. On a particularly bloody week in 2018, PJC-based narcotraffickers killed eleven people associated with opposing narco-bands, including their accountants and pilots.

The drug trade requires and complements an illegal trade of arms. That is the case in Paraguay, where the same groups that dominate the drug trade also control the arms trade. The vast majority of arms traded in Paraguay come from the United States en route to Rio de Janeiro's favelas, the heart of Brazil's drug violence. Other arms are shipped to Paraguay for safekeeping.

The trade has grown so fast that in May 2018 the U.S. government banned the exports of arms to Paraguay in an attempt to decrease it. But the Paraguayan authorities responsible for border control and oversight of armories are not up to the challenge. Three months after the U.S. government's ban, an inspection at a police armory found that officers on the narcotraffickers' dole had replaced forty-two automatic rifles with wooden and plastic replicas.[62] In this context, the U.S. Drug Enforcement Administration has to vet and pay salaries to a special investigative unit within the national police because they do not trust regular police units to do their jobs without leaking information or otherwise helping narcotraffickers. Likewise, the Paraguayan police cannot match the narcotraffickers' firepower. On the night of April 23, 2017, a sixty-strong assault unit of the PCC took CDE by assault and executed a large-scale robbery. The highly trained group divided into three groups: one group took up positions downtown, burning vehicles and blocking streets; another group cordoned off the site run by a private security company where the vault was located; and the third one slaughtered the one officer guarding the vault and blasted it open, making out with over $11 million in cash.

Paraguay's way of doing business also provides a fertile ground for the radicalized youth and university graduates dreaming of revolution. In the case of Paraguay, the revolutionaries formed the Paraguayan People's Army (Ejército del Pueblo Paraguayo, EPP), a ragtag guerrilla group of no more than forty members bent on overthrowing the government by way of armed operations, extortion, kidnapping, and straight up thievery. In its early stages, the group received training from the Revolutionary Armed Forces of Colombia (FARC, in Spanish), who counseled dividing up the group between a southern and a northern division. While the southern division never made it past the incubation stage, the remaining northern division was able to find sanctuary in the North's thick bush and the surrounding state-less areas. So far, the EPP's actions have caused more than sixty fatalities between civilians and police, though the group's leader remains in jail, where he listed his profession as "guerrillero" (guerrilla). To confront the EPP, the Paraguayan government has deployed a Joint Task Force that includes police and military personnel but so far it has been ineffective. In fact it has been a source of human rights violations against the population living in areas of EPP influence. To be fair to the Paraguayan forces, the EPP members move around in an area of almost 500,000 acres that includes thousands of acres of hard-to-patrol primary forest. What's more, in their stomping grounds the EPP members have some acquiescence from the local population based not on ideological agreement, but stemming from indifference and fear. It is estimated the EPP has extracted around $3.7 million from twelve kidnappings; its main source of income is money obtained from kidnapping Mennonite farmers. Why does the EPP kidnap Mennonites? As infamous criminal Willie Sutton explained why he robbed banks, "that's where the money is." The EPP snatches Mennonites because they are able to pay upwards of $500,000 in ransoms. Unlike their Colombian brethren, the EPP has not been able to put itself at the center of the drug and arms trades, and so its capacity to challenge the Paraguayan security forces remain quite limited.

What remains less clear is the capacity of Middle East–based terrorist groups to profit from Paraguay's way of doing business. Although a lot of ink is spilled over the potential for these groups to use CDE as a base to launch terrorist acts against enemies across Latin America, the fact remains that Hezbollah or other terrorist groups are largely absent from Paraguay when it comes to operations on the ground. What studies and visits from an inordinate number of intelligence officers, diplomats, congressional delegations, and impressionable journalists have revealed is that in CDE there is fund-raising and proselytizing for Hezbollah intended for activities outside CDE. The city offers the underworld the capacity to swap dollar denominated funds with the three local currencies, has lax border controls with little cooperation among neighbors, and three different legal frameworks full of loopholes. Until recently, Paraguay was still accepting "bearer" shares, the type that allows issuing firms to neither register the owner nor track transfers of ownership. How much fund-raising takes place? Hard to tell. The city hosts a large Lebanese community of Kirznerios that profit from the Tri Deal like few other groups. Among them there are undoubtedly some people that abet Hezbollah's financial operations, but in general the Hezbollah-supporting Lebanese people of CDE resemble the early twentieth century Nazi-supporting Germans of Asunción; they seem to largely sympathize out of affection for the old country and not because they believe in Hezbollah's core principles. By and large, they are a diverse bunch that like all the other social groups in Paraguay face unique circumstances and common challenges, as we will see next.

V

Labor Forces

Mennonites, Brasiguayos, Indigenous, and the New Urban Class

It is Saturday afternoon in San Lorenzo, one of Asunción's suburbs. Inside a strip mall young Paraguayans crack jokes in the half Spanish, half Guarani dialect called "Jopará." Some of them carry McDonald's fare, others head to the movies. Not far from the mall, their middle-class parents watch cable TV at home, drink tereré, or tidy up the backyard. A lot of them are first generation urban dwellers, the children of generations and generations who toiled the fields without much change to their economic well-being. Their forefathers endured bloody wars, dictatorships, and watched Europeans and some Australians in the Utopia-building business come, falter, perish, and disappear. For most of them, not much had changed since independence; they were poor, strangers to formal education, with low life expectancy, and scattered around a land far away from international markets. The bourgeois lifestyle was forever a luxury of a few well-connected individuals. Now smartphone-tapping, car-driving Paraguayans are everywhere.

But there is also La Chacarita. The area, formally named Ricardo Brugada but popularly known as La Chacarita, is Paraguay's largest shantytown, where more than 10,000 people live in close quarters and in the country's direst conditions. Most people's houses consist of a mix of brick and wooden walls attached to a corrugated tin roof. The whole neighborhood is located in the low-lying area where the Paraguay River spills over every time it rises; flooding is La Chacarita's middle name. A great many of its inhabitants are also rural migrants who almost by default are lured to the area's few urban regulations, light policing, and overall lack of services, where it is easy to set up residence. Still, the police regularly raid La Chacarita in search of drug traffickers, petty thieves, or the usual suspects.

127

Both San Lorenzo and La Chacarita embody the uneven transition that most Paraguayans are undergoing from rural living, with its subsistence agriculture and traditional social arrangements, to life in the city, with its informal employment and the disruption of those social arrangements. The transition is accelerated by the two-pronged force of a dynamic economy and a young population, and it is made worse by a state that struggles to provide basic services. In this context, the old elite is thriving and expanding while it cohabitates with a middle class that is growing, albeit at a snail's pace, having recently reached 40 percent of the population.

Although this trend describes the majority of the population, it's not the only one shaping Paraguay's society. Two groups, Mennonites and Brasiguayos, have risen to the economic top at the same time that the original Indigenous people have been left behind. Furthermore, the diverging economic accomplishments of Mennonites, Brasiguayos, and the Indigenous reveal the complexity of the Paraguayan society and at the same time the ineffectiveness of simple stories to explain a country's given development stage. These three groups all co-existed with given (or imposed in some cases) economic and social conditions and have had to survive with different degrees of political clout. In economist Albert Hirschman's classic definition, citizens have two options when confronting poor government services, they can either *voice* their dissatisfaction through political channels and activism or they can *exit* by building their own institutions or altogether emigrating.[1] Mennonites, Brasiguayos, and the Indigenous all lacked *voice*, so they had to find ways to somehow *exit* their realities and find redemption in rural areas. The fact that some thrived and others could not, even though they all faced the same set of constraints, is what makes political economy interesting.

Last but not least, there's also the fascinating case of the Lebanese, Japanese, and Korean immigrant communities. While the original Lebanese who moved to Paraguay were Christians, the last waves of immigration have also brought Muslim Lebanese, who mainly located in Ciudad del Este. Like other Lebanese immigrants to Latin America, they have thrived on commerce and politics, two areas where their numbers punch above their demographic weight. The Japanese and Koreans came to Paraguay in waves starting in the 1930s and after World War II to colonize rural areas. Many years later their descendants are thriving and beat the Paraguayan average on every indicator, including educational achievement, per capita income, etc. Just like the Mennonites and the Brasiguayos, these three immigrant groups came to a land with significant economic and social challenges and without the capacity to express *voice* but were still able to move up the economic ladder. In modern Paraguay, President Mario Abdo Benítez (2018–2023) is of Lebanese origin, one of the country's top TV and radio personalities is a Korean-Paraguayan woman, and one of the wealthiest individuals is a Nikkei (Japanese descendant) woman.

Come, Ye Faithful, Raise the Urban Strain

When General Andrés Rodríguez forced Alfredo Stroessner out in 1989, less than 50 percent of the population lived in urban areas, a proportion not different from other developing economies. Only in 2008 has the world's urban population become larger than the rural population for the first time in the history of humankind.[2] Paraguay reached that milestone ahead of time in 1992, but much later than Latin America and the Caribbean's urban-majority inception in 1961. As of 2017, 61 percent of Paraguayans were urban dwellers, making the country one of the least urbanized countries in South America.[3] All evidence indicates the number will continue growing at the very least until it approaches the region's 80 percent average.

The Paraguayan transition is evident in all major urban centers, but particularly in the capital Asunción. You can see the plight of the new urban class every time you stop at a major intersection in Asunción. There, as vehicles wait for the green light, young entrepreneurs sell fruit, chipas, perform juggling routines, and push window washing to averse drivers. Many of these young informal laborers come to the city all by themselves. Indeed, the move from rural to urban areas does not take place in a *Grapes of Wrath*–style pack-the-family-in-the-car-and-go. Instead it involves the male head of household leaving the family behind to seek job opportunities

The new urban class is on the move, rain or shine (courtesy *Última Hora*).

on his own. In some rural districts, an average two out of three households are headed by women, usually with extended families including several children and elderly individuals under their care. Most of these households survive on subsistence farming, with teenagers and sometimes children serving as key laborers for their families. When the whole family comes to the city and both parents have to work, children and teenagers are typically left alone at home or with a relative. Those are not the worst-off kids. When the parents' housing situation is unstable, children (mostly boys) end up roaming the streets, begging for money or lured to petty crime and drug addiction. The roaming bands can sometime reach 400 kids,[4] resembling Brazilian Jorge Amado's novel *Captains of the Sands*, where street children are forced into adulthood, ready or not.

Young girls do not have it easy either. They are the main victims of an old practice called "criadazgo," originating long ago but still enduring in the twenty-first century. The practice typically involves parents from a poor rural household that due to economic hardship have to send one of their children (generally a girl) to live in an urban household. She stays under the care of a family with either weak or no links to the child or community where she comes from. A common justification for criadazgo is that it allows a young girl who otherwise would have not been able to attend school and have proper shelter and food to have the chance to experience a different life in exchange for a few hours of domestic work. In practice, criadazgo is a source of child labor and abuse. Many victims do not receive pay at all in spite of working long hours, often suffer from sexual exploitation, and generally are in no condition to pursue an education. According to a United Nations Special Rapporteur on contemporary forms of slavery that visited Paraguay in 2018, the number of criadazgo cases reached 46,933, amounting to 2.5 percent of the country's total number of children under eighteen years of age.[5] The U.S. Department of Labor's report on worst forms of child labor from 2018 reported that criadazgo was "pervasive" in Paraguay.[6]

The World Bank estimates that 66,000 new workers will enter the Paraguayan labor force every year through 2030. The number seems attainable if we consider the country created jobs at an annual rate of 110,000 in the 2008–15 period.[7] The problem is that almost all new jobs are created in towns and cities and require skills that rural workers often do not have. Moreover, the process of urbanization is necessary to achieve higher average incomes at the national level. On one hand, greater urbanization correlates with higher productivity and faster economic growth. On the other hand, the mechanization of agricultural production with its massive productivity improvements means less employment and all sorts of negative economic cascade effects for rural dwellers. To appreciate productivity's impact, consider these numbers: Paraguay had 494,000 workers in the agricultural sector in 1980, increasing to 811,000 in 2008,[8] a 64 percent increase. Meanwhile, population growth went from 3.1 to 6 million during those same years, a 90 percent increase. Soybean production in those years increased from half a million to 6.3 million tonnes,[9] a whopping 1,160 percent growth on the heels of mechanized production. While higher levels of mechanization in agriculture have brought higher economic growth rates, it has also brought higher rural poverty rates, as those formerly employed in agriculture are left without a steady income.

The skill-based mismatch between jobs created and jobs fulfilled affect both rural migrants and urban laborers. Job fairs in Asunción are consistently oversubscribed, with lines of young aspiring workers curling around the block. When I take the flight from Asunción to Montevideo to visit my extended family, many of my fellow passengers are middle-aged Uruguayan men employed in management positions in the Paraguayan private sector. They are in Paraguay to fill a significant gap in the local force between low-skilled labor and highly qualified business-owners. The gap is what the World Economic Forum calls an "inadequately educated workforce" and it constitutes the second most problematic factor for doing business in Paraguay.[10]

Although the official unemployment rate has remained low for many years, informal and under-employment is high. What most job seekers want is a formal employment with benefits, but most toil instead in the informal sector's myriad small and medium sized enterprises that generate most of Paraguay's jobs. Businesses owned and operated by a single person ("cuentapropistas" in Paraguayan parlance) account for almost a quarter of all businesses in Paraguay, and they operate mostly in the informal sector.[11] In rural areas, informality takes the more traditional form of subsistence farming. Three out of four rural households are engaged in subsistence farming, with a lifestyle and economic conditions not too different from eighteenth-century rural families, save for cellphones and motorcycles. And neither of those new technologies help them when rains isolate their communities for days. In urban areas, having a motorcycle is not necessarily a blessing either. The lax enforcement of laws mixed with bad road conditions kills around 1,200 Paraguayans every year, making traffic accidents one of the country's top causes of death among young adults (eighteen to thirty-five years old). According to WHO, in Latin America only the Dominican Republic has more motorcycle accidents per 100,000 population than Paraguay.[12] In more than half of motorcycle accident deaths, the victim was not wearing a helmet.[13]

The rapid transformation of the old social order with its base in the countryside sometimes flares up when it involves land tenure conflicts.

Informal workers, like this street vendor, constitute the majority of Paraguay's labor force (courtesy Oscar Rivet).

Any Paraguayan with historical awareness knows this is not a trivial matter; lesser social order transitions have triggered bouts of political violence in the past. The old "encomienda" system, which granted land and its inhabitants to encomienda title holders, was long abolished, but the actual practice of inheriting Indigenous people with land purchases never quite expired. The majority of current land-related conflicts involve Indigenous people that lived in a rural area for a long time yet never secured the corresponding title because, of course, they consider those lands sacred territory unbound by any document. To make matters worse, the obscure and corrupt way in which the Stroessner regime gave away land to its cronies added extra legal uncertainty to land tenure conflicts. Many times Indigenous groups or those seeking land to live near the capital are left with no legal recourse and carry out land invasions. Fraudsters are often the land invasions' instigators; they charge the landless a "commission" to find the land and provide an (informal) electricity connection and access to water. When problems arise, these intermediaries are the first to flee. As a result of the legal uncertainty, fraud, and people's desperation, the raids and evictions of occupiers are always on the brink of flaring up into another Curuguaty.

The Curuguaty incident[14] embodies many of the problems associated with land tenure. It started when a private company owned by a former

Colorado senator filed a claim to land occupied by landless farmers before a Curuguaty court, in spite of not having any formal legal title to the lands in question. In turn, the court, acting under dubious legal authority, sent a police force to vacate the property. Once at the site, the police acted with unwarranted aggressiveness and tried to dislodge the farmers by force. Nobody knows who fired the first bullet, but by the end of the ensuing skirmish, eleven campesinos and six police officers were dead, with several others injured. No police officer was ever investigated or charged, yet twelve campesinos were charged with a number of crimes. The judicial investigation was lacking to say the least. Fernando Lugo, the president who was impeached as a result of the Curuguaty incident, would later become president of the Senate and try to prevent an investigation into the incident from becoming public. In the end, the Supreme Court annulled the convictions on the basis of the prosecutors' failure to demonstrate a direct link between the defendants and the alleged crimes. The Curuguaty case demonstrates Paraguay's challenges when it comes to land issues, ranging from weak rule of law, unequal access to land, to undue political influence.

These challenges underpin another way in which the Paraguayan state is dealing with the rural-urban transition: by locking up young low-income men. There are large numbers of unemployed young men from dislocated families who have not coped well with the temptations of illegal activities in a context of limited community support and a lack of government services. According to the government watchdog agency the National Mechanism for the Prevention of Torture, the total number of inmates from 1996 to 2019 grew by a factor of five,[15] a number that is completely disconnected from the country's population growth. If the numbers of inmates were correlated with demographic growth, Paraguay's population would have reached around 22.5 million in 2019 instead of 7 million. It is not an exaggeration to say they are locked up; three quarters of male prisoners are held in pre-trial detention. Paraguay has one of the world's highest percentages of prison inmates in this legal status. To make matters worse, detention centers are overcrowded and force inmates to endure inhumane living conditions. Based on international standards, Paraguayan prisons cram three times more inmates than the available capacity.[16] But that's not all. So-called VIP inmates get special treatment, including private cells with amenities such as cable TV and a fridge. And because the country does not have proper maximum-security prisons, crime syndicate leaders constantly escape. Unable to cope with these mostly Brazilian prisoners, Paraguayan law enforcement authorities hand them over to Brazilian authorities.

Whereas too many young males are locked up, too many women are overworked and underpaid. Starting in the early 2000s, women started joining the labor force in higher numbers, helped by the transition to urban employment in the services and manufacturing sectors. Although they left behind backbreaking work in the fields, their urban employment is far from idyllic. Large numbers of women work in housekeeping, the lowest paid job with the greatest informality rates. Nonetheless, their employment numbers remain below men's. The employment rate for women aged 25–64 years has hovered around 60 percent since 1990 with a slight upward tendency; the figure for men has always been above 90 percent.[17] These numbers, however, do not reflect the additional work that women carry out day in and day out across Paraguayan households. In Paraguay, women are responsible for housework and for the care of family members either too young or too old to work or otherwise incapacitated. On top of everything, femicide is rampant in Paraguay; a woman is killed every few days (in 90 percent of cases by her partner) and almost all the abuse cases go unreported. Although not all cases reach this extreme, machismo is generally traced as a source of all types of emotional and physical abuse women suffer.

The basic division of labor after childbirth consists of women staying at home to raise the new household member and performing house chores and men attaining gainful employment. Why Paraguayan couples fall back to traditional gender roles requires a full sociological study. In Paraguay, higher years of schooling correlate with higher income. However, the preference for male employment does not result from actual human capital as both genders have similar levels of schooling. The fact that Paraguay has a high proportion of Catholics also points to the influence of traditional gender roles. The data, however, are clear: women with children under one year of age have the lowest employment rate, and men under the same circumstances have the highest employment rate (under 40 percent versus close to 100 percent).[18]

The expected corollary of cultural and economic barriers to women's empowerment is their low participation in corporate structures, with few women holding leadership positions in private businesses and business organizations. It is uncommon to find female CEOs and the number of female corporate managers amounts to 45 percent of the total, according to an OECD survey that probably overstates the number.[19] A 2013 study by the Economist Intelligence Unit ranked Paraguay nineteen out of twenty Latin American countries in terms of overall environment for female entrepreneurs. The study described Paraguayan women's participation level in business networks and organizations as "poor."[20]

Paraguayans, young and old, still find time to worship deities (they also worship their favorite soccer teams). Notably, the country's social transformation is taking place in the context of high religiosity. Not only the average Paraguayan is a church-going Catholic, but also the Mennonites and the Brasiguayos embrace Christian beliefs with strong impetus. There are also around 90,000 members of the Church of Jesus Christ of Latter-day Saints and growing. According to a Pew Research poll, 82 percent of Paraguayans say they pray daily.[21] Legislators find nothing wrong with starting congressional sessions with a prayer, even though the constitution establishes the separation of church and state. According to the Latinobarómetro survey, Paraguayans trust "the church" more than any other institution; between 1995 and 2017 on average 82 percent of Paraguayans responded they either trust "the church" or trust it a lot. Paraguay gets a positive nod in the U.S. Department of State's 2018 Religious Freedom Report (I know, because I helped write it). Although the Catholic Church enjoys some prerogatives due to its obvious historic role and high membership among the population, other religious groups are free to operate on equal terms.

The biggest expression of Paraguayan religiosity is the annual Caacupé festival. Held over nine days ending December 8—the Feast of the Immaculate Conception—the festival is a religious Woodstock worshipping the town of Caacupé's wooden virgin, "Our Lady of the Miracles." It brings together a procession of devotees that during the whole week of festivities can reach more than a million people (city's population is around 50,000). Most people, like my housekeeper or my Guaraní teacher, walk the thirteen miles from the closest bus junction to the town; many others walk or bike from all over the country. The religious journey does not stop after reaching the destination, but continues through the night with mass, public prayers, concerts, and various talks on the evils of "gender ideology."[22] Participants can track events, find their way around town, and search other relevant information by downloading the festival's app. The main homily is broadcast live to the whole country via TV and radio and works as a fatherly reprimand, decrying the country's corruption and lack of honesty and good will on the part of politicians. Alas, the reprimand is utterly ignored if measured by politicians' behavior. Overall, the Catholic Church manages to deal with around a tenth of Paraguay's population coming to town without major disruption; they run a smooth logistical and security organization capable of managing every detail, including the 150,000 pieces of sacramental bread that parishioners swallow during the event's last day.

And thank God, whatever her affiliation might be, for Paraguayans' religiosity, because without it the country's societal changes would probably be more troublesome and discomforting. The certainty of religion seems to work as an emotional anchor holding forth against societal changes and the inability to repay debts and favors: faced with uncertainty the typical answer is "Dios proveerá (God shall provide)" and when short of monetary currency the reply is "Que Dios se lo pague (May God repay you)." Furthermore, by putting their lives in the hands of a superior power, young

The Virgin of Caacupé Festival every December 8 attracts thousands of worshipers, who make the pilgrimage from all corners and use every transportation mean, including horse carriage and bare feet (courtesy *Última Hora*).

males specifically, can overcome what constitutes the biggest economic and social transition since the Triple Alliance War without malicious thoughts toward the transition's substantial inequalities. If I were in the shoes of one of the rural migrants and had to separate from my wife and children, work under informal conditions, and live in a shack with limited access to water and electricity services and prone to flooding, I would also need a heavenly force to carry me through the day without starting a riot. Already, watching the average Paraguayan tolerate the politicians' crass behavior makes me hope for a Divine Plan.

Paraguayans also value religious institutions because they step up to provide the services the Paraguayan state fails to deliver. The usual protections of a welfare state are not covered by the state: 78 percent of the population does not have social security coverage, more than half work without labor protections, and over a third do not have health insurance. The government fails mostly those Paraguayans that need social services the most—the urban poor, rural, socially excluded groups, and Indigenous communities. In turn, religious institutions are key suppliers of health services, education at all levels, and a whole host of other social services such as shelters for victims of human trafficking and violence, daycare centers, and food banks.

In fairness to the Paraguayan government, youth unemployment is a global problem that affects developed and developing countries alike. Greece, Spain, Italy, and South Africa all have at least a quarter of their youth unemployed, a persistent problem with no easy solutions regardless of available government resources. Paraguay's advantage is exactly its challenge; the country's youth, unlike in developed countries, shows a higher willingness to move to new markets and explore new opportunities. In part, the Paraguayan youth's eagerness to move is associated with low human capital. Because of low salaries and equally low earning expectations, workers are more flexible. Alas, not only do a large number of workers, young and old, fail to impress employers with their skills, but the future workers are not being educated to meet the demand for more skilled labor.

Young and Unskilled

Ask any Paraguayan above fifty years old how many siblings he or she has and the answer will probably be "over four." Ask the same question to a thirty-year-old and the answer will probably be "just two." According to World Bank data, in the late 1960s Paraguayan women had on average nearly seven children; during the 1980s the average decreased but remained a vigorous five kids per woman. Only in 2016 the average started to align with developed countries when it went under 2.5 children. Family gatherings in Paraguay can be crowded, raucous affairs.

As a result of these demographic trends Paraguay has earned a fat demographic dividend (DD); this is the extra oomph to economic growth derived from having a large young working-age population and low fertility rates. In general DDs have proven to provide enormous benefits to countries, but they must be built on strong foundations. In particular, to fully profit from this dividend a country needs a steady economic expansion in order to absorb the new working-age individuals into the labor market and improving educational attainment to match the labor demand with a skilled working force.

Paraguay's DD is clearly seen in its low demographic dependency ratio, the proportion of non-working population ("dependent" or those under fifteen and above sixty-five years of age) to working-age individuals. This is an important future-oriented measure to calibrate the burden on a population's productive labor force and its capacity to sustain positive economic growth rates and shoulder fiscal burdens. By its dependency ratio, Paraguay is a true DD champion, with a current low ratio of two workers per dependent and expected to steadily decrease in the next twenty years adding more workers per dependents (compare to aging Japan's current 6.6 dependents for every 10 workers). Most importantly, the proportion of those older than sixty-four and presumably not engaged in productive labor in Paraguay is among the lowest in the world; only one out of every ten Paraguayans are in that category (in the United States 2.3 out of 10 are above sixty-four years old). Furthermore, Paraguay's share of the prime working population (ages twenty-five to forty-nine) is expanding and expected to peak in 2030 at 37 percent of the population.[23]

The DD effect greases the economic wheels through two mechanisms: (1) it lowers the number of workers per retiree and thus increases capital available for investment; and (2) it boosts labor productivity by bringing in younger workers and new skills. Already, the Paraguayan DD contributed on average 0.8 percent growth in 2004–2016 and accounted for 20 percent of the poverty reduction.[24] DD can also have positive effects on the public purse when a large proportion of workers are bringing in tax receipts instead of draining the treasury. However, if the majority of the workers are not contributing to the social security system and/or are not managing high household savings rates, DD can be ineffectual to the government's coffers. Either one of those two conditions must take place for DD to have a positive fiscal impact. Absent those conditions, the only way to avoid a

Children in urban poverty constitute a large portion of Paraguay's "demographic dividend" (courtesy *Última Hora*).

fiscal crunch is for future generations to manage above-average productivity growth or for foreign creditors to become extra generous. Alas, Paraguayan households have some of the lowest savings rates in Latin America[25] and the country's gross savings rate (which includes households, government, and firms) is below the regional average.[26] Less than half of Paraguayan adults have a bank account, and of those, only 12 percent use it for savings purposes.[27] There is still a silver lining for Paraguay, as countries tend to save more as their populations become wealthier, older, and better educated. This is a big "if," principally because in Paraguay the trinity is working for wealth and age yet failing at education.

Every start of the Paraguayan academic year brings back the same ritual: TV cameras visit an average school with its dilapidated infrastructure, collapsing roofs, lack of electricity or running water or both; public outrage follows but soon fizzles out. When I observed the 2018 elections, I visited a number of these schools in Asunción (which served as polling stations) and witnessed their utter neglect. And the schools I visited are some of the country's best; the state of rural schools is even more depressing, with students that have to walk a couple of miles to sit in bare shacks typically overcrowded with children of varying ages. Official and unofficial reports lowball that nearly a third of public schools are in a critical state in terms of infrastructure quality.

The educational attainment numbers in Paraguay are staggering: only four out of ten students finish high school; 70 percent of Paraguayan students in basic education do not have bare minimum math and language skills. A 2015 study by the Ministry of Education that tested 500,000 students of third, sixth, ninth, and twelfth grades revealed that only 6 percent of the students were able to pass a satisfactory score in mathematics and language.[28] The respected Programme for International Student Assessment (PISA) assessed the performance in math and science of Paraguay's fifteen-year-old students and found they were the worst performers among Latin American peers. The failure to educate has concrete consequences. For example, according to the World Bank's Human Capital Index (HCI), Paraguayan children are not reaching their full capacity by the time they reach eighteen years of age due to deficient education and health; the index calculates a 47 percent productivity loss for not having complete education and full health. Paraguay's HCI score is lower than the average for Latin America.[29]

Schools' poor infrastructure poses a challenge to the average student, but even more so to those with disabilities. The NGO Fundación Saraki estimates that one in five school-aged persons with disabilities attend school. This low number also points to a lack of suitable urban infrastructure. Persons with disabilities in Paraguay have to make a heroic effort every day to move around cities without basic accessibility features such as wheel-chair ramps, uncluttered sidewalks or disabled-friendly public transportation and bathrooms. Add minimum public transport connectivity and the challenges for people with disabilities to get an education become almost insurmountable.

For older kids, cost further limits attainment. An IADB study of 1,536 Paraguayan Millennials found that only a third of them can afford to study without working at the same time, the lowest proportion of Latin America. At the same time, a quarter of them only work, Latin America's largest proportion. And of those that only work, fully three quarters work in the informal sector, yes, the highest Latin American proportion too. A fifth of Millennials in Paraguay are considered "ninis" (ni trabaja, ni estudia), people who neither study nor work. The number gets worse when only women are counted, reaching 27.5 percent. What do these women do all day? On average, Millennial women spend more than seven hours a day doing house chores and taking care of family members or their own off-spring.[30] The challenges increase for students living in far-away rural areas. The first ever Maskoy Indigenous person to graduate from college had to move from her faraway community in the Chaco to a place closer to Asunción in order to attend school, yet she still had a two-hour commute by bus each way, every day.[31]

There is an incalculable threshold between learning that is reliant on basic infrastructure (school buildings, teachers, books, etc.) and learning that is ingrained in the cultural fabric of a society. In some countries, education represents a higher value and no matter the political, social, or economic circumstances, students are schooled. In Maoist China, for example, most books were considered "poisonous weeds," universities were shut down, high school teachers with critical thinking tendencies were jailed, and yet families still clung to the notion that education is the path to a better life. A 2018 story from *The Economist* reported that some Chinese mothers now go as far as spending about one-fifth of their household's monthly income in order to provide quality education to their children.[32] In South Korea, teen suicide has become pandemic mostly due to the pressure on students to get good grades. In other countries like Paraguay, education and learning in general are not seen as priorities that young people need to pursue at all costs. To be fair, parents in Paraguay never had a reason to invest in education; for most of its history the key to survival and limited prosperity was farming skills. In Guaraní culture, the arandu ka'aty, the practical "knowledge of the jungle" or "folk wisdom" was the desired education. Paraguayans living in rural areas continue to value subsistence agriculture as the primary goal for their children and so they neglect schooling or learning new skills outside basic farming. The local publishing market reflects this reality. In 2009, the novel ¿*Dónde estará mi primavera?* (Where's my spring?) by Carlos Martini broke historic records in the Paraguayan literary market after it sold 500 books.[33] One of the times I visited Asunción's annual book fair, a bookstore owner confided to me that based on research by local publishers, Paraguayans read on average less than one book a year; the Paraguayan Chamber of Publishers and Booksellers estimates that only two out of ten Paraguayan households possess books.

To what extent societies value education is relevant because international studies show that higher public spending does not necessarily correspond with equal improvement in educational attainment at the national level. Paraguay is a case in point. Already, the country's constitution (article 85) mandates at least 20 percent of government's expenditures must go to education. Yet as we have seen, the Paraguayan state's capacity to allocate funds efficiently and with probity is modest. Spending in education went up by more than 300 percent between 2003 and 2016, mostly to pay public teachers' salaries. The public teachers' union remains a powerful constituency and is able to get increases without providing any result-based accountability. Consequently, as of 2018, the Paraguayan government spent annually $1,092 per student in education (the category with the highest annual spending per beneficiary is burial services, around $14,500).[34]

A massive 216-page World Bank study on international education policies found that "unhealthy politics" derail public policies intended to improve educational outcomes. Specifically the Bank said, "powerful individuals or groups can make others act in ways that serve private interests rather than the collective good."[35] Welcome to Paraguay, education experts. In 2012 Congress passed a law creating the FONACIDE (National Fund for Public Investment and Development), aimed at transferring funds from Itaipú dam's deep pockets to public education. The law mandated that half of the funds had to go to educational infrastructure, mostly school buildings, maintenance, and upgrade. In 2012–2018, the transfer to local and provincial governments for school infrastructure amounted to $225 million. That is a lot of money for Paraguay and could have gone a long way towards solving most of the country's educational infrastructure needs. However, few guaraníes made it to the allotted purpose; the bulk of the money went to hire politically connected administrative personnel at best and to the pockets of corrupt politicians and their families in most cases. The Ciudad del Este–based NGO reAcción scrutinized publicly available information and exposed how in one year (2012–2013) $200,000 in FONACIDE funds disappeared without explanation from the city's coffers.[36]

Likewise, international studies show higher public spending in education does not correlate with higher economic growth rates. There is, however, little doubt that education understood as superior cognitive

School infrastructure in rural areas can be lacking (courtesy *Última Hora*).

skills determines an individual's capacity to earn a higher income and overall pursue a more prosperous life. There is strong evidence showing that private schools in developing countries deliver small but tangible increases in achievement and at a lower cost per student compared to public schools. This is not news to Paraguayan parents; those who can afford it (and that includes most of the senior leadership at the Education Ministry and Congress members) send their children to private schools. The challenge is allocating public funds in a way that helps recipients contribute to higher national growth rates. Hence, the countries that have spent the most on education over the past fifty years are not the countries that have grown the most. A different but equally huge World Bank study of education quality that included 163 countries for the 1965–2015 period found that "Learning outcomes in developing countries often cluster at the bottom of a global scale."[37] In other words, measurable educational outcomes tend to correlate with national per capita incomes. What seem to matter the most for economic growth is not so much years of schooling, but learning new skills, particularly the type workers acquire on the job.[38] Education-as-skills-acquisition over education-as-schooling. In Paraguay, the latter has been improving in the sense that on average more Paraguayans attend school than in the past. What is really happening is that students are being placed in buildings called "schools" in large numbers, but they are not learning much. In the skills-acquisition sense, education has completely failed at least the past two generations of Paraguayans, as evidenced by students' lack of basic language and math skills.

In Paraguay this education-is-not-schooling principle is real. For example, according to a study by the think-tank CADEP, in the decade from 2002 to 2010 the number of years in school grew for all workers, and the unemployment among youth with secondary and tertiary education decreased.[39] The paradox is that the unemployment rate of this group was higher than the unemployment rate of youth with just primary education. The authors contend this difference between more education and higher unemployment might be caused by a difference between the type of labor supplied and the type of labor demanded, which is another way of saying that employment-worthy skills are not necessarily acquired at school.

Similarly, when Paraguayans emigrate, they earn high incomes in spite of their low educational attainment or poor education quality. Paraguay is the Latin American country that sends the least immigrants to the United States; according to U.S. Census estimates, 323,127 Paraguayans lived in the U.S. as of 2016.[40] Only 382 Paraguayans obtained permanent U.S. residency in 2015.[41] Nonetheless, Paraguayan households in the United States earned an above average income of $60,210 in 1999, the latest year data are available.[42] There are around 1.5 million Paraguayans in Argentina and 100,000 in Spain who by the most part earn wages well above the average salary in Paraguay. And there is also a group of immigrants to Paraguay who earn salaries available only in developed countries.

Menno Knights

I am standing at the intersections of Friedhof-Strasse and Harbiner-Strasse; any direction I walk there are large houses with equally large yards, manicured lawns, and 4x4s parked in the garages. Except for some big dogs, the houses have no security fences, gates, or anti-burglary devices whatsoever. Kids ride their bikes and older folk do yard work. The place could pass for a rural neighborhood in northwestern Germany or a quiet California suburb, with dusty roads. It is neither. It is a Mennonite neighborhood in Filadelfia, a city located in the middle of Paraguay's Chaco region, the most isolated place in the country.

If an evil economic development project were to test the endurance of a group of people in one of the earth's most challenging environments it would look a lot like the Mennonite experience in Paraguay. In the Chaco region, almost nothing useful for human existence grows—mostly palm trees, silk floss trees, and scrub vegetation. Its sandy soil together with scorching average temperatures and little rainfall that floods the place with scattered furious rains requires a special talent to survive and flourish. And let's not forget about the mosquitos swarming with ugly tropical diseases.

Before coming to Paraguay, Mennonites were familiar with life-or-death predicaments. There were challenges from the beginning in 1525 in Switzerland, when, following Martin Luther's reformation, a small group of adults baptized each other and laid the foundations of the Anabaptist movement. As the name implies (and as the group's actions demonstrated) they were against infant baptism and believed in the need for baptism to be a conscious decision. Their Swiss religious authorities did not like the proposition and went on to persecute and execute the Anabaptist leaders. It did not help that the Anabaptists for the most part were strict pacifists who did not take up arms or fight back by violent means. However, the Anabaptist approach spread north along the Rhine, all the way to Friesland, a region formerly inhabited by Germanic people and today situated in the Netherlands. There it reached a Catholic priest by the name of Menno Simons, who decided to switch sides and codified the Anabaptist credo. In order to survive, some of the Anabaptists started calling themselves "the followers

Roads in the Chaco region could use more civil engineers (courtesy *Última Hora*).

of Menno" and the name evolved to "the Mennonites," which somehow did not trigger the violent reactions of their former name. Still, the Mennonites' pacifism, with their refusal to join armies, together with their support for the separation of state and church, meant they were not welcomed along the Rhine. In turn, they moved en masse to the Polish city of Gdansk and the nearby Vistula river delta. As fate would have it, in the late 1770s their community became part of the Prussian Kingdom. The new overlords found the Mennonites' pacifism a nuisance and decided to increase the fees imposed to avoid military service. Around that time, an opening came when the Russian tsarina Catherine the Great, flush with new land after defeating the Ottoman Empire, offered the Mennonites the opportunity to populate territories located in modern-day Ukraine. The Mennonites took the offer, and once again moved to a new land. They thrived for a century until different Russian authorities abjured their commitments. Specifically, the Russians also were not willing to tolerate anymore the Mennonites' military service exemption. At this stage, some Mennonites negotiated a new deal under which they could do community service instead of serving in the military. Others found the agreement to be a step too far from their convictions and migrated to Canada. The new agreement lasted until the Russian Revolution first and the establishment of the Soviet Union later made it impossible to not only preserve their faith but also their lives. The last straw to Mennonite communities in Russia came with World War II and the persecution of German-speaking people that followed it. Meanwhile, in Canada around the 1920s, the Mennonites were under pressure to attend English-language public schools, a mandate that denied their educational autonomy to teach their faith and to do so in their own language.

And so a group of Canadian Mennonites set off looking for new lands to settle and eventually learned that a country in the middle of South America was looking for immigrants to colonize uninhabited lands. The Mennonites sent a group of scouts to Paraguay who negotiated the basic conditions for their settlement in the country, which included autonomy to practice their religion and educate their community in their own language, no taxes for the first ten years, autonomy to manage inheritances, and exemption from military service. They bought the land from one of the country's largest landowners, Argentine Carlos Casado. The land included scattered Indigenous communities who were somehow consulted and, according to the official Mennonite story, gave their approval to have the Mennonites as neighbors.

Of the first 1,765 Mennonites that arrived from Canada on December 1926, one in ten died within the first two years, mostly due to typhus.[43] Within the first months, many Mennonites who could afford the trip back returned to Canada or otherwise fled from the Paraguayan green hell. Mennonite pastor Ricardo Frisen put the Chaco pioneers' onus in stark terms: "those that did not make an effort would die."[44] An effort they made; with basic farming and construction tools in hand, tents, and a work ethic tempered through centuries of labor-intensive new beginnings that those early Mennonites had plowed through. The Chaco geography had one more survival test for the Mennonites. Only eight years after their arrival, the Chaco War commenced, bringing Paraguayan and Bolivian troops in direct contact with the weary settlers. Although no major battle took place in Mennonite lands, the war's outcome was uncertain and thus their survival was once again imperiled.

Decades later, after taming the Chaco and enduring the war, the Mennonite population swelled and set on a steady path of economic progress unmatched in the rest of Paraguay. By the time the last wave of Mennonite immigrants arrived in 1950, there were 9,950 Mennonites in Paraguay, 0.7 percent of the total population.[45] Current estimates based on the latest census put the number of Mennonites at nearly 50,000, also 0.7 percent of the total. Although the percentage is low, it constitutes the highest proportion of Mennonites in any country. They are mostly concentrated in the Chaco, but other small communities with different degrees of religious orthodoxy live scattered around the country. For instance, there are some Mennonites who emigrated from Mexico and follow an Amish-type lifestyle, including wearing traditional dresses and eschewing modern conveniences such as cars and farming machinery. Still, in modern Paraguay, the average per capita income of Mennonites is estimated at $55,000 per year. The figure is more than ten times higher than the national average and comparable to the top high-income countries' average. Mennonites possess around 2.5 million acres of land,[46] an extension larger than the size of Delaware and Rhode Island combined. They process about three quarts of the national milk consumption, are top beef exporters, and employ the majority of formally employed Indigenous people in Paraguay.

The three Mennonite colonies in the Chaco region—Loma Plata, Filadelfia, and Neuland—are run almost independently from the central government. Loma Plata was founded by the first Canadian group to arrive, Filadelfia by a group from Ukraine who arrived in the early 1930s, and Neuland by a group of Russian refugees that came after World War II. The Mennonites created cooperatives that group together their supply of products and services and at the same time provide social services to members and the Indigenous communities. The top three cooperatives are the Loma Plata–based "Choritzer," Filadelfia's "Fernheim," and Neuland's eponymous cooperative. The cooperatives police the streets, provide electricity and water, upkeep streets, and run the schools, hospitals, and retirement homes. Each cooperative taxes its members a percentage of their salaries and from those funds come cradle-to-the-grave services. They are a successful welfare state within an ineffectual national state.

Because they grow up speaking German at home and attend German-speaking schools, almost all Mennonites speak Spanish with a heavy accent. Everything in Mennonite areas, from street signs to businesses signage to radio commercials, are in both German and Spanish. Men dominate all corporate leadership; the three CEOs of the largest cooperatives are all cut from the same cloth: almost sixty years old, well groomed but lacking any swagger, they all started young and spent years moving up the ranks. In Mennonite-land there is an informal caste system consisting of Mennonites, Latinos (non–Indigenous Paraguayans), and Indigenous. While the system is largely merit-based and non-discriminatory, the different groups do not intermarry or share social activities. Work brings them together and their ethnic and cultural differences keep them apart. A Mennonite from the Chaco region explained to the British newspaper *The Guardian* the basic differences between his kin and the locals: "The first [concept] is that people from the north[ern hemisphere] need to stockpile. They work from sunrise to sunset, investing, so they can survive the winter. But a person from the south, to put it crudely, can sit under a mango tree and wait for a mango to fall on his head. Nature provides security."[47]

Brazil in Paraguay

"Procuramena otro chuveiro, chera'a (Please look for another shower nozzle for me, my friend)." The phrase spoken in almost equal parts Spanish–Guaraní–Portuguese at a border town store encapsulates the distinctive flavor of the vast borderland between Paraguay and Brazil. This is where the so-called "Brasiguayos" have lived and prospered for more than fifty years. Their presence is both a source of economic dynamism and social conflict. Brasiguayos brought agricultural expertise and capital to a region that consisted of native forest and turned it into one of Paraguay's economic engines. On the heels of soybean and, more recently, cattle exports, they ploughed through with little consideration for environmental concerns or the rights of local Indigenous communities. Although Paraguayans are exceptionally hospitable and welcoming of foreigners, their laid-back demeanor is transformed when sovereignty issues relating to its neighbors Argentina and Brazil emerge. I have heard smart Paraguayans who otherwise express sensible views completely lose their balance when talking about Brasiguayos. Of course, they have good reasons to get upset;

the establishment of binational borders has always been determined unilaterally by Brazil. In turn, many Paraguayans see the Brasiguayos as a fifth column that—like Russians in eastern Ukraine—will one day aid a Brazilian conquest of Paraguayan land. The reality on the ground seems more benign, if still beset by real challenges.

Brasiguayos is a term not always straightforward or consistent. It refers to both Brazilians and their descendants who reside in Paraguay. Some of them have both nationalities, others have one but move about as if they had both. As a result, their numbers are not exact; they are estimated to number between 300,000 and 500,000 people. They are largely clustered near the border with Brazil, but they are also found in other areas farther away such as the Chaco region. Depending on how you count them, Brasiguayos are either the first or second largest population of Brazilians abroad. They are the largest immigrant group in Paraguay by far. In some border towns, Brasiguayos make up the majority of the population, and Portuguese is the lingua franca in those regions. To a great extent, many of them are dual immigrants, many having ancestors originally settled in Brazil from Germany, Italy, and Eastern European countries. Others came from the poorest states in Brazil's northeast, many of them descendants from slaves and oppressed Indigenous groups.

When Brasiguayos started pouring in during the late 1960s, they came with fresh cash and bought up vast amounts of cheap land. At the time, only the scattered Indigenous tribes living in eastern Paraguay noted the new neighbors' arrival. For most Paraguayans the lands close to the Brazilian frontier consisted of inhabitable bush. The selling point was straightforward: "For the price of one hectare in Brazil you can buy five in Paraguay."[48] A similar process of land consolidation into big agribusinesses aimed at economies of scale that characterizes modern Paraguay was what pushed many Brasiguayos out of Brazil in the 1960s and 1970s. In those years the Brazilian state was already deep into import-substitution agitation and other policies of deep political intervention in economic areas and high taxation, which made Brazilian entrepreneurs flee for laissez-faire Paraguay. In addition, Paraguay's state-owned bank provided credit to Brasiguayos at lower interest rates than in Brazil; since they had land titles, unlike many Paraguayan farmers, they were able to benefit with little competition.[49] Brasiguayos then proceeded to do what they were trying to do in Brazil: clear forests to plant commodity crops and operate cattle ranches. Many of those newfangled landowners hired others like them to work on the farms.

For the Stroessner regime, Brazilian immigration to Paraguay was part of a policy of greater overall engagement with Brazil that included the construction of the Friendship Bridge and the Itaipú dam, as we will see in the next chapter. The fact that both countries had military dictatorships was obviously a crucial factor in bringing the two governments together in a quick, purposeful fashion that did not require much consultation with concerned parties or local communities. Many Paraguayan military men benefited from the sale of lands to Brasiguayos, which they acquired either through "insider trading" type of deals or simply by reselling land illegally appropriated for themselves.

From the beginning, the Brasiguayos' key competitive advantage was their use of better farming technologies, mostly in the form of machines. It is also this mechanization of agriculture that is at the center of most social conflicts with Brasiguayos, as small farmers can neither compete nor get hired. During the Stroessner regime, small farmers and landless peasants had no legal recourse when Brasiguayos bought their lands and they were forced to move out. With the onset of democracy, legal recourse did not improve much for these farmers, but at least they could protest without being violently repressed. In turn, there has been a constant if fluctuating struggle between excluded farmers and Brasiguayos. Most of the time it is the farmers who protest against the Brasiguayos by cutting down fences, burning down fields or blocking roads. The Brasiguayos protest just as well; they typically take their tractors for rides, blocking highways or central roads in urban areas.

In spite of what the current average Brasiguayo looks like, the first ones for the most part were farmers of limited economic means, who could not afford Brazilian lands and economic conditions. They came with what little financial resources they had to a land that was more affordable largely because it was undeveloped, lacking road infrastructure and a skilled labor force. Their early investment in Paraguayan agriculture generated a virtuous circle where greater yields and corresponding incomes bolstered land prices, bringing significant wealth to many Brasiguayos.

A few earned vast amounts of wealth, like Tranquilo Favero. In spite of what his first name suggests, Tranquilo is an energetic Brasiguayo of Italian descent who moved to Paraguay in the late 1960s, bought land with cash and on credit, and introduced mechanized agriculture to great success. Today he is the known as the "Soybean Tsar" in Paraguay because his company is the country's biggest soybean exporter. Also, his Grupo Favero stands as Paraguay's third largest landowner with nearly 400,000 acres and one of the largest employers and taxpayers; one of his many agribusinesses earns more than $40 million annually from grain exports. Because of its size, the Grupo Favero is usually involved in land conflicts, either with Indigenous communities evicted from their lands or small producers pushed out of business by Favero's companies. While Tranquilo is guilty of unfortunate pronouncements about Paraguayan farmers' work ethic, he is also unfairly portrayed as a Brasiguayo Scrooge McDuck unconcerned with Paraguay's traditional ways.

Certainly, many Brasiguayos avoid putting down roots in Paraguay. The geographic proximity with Brazil gives them an incentive to go back and forth between the two countries, keeping their Brazilianness intact. In terms of everyday living, Paraguay for a Brasiguayo is not much different than the Brazilian states bordering Paraguay. They can gain from the productivity of Paraguayan lands, but at the same time enjoy the better health and educational opportunities available on the Brazilian side. Because they are domiciled in Paraguay, their tax burden is low, but they can nonetheless take advantage of Brazil's better physical infrastructure without paying its much higher taxes. For example, in 2013, a group of Brazilian investigators interviewed thirty-nine Brasiguayos residing along the border and described how they move back and forth between the countries. In general, they worked in Paraguay and owned land there but utilized social services such as medical facilities and education on the Brazilian side.[50] Furthermore, even before modern communications technologies existed, Brasiguayos were plugged in to Brazilian radio and TV, so their Paraguayan cultural imprint has always been low.

In the traditional media, particularly in social media, the Brasiguayos-versus-farmers rhetoric sometimes turns jingoistic, sometimes portrayed as a clash of civilizations. From one perspective, there are the new bandeirantes taking land by force and subjugating Paraguayan rural folk. Taken from another perspective, there are the hard-working pioneers moving ahead in spite of the locals' indolent habits. In a more sober analysis, investigator José Albuquerque explained the different views in terms of development cultures. On the one hand, there is the Brasiguayos' "capitalist spirit" with its focus on work ethic as the mechanism to accumulate wealth. On the other hand, there is the local farmers' community-based agricultural methods, derived from the Indigenous notion of productive activities as solidarity and subsistence practices.[51] It is important to note this dichotomy is biased, as all immigrants are on average more willing to take risks, innovate, and engage in productive enterprises. In addition, the Brasiguayos share more traits with the Paraguayans living in Buenos Aires, for instance, than with many other Brazilians living in Brazil.

Indigenous Language, Indigenous Problems

Jorgelina (not her real name) is only ten years old but already speaks three languages. She attends school every day, lives in a small community surrounded by supportive family members, attentive government officials, and caring religious communities. When I visited the Indigenous community where Jorgelina lives, deep in the Chaco region, just three hours driving to the border with Bolivia, I realized how meaningless some development indicators can be. For Jorgelina is a native Nivaclé speaker, with good Guaraní and Spanish, all language skills that will *not* take her far from her community. Indeed, her community and family network were supportive, but in a way that did not always help her break free from poverty; not finishing school or getting pregnant at fifteen years of age were still common practices passed from generation to generation. As for public services, they were far away and too scattered to alter the cycle of poverty. Jorgelina's school quality was above average in terms of Paraguay's rural schools thanks to Catholic Church support, even though it had the bare minimum infrastructure.

One of Paraguay's key distinctive features is that its people are a non–Indigenous people that speak an Indigenous language. Perhaps as high as 75 percent of Paraguayans are bilingual Spanish–Guaraní speakers. Although the last census from 2012 indicated that 7.9 percent of Paraguayans spoke only Guaraní, researchers have criticized the census's methodology and estimate the percentage to be around 25 percent. Paraguay's Indigenous people were for a long time, like in the rest of Latin America, called "Indians" due to Christopher Columbus's utter confusion about his 1492 landing site. The Paraguayan constitution defines them as "groups of culture preceding the formation and organization of the Paraguayan State." According to the better-crafted 2012 census of Indigenous people, these groups of preceding people totaled 112,381, amounting to 1.7 percent of the Paraguayan total population.[52] They were distributed across five distinct linguistic groups: the Guaraní, Mataco Mataguayo, Zamuco, Maskoy, and the Guaicurú. Among the largest of them, the Guaraní, there were six other groups: the Pãi-Tavyterã, Aché, Avá-Guaraní, Mbyá-Guaraní, Guaraní-Ñandeva, and the Occidental-Guaraní. Overall, they are a diverse group, speaking different languages and featuring equally distinct lifestyles, from the Ayoreo living in voluntary isolation to the multinational Mbyá spread out across Paraguay, Argentina, and Brazil.

The remaining 98.3 percent of the Paraguayan population is a mix of a mix of a mix. The early mix happened in colonial times between the original peoples' women and the male colonizers, plus an infusion of slave population of African ancestry; a further mix happened after the Triple Alliance War when most of the Paraguayan male population was decimated and immigrants and returning Paraguayans procreated with the surviving females; and a last mix took place during the first half of the twentieth century when immigrants from Japan, Korea, and the Middle East together with various European immigrant groups escaping the continent's madness of wars and communism joined the few Paraguayans left. By the 1960s, Paraguay's anthropological profile was unrecognizable from anything that existed before, with only the Guaraní language serving as a cultural glue. Even then, the country's population was under 2 million inhabitants; today's estimated 7 million Paraguayans constitute a brand-new cultural entity. Based on gene studies, Paraguayans have a strong connection to the first Indigenous peoples to settle the land. A 2018 DNA analysis of 550 Paraguayans found that on average they are 85 percent native to South America, 7 percent European, and 7 percent African.[53]

Unfortunately, little is known about the Indigenous people that inhabited Paraguay long before the Spanish colonizers arrived. Bartomeu Melià, the country's foremost expert on Guaraní culture, concluded that "the Guaraní people are still that unknown. [There is] little we know about their economic system, the real causes of their migrations, their psychology, the types of religion practiced amongst them, the role of the boss. Even the Guaraníes' pre-historical and historical physical look escapes us."[54] This void of knowledge generates innumerable urban myths and interesting stories about Paraguay. A great deal of bad armchair anthropology traces the country's current problems to the original inhabitants' traits. A lack of empirical data or unfamiliarity with the latest research exacerbates the problem. Typically, Paraguay's most intractable problems (informality, corruption, etc.) are ascribed to the Guaraníes' nomadic traditions and their preference for short-term over long-term gains, their propensity for picking the low-hanging fruit, and their predisposition to flexible human relationships. Add the Guaraníes' penchant for eating their enemies' corpses and the silliness of social analysis goes through the roof. While in some cases these anthropological traits are relevant, the Paraguay that emerges from the data and as viewed through a social science lens is a country that behaves like any other country, in the sense that it shares problems, challenges, and strengths observed in other societies with varying development levels.

Unquestionably, there are uniquely Paraguayan geographical and cultural elements. Augusto Roa Bastos, the country's most celebrated novelist, hit the cultural nail on the geographic head when he defined Paraguay as "an island surrounded by land." The resultant isolation set the conditions for the existence of the Guaraní language. For most of history, the Paraguayan population was largely rural and educated by Guaraní-speaking women. For decades, the few public schools scattered around the country forced Guaraní-speaking children to learn the curriculum in Spanish, limiting the students' ability to gain new skills and further deepening their cultural isolation.

It remains a puzzle to what extent the use of the Guaraní language serves as an explanatory variable for the country's current condition. While Guaraní use defines Paraguay as a nation, its survival and widespread use among the population explains little about modern Paraguay. Paraguayan scholar Alfred Neufeld described a "fatalism" in Paraguayans that prevented them from improving their lot given destiny's fixed nature.[55] If fate is given, why change behavior at all? Neufeld found Guaraní phrases and attitudes to explain his thesis, but conceded it does not explain modern Paraguay; as he told me, "It was accurate for the Paraguay of twenty-five years ago but does not explain today's Paraguay."[56] In the same vein, cultural commentator Aníbal Romero spoke of a "loathsome resignation"[57] that makes Paraguayans tolerant of their country's problems. Romero observed that Paraguayans when faced with a corrupt politician simply uttered, "To'úna pero tojapo (let him take advantage, but let him do something)." In any case, knowing there was a group of people called "Guaraní" and that their language survived to the twenty-first century is a poor tool to understand modern Paraguay's political system, per capita income, demography, or judicial system. If the only thing that Paraguayans had done different throughout their existence was to give up the Guaraní and speak only Spanish, modern Paraguay would probably look much the same.

What is not a puzzle is the fact that those who only speak Guaraní, or any other Indigenous language, are among the Paraguayans with the lowest per capita income, least years of schooling and access to health services, and in the bottom of any other social and economic wellbeing figure. Almost three out of four Indigenous people younger than eighteen years live in poverty, a proportion three times higher than the rest of the population.[58] In the more isolated communities, alcoholism, drug addiction, and high suicide rates are common. There is also violence between youth gangs; in an Indigenous community in the Chaco region, one gang associated itself with an Argentine cumbia band and battled another group associated with a German heavy-metal band. Victims of their street brawls have ended up in emergency rooms. Local police units are often too afraid to enter Indigenous communities for fear of reprisals.

In 2014, a United Nations Special Rapporteur on the rights of indigenous peoples visited Paraguay and recommended the Paraguayan state declare the Indigenous people's situation an emergency due to "widespread lack of legal protection for Indigenous peoples' rights over their lands, territories and resources, which are vital to ensure their survival and uphold their dignity."[59] Yet, the Paraguayan state is neither interested nor does it have the resources to improve the situation. If the government's Instituto Paraguayo del Indígena (Paraguayan Institute for the Indigenous) serves any purpose at all, it is as a symbol for how much the Paraguayan state cares about the Indigenous population. The institute's office is decrepit, with

paint peeling off the walls, and smelly bathrooms. One of the latest direc-
tors of the institute did not even speak an Indigenous language, not even
Jopará.

What the Paraguayan government has done more consistently is give
land to Indigenous groups, either by returning lands that belonged to communities from ancient times or by relocating communities to former public lands. The process of granting public lands has been rather arbitrary,
with recipients chosen based more on political clout or capacity to mobi-
lize than actual needs. Because the country's judicial system has failed them
repeatedly, Indigenous communities have taken their land-ownership cases
to international courts. Three out of the seven cases filed against Paraguay
before the Inter-American Court of Human Rights deal with failure to provide access to ancestral lands for Indigenous communities, as mandated
in the national constitution. In 2019, after more than two decades of litigation, the Paraguayan government finally complied with the court ruling
and paid its dues to the Xákmok Kásek community. The government had
already returned most of their ancestral lands located in the Chaco region
in the previous years.

The policy of returning lands to Indigenous communities is clearly
just and necessary, but limited when it comes to improving their economic
wellbeing. Many Indigenous communities remain in their ancestral lands
and pursue their traditional way of life with modern tools, including satellite TV, cellphones, and motorcycles. Yet because their communities are
isolated and their members' human capital is limited, they have little chance
for economic improvement. Many Indigenous groups in their desperation
cut down trees in restricted areas or sell their "derechera," the right of possession to a land, to investors. Others travel miles to the capital, away from
their communities and way of life, and camp in one of Asunción's downtown plazas for months to get what many Asuncenos call a handout, but
what the Indigenous consider their due after centuries of discrimination
and persecution. Families with little kids eat, defecate, beg, move about
aimlessly across public spaces in Asunción, enduring foul weather conditions and mosquitos. They are almost never removed by force but stay until
their desperate living conditions move a public officer or politician to help
them. To a great extent they are there due to the transformation of Paraguay's agriculture and the limits of its clean energy resources.

VI

Big Agriculture Versus the Green Energy Utopia

John Parish Robertson, a British explorer, came to Paraguay from Argentina in the early nineteenth century and made his way north on foot all the way to Asunción. Based on what he saw, he gushed, "[Paraguay is] a country so substantially favoured, and so highly adorned by Nature."[1] Even Thomas Carlyle, the famed Scottish essayist, opined without visiting the country that Paraguayans "lead a drowsy life, of ease and sluttish abundance."[2] These portrayals have been around for centuries, and illustrate a reality that in spite of the wars and social conflicts has not changed. Paraguay is still blessed with some of the most productive lands in the world, has a high average of sunshine hours a year yet with a good average rainfall, and to top it off a subtropical weather that allows more than one harvest per year of many crops.

What's more, the whole place is one big emptiness. The contrast with Vietnam, my previous place of residence, is striking. Vietnam is a country that has almost the same geographical size as Paraguay[3] yet packs more than 90 million souls in it (compared to Paraguay's 7 million). In Vietnam, you cannot drive anywhere without bumping into people; Vietnamese rural areas are full of busy small towns. Not so in Paraguay, where outside of Asunción you can drive for long stretches without seeing other human beings. Although Paraguay is not among the least densely populated countries in the world, the demographic distribution makes it look emptier. More than 95 percent of Paraguayans live within the 40 percent of land located east of the Paraguay River. Less than 5 percent of Paraguayans live in the Chaco region, which comprises 60 percent of the territory. Likewise, no matter where you go in Paraguay, the land is sure to be flat, except for rolling hills here and there. Before Vietnam, I resided in Ecuador, a country slightly smaller than Paraguay but with a testing topography, traversed by the Andes' rugged mountain range and its snow-covered volcanoes, but also interspersed with deep primary jungles. Paraguay cannot be more different: it presents no significant topographical challenge to farming, and almost the whole territory is suitable for agriculture.

The cherry on Paraguay's natural cake is the vast amount of hydroelectric energy available. Paraguay is one of only a few countries in the world that generates nearly all of its electricity from falling water. It has an enormous surplus thanks to two large dams situated in the Paraná River—Itaipú, shared with Brazil, and Yacyretá, shared with Argentina—and a smaller one of its own in the Acaray river. As a result, Paraguay benefits from clean energy at a low price that generates no side effects. What's more, it has an enormous yet tangible potential to build its economy around its clean energy. The potential is not only in the numbers, but also in the incredible feat that building these large dams represents. When I visited the Itaipú dam, I could not believe my eyes; its sheer size, the amount of concrete poured, and the whopping amounts of land and water removed to build it. I readily concurred with the American Society of Civil Engineers' decision to select the dam as one of the Seven Wonders of the Modern World.

Yet, agriculture and environment do not always go hand in hand in Paraguay. In particular, the rapid expansion of soybean and cattle production means large swaths of lands have been deforested. In addition, the country's economic expansion means many rivers have been contaminated. Although the Lorax has not lifted himself up yet, the Truffula forest has been decimated. The tradeoff between agricultural expansion and environmental degradation is neither new nor unique to Paraguay. But it has reached a boiling point in a country where environmental considerations and an emerging social activism are coming together to stop the further

The American Society of Civil Engineers named the Itaipú Dam one of the "Seven Wonders of the Modern World" (courtesy *Última Hora*).

development of environmentally degrading agriculture. Meanwhile, big companies still rely on diesel-run generators to supplement their electricity capacity, Paraguay's biggest import item is refined petroleum, and one of the top sources of energy is biomass, the technical word for "burning wood and charcoal obtained from nearby trees."

The Agricultural Golden Geese

Nineteenth-century explorers and faraway scribes were right: Paraguay has highly favorable conditions for agriculture. Whatever elements are involved in an optimal ecological foundation to achieve high agricultural productivity, the land east of the homonymous river has them. It boasts bedrock geology with natural soil fertility and overall high arability rates, abundant rainfall with extremely low probabilities of drought, and allows for a summer–winter crop system. Paraguay sits on top of the Guaraní Aquifer, the world's second largest known aquifer and one of its largest reservoirs of fresh water. Paraguay shares the aquifer with three other countries—Argentina, Brazil, and Uruguay; it is regulated by an international treaty based on United Nations recommendations, the Guaraní Aquifer Agreement. In addition, across Paraguay the incidence of natural catastrophes is low, which is comforting when your annual income is contingent on a normal harvest.

The Chaco, the region west of the Paraguay River, has more difficult conditions for agriculture. For example, it lacks natural drainage, a significant impediment to agricultural development. Add an impermeable sub-soil to its heavy seasonal rains and the profit calculation becomes tight. For a long time, only cattle raising and the production of quebracho extract for tanning purposes made economic sense. Still, a key advantage for cattle production in the Chaco is the extensive availability of guinea grass (*Megathyrsus maximus*), a foraging grass liked by both ranchers and cows due to its nutritional value and palatability, where its average yield is higher than in Argentina and Uruguay.

Favorable agricultural conditions are not enough for success; as American economist Julian Simon explained, the ultimate resource is the human mind.[4] In the 1950s, American anthropologists Elman and Helen Service noted Paraguayan agriculture had low productivity due to "antiquated methods and failure to use fertilizer, insecticides and proper crop rotation and seed selection."[5] However, in the past fifty years in particular, Paraguayan and foreign minds have been able to utilize the country's natural resources to make the agricultural sector its economic engine. The proportion of agricultural to total land has gone up from around a quarter in the early 1960s to more than half in 2019.[6] Most importantly, the productivity of land has improved as well; in 1967, Paraguayan farmers yielded less than 3,000 pounds of cereals per hectare and in 2017 the number escalated to almost 10,000 pounds. On average, each Paraguayan person produces one ton of cereals every year. Not surprisingly, when it comes to exports, Paraguay is a world champ, ranking among the top ten global exporters of soy, rice, sesame, organic sugar, and stevia. Best of all, everywhere you look there is potential for growth. Only 55 percent of Paraguay's total land is used for agriculture, while in Uruguay it is 85 percent.

Paraguay's outstanding agricultural numbers would not look the same without soybean production. All the major trends related to agriculture and its environmental side effects can be explained by soy production alone, which at more than 10 million metric tons is gigantic. In the fifty years from 1967 to 2017, soybean production went from 31,700 to 8.4 million acres, a percentage increase so great it's meaningless.[7] Paraguay is the fifth biggest soybean exporter in the world and brings in $1.5 billion, the country's largest source of foreign currency. Soybean dollars are so powerful that their transfer into the local economy shifts the overall level of credit.[8] The main market for Paraguayan soy is Argentina, which absorbs two-thirds of all exports. Granted, not all the production ends up in Argentina. An unknown percentage heads to China, a country that as we will

Paraguay is one of the world's top producers and exporters of soybean, reaching productivity levels similar to high-income countries (courtesy *Última Hora*).

see in the next chapter does not have diplomatic relations with Paraguay. The company that exports the most soybeans from Paraguay is the Chinese COFCO International. But Paraguay does not just milk Mother Nature's gifts. The Paraguayan soybean producers are top-notch as well, yielding close to three metric tons per hectare, on par with the most productive countries. Paraguay's soybean yield at 31,000 hectograms per hectare

… yet, overall agricultural productivity has significant room for growth (courtesy Oscar Rivet).

is close to world leaders United States' 33,000 and Brazil's 33,800. Furthermore, the Paraguayan soybean is protein rich, higher than Argentina's and Brazil's, and thus fetches a price premium. The protein difference is not big, but one or two percentage points can make a huge difference in terms of costs and profits.

The production of soybeans is so large and profitable in Paraguay that multinational agribusinesses operate their own navies, featuring large fleets of barges and modern ports. The American commodity trading giant Archer Daniels Midland (ADM) alone has 200 barges. ADM and other commodity trading companies, however, do not own the land nor plant the soybeans. They simply buy it from local producers. Their capital footprint is composed of the silos to store the production, the barges to move it out, and the ports in Paraguay and in the region to export it to global markets. Some companies also have processing plants where around 40 percent of soybean production is turned into soybean meal, oil, and hull pellets.

In Paraguay's agricultural machine, beef production comes close behind soybeans in economic importance. For starters, there are more than two cows for every Paraguayan.[9] When slaughtered, these cows yield beef at international standards. For instance, Paraguayan cattle ranchers achieve quality and productivity numbers equal to beef-producing leaders

Paraguay's barges, the world's third largest fleet behind the United States and China, move three-quarters of the country's foreign trade (courtesy *Última Hora*).

Brazil and Argentina. In the past thirty years, beef production quadrupled, reaching more than 400,000 tons; exports have grown apace, making Paraguay a leading player in the global market and bringing in upwards of $1 billion every year. Remarkably, Paraguayan beef exports have diversified, with Russia and Chile as its top buyers. Other important markets are Vietnam, and Israel. Starting in 2015, the customer-friendly Qatar Airways has been offering Paraguayan beef on its flights. Just as important, the potential for further growth is significant, as both the Chinese and the U.S. markets remain largely closed to Paraguayan beef. Cattle ranchers in Paraguay salivate when they hear about the Chinese middle class growing in size and demanding more beef, or when orthodox Hindus in India (the world's second biggest beef exporter) seek a national ban on the slaughtering of cows and the export of beef. There is also room for productivity growth as Paraguayan cows are still under-producing calves compared to other major producers. For example, Paraguay's number of calves born relative to the number of cows bred, 4.5 per 10, is lower than Uruguay's 6 per 10 or the United States' 8 per 10.

Both soybean and beef production have attracted levels of foreign direct investment that the rest of the economy could only dream of. Large American companies such as Cargill, the aforementioned ADM, or Russia's Sodrugestvo are leading exporters, but also manufacturers, turning soybean into oils for exports. Similarly, large Brazilian meatpacking companies have moved to Paraguay and become key producers and exporters. In addition, taxation of agricultural exports in Argentina, political uncertainty in Brazil, and high prices in Uruguay have been the great gifts to Paraguayan agriculture in the past twenty years, attracting investors from the region and their critical know-how to compete in global markets.

In spite of its prowess, the agricultural sector's contribution to the Paraguayan GDP has been on a steady decline. It used to comprise almost half the economy back in the 1960s, but now it only contributes 10 percent of GDP. To be clear, agriculture's smaller GDP contribution says more about the rest of the economy, particularly its service and manufacturing sectors, than anything else. It could be argued that the economic growth brought about by agriculture gave rise to a bigger service economy and a larger manufacturing base.

In this sense, the most consequential change in Paraguay's agriculture has been the transition away from small-scale production largely intended for domestic consumption to large-scale, mechanized production aimed at global commodity markets. Paradoxically, the transition is responsible for both high economic growth and high unemployment. Informal estimates indicate that mechanized agriculture employs one worker per 200 hectares (494 acres), the same area that can hold twenty families engaged in subsistence agriculture. There is nothing particularly evil about Paraguayan soy producers; they use equal amounts of technology (including pesticides) and labor per given land as a producer in Iowa or the Argentinian Pampas.

However, there is also a problem that is uniquely Paraguayan, which affects land ownership and its distribution. Since the times following independence, Paraguay has allocated land neither fairly nor transparently. Under the reign of Rodríguez de Francia, the Paraguayan state inherited the lands of the Spanish Crown and kept them. Following the end of the Triple Alliance War, the government decided to attract immigrants with the country's only available resource, which was land. Argentines, Brazilians, Mennonites, Koreans, Japanese, and Eastern Europeans were lured to Paraguay by the promise of land ownership. But the Indigenous living within those large extensions of land sold at fire sale prices never had a say over the transactions. The lands where they lived from time immemorial were first forcefully taken from them by Spanish conquerors and then sold by the politicians of the independent Paraguay. Meanwhile, those Indigenous people that melted in the Paraguayan stew of ethnicities were not favored with lands either. Most of them remained in rural areas where their claims to ownership were flimsy at best, even though they were not typically challenged in court. Those holding political power and their beneficiaries acquired official public titles generally to the detriment of people with no political sway or inside knowledge of land deals. The Stroessner regime's Instituto de Bienestar Rural (Rural Welfare Institute) was born with the intention of populating rural areas and giving land ownership to more people, but it quickly became a vehicle to give away thousands of acres to politically connected individuals or those willing to pay a bribe, or to challenge land ownership claims of political rivals. In 2012, the government realized how grave the situation was—the sum of all titles added up to almost 60 million hectares, 20 million more hectares than the country's real size![10] Only with the advent of GPS technology have courts and private attorneys been able to settle land disputes in a more technical fashion, without resorting to political maneuvering, even if legal chicaneries still tend to favor those with powerful connections.

As a result, small farmers were never able to utilize their land to generate capital and finance a profitable enterprise. And unlike many Asian development success stories where land reform played an important role,[11] Paraguay's low demographic density meant that the small farms' actual production remained for subsistence only and did not reach markets. With the advent of commodity crops in the 1970s and the opening of the frontier to Brazil, the government came under pressure to provide clear land titling. Unfortunately for small farmers, only those businesses big enough to hire lawyers and lobby policy makers benefited from the drive to formalize land titles. The consequence for modern Paraguay is that around 40 percent of rural properties either do not have title or hold titles of limited legal validity.[12]

A predictable outcome of unfair land distribution is heavily concentrated land ownership. The British NGO Oxfam estimates 12,000 owners concentrate 90 percent of land ownership.[13] According to a World Bank report, 1 percent of all ranches in Paraguay control more than 70 percent of the productive land.[14] The late Sun Myung Moon's Unification Church is Paraguay's biggest landowner, with close to 1.5 million acres, which amounts to an area similar in size to the State of Palestine. Moon bought lands from Carlos Casado's holdings, a top beneficiary of post–Triple Alliance War land sales. Other big landowners include Brasiguayos and the families of politicians and business owners who were close to the Stroessner regime.

However, there has been some land distribution based on fairer procedures, but the results in terms of economic achievement have been poor. Most small farmers and so-called landless peasants who were able to access valuable lands have either failed to use them productively or ended up selling them to investors. Often, they trade their derechera, a right of land possession dependent on full payment for ownership. Because at the time of the sale the land is not fully paid and cannot be sold for ten years after occupancy, the transaction is informal and the land use prone to illegal exploits. Similarly, many Indigenous chiefs take advantage of their communities' tax-free lands and rent them to outside producers, gaining a large rent. The land-use conditions in these transactions are also set to low standards and become a source of deforestation and illegal logging. And the proceeds from the rent are not always distributed fairly inside the community.

In an ideal world, land would be largely allocated to its most productive uses based on clear land titles and strict environmental controls. Or it could be returned to the Indigenous communities so they can go back to their traditional way of life, including lives that were "poor, nasty, brutish, and short," to paraphrase Thomas Hobbes. In Paraguay, land is gradually being allocated to its most productive uses, but with little environmental controls. Soybean and cattle ranching are indeed the most productive uses of Paraguayan land, requiring scale in order to reach their productivity sweet spot. More and more, size matters to beat marginal cost and achieve financial sustainability. Thus, absent a labor-intensive crop that can fetch a high price in global markets, rural workers and their families have few options to earn currency. Cotton used to play that role, but since its price fizzled around 2010, there has been no other crop substitute. For a while sesame looked like such a power crop, but it was never able to pick up the cotton slack. Japan was the main buyer and requested tough quality standards that small Paraguayan farmers were not able to deliver. In addition, the welfare calculus for farmers has changed. For example, most farmers have added two expenditure items to their budgets that did not exist before, namely gas for their motorcycles and pre-paid airtime for their cellular phones.

Unable to meet productivity and quality standards, farm income has crashed and bled labor to the cities. The traditional farm size shrank as well. It went from 173 acres in the 1960s to less than 15 acres in 2017.[15] Rural household members tend to be older too. Those left behind must eke out a living solely on subsistence agriculture. On the other hand, those few who find gainful rural employment are like some of my Uruguayan friends, professional individuals with both technical and managerial skills able to administer large agricultural operations with few human resources. Their families reside in the city while the spouse travels to rural areas periodically.

At the end of the day, all rural producers need to beat the weather and international prices with steady productivity improvements; absent these there is no realistic escape from poverty. While the small farmers organizations' demands for land ownership, better titling, and government intervention are altogether righteous causes and potentially helpful for their economic wellbeing, they still need to produce by means of extracting greater value and using fewer resources. And while land reform remains the top demand for protesters who have rallied in Asunción annually since 1994, its attainment may not necessarily solve farmers' economic problems. Without a labor-intensive and high-demand agricultural commodity that can match the higher incomes available in cities, rural families have few economic incentives to stay put. Likewise, Paraguayan rural areas lack basic services available in cities such as internet connection, paved roads, and access to a cheaper and more diversified basket of basic goods and services. Furthermore, cities offer educational and health services that in rural areas are either unavailable or modest.

The Green Energy Utopia Gives Three Dams

When it comes to electricity production and consumption, Paraguay is like a thirsty person in a desert sitting by a huge bottle of high-end water but lacking an opener. Here is the paradox: thanks to a large hydroelectric infrastructure, nearly 100 percent of the electricity produced in Paraguay is clean and renewable. Furthermore, at 6.2 cents per kilowatt, Paraguay has one of the lowest electricity prices in the world (for example, compare to 8.8 cents in Argentina, 16.9 in Sao Paulo, 20.4 in Rio de Janeiro and 23.1 in the United States).[16] Except for absurdly subsidized Venezuela, Paraguay has Latin America's lowest electricity rates for both residential and industrial consumption.[17] Furthermore, no other country in the world exports more clean energy than Paraguay.

Alas, Paraguay does not take advantage of its clean energy. Not long ago, the government was bragging in a public relations video[18] that Paraguay "only" consumes 13 percent of the electricity it produces. The scare quotes are mine and let me explain why: it means both that the country has large production and that it consumes at developing-country levels. The data on electric power consumption[19] for Paraguay is clear; the country is placed among the lowest per capita consumers in the world, below the world and Latin American and Caribbean averages. Paraguayans consume 73 percent of the electricity Latin Americans consume on average and 12 percent of the electricity consumed per person in the United States.

In addition to a low per capita income, another culprit of Paraguay's low consumption rate is the lack of a suitable infrastructure. Because of it, Paraguay's bounty of clean, cheap electricity does not reach all corners of the country. Data from the World Economic Forum's "Global Competitiveness Report"[20] show that Paraguay's quality of electricity supply is poor; less than twenty countries in the whole world have a worse quality than Paraguay. It has one of Latin America's smallest electricity transmission capabilities, with only one high-voltage line installed for the whole country (the government plans to add two lines by 2022). As a result, other energy indicators are out of whack. For example, the country's consumption of renewable energy is scant; it constitutes 15.7 percent of the total, with biomass (mostly wood and charcoal) amounting to 44.2 percent and fossil fuels 40.1 percent.[21] Without infrastructure and wood available nearby (as is the case in Paraguay), there is little incentive for companies and households to use renewable energy. The energy-use breakdown has not changed much in the past decade. However, use of biomass has decreased compared to the 1980s when Paraguay derived more than half of its total energy from firewood and ranked as the top per capita consumer of firewood in Latin America.[22]

Additionally, Paraguay lags behind Latin America and the Caribbean in access to clean fuels and technologies for cooking; 64 percent of Paraguayans have access, compared to 86 percent in the Latin American region or 100 percent in the United States.[23] Paraguayan companies are not energy efficient either; the quantity of energy they need to produce one unit of GDP growth is low by regional and developed-world standards.[24] The electricity infrastructure deficit is plainly apparent without crunching numbers—look at the thousands and thousands of gas stations across the country. With suitable infrastructure, Paraguay should be a land of electric cars. In turn, Paraguay is not making as much progress in reducing the gases that cause global warming. When I drove my car with the windows down or walked near a public transport bus in Asunción, I realized as I inhaled diesel fumes that the green revolution had not totally arrived yet. In the 2017 Social Progress Index,[25] Paraguay received bad grades for its greenhouse emissions, with an indicator ranking of 106 out of 128 countries.

It can certainly get hot in Asunción during the summer, with temperatures averaging about 82°F (28°C) in January and usually reaching 100°F (38°C) in the middle of the day. Unfortunately, on those days when the thermometer hits 100°F, the electricity consistently goes off. Not surprisingly, Paraguayans hold the National Administration of Electricity (ANDE in Spanish), the state-owned electricity utility, in utter contempt. The entity is the butt of many jokes simply because otherwise its operations would be infuriating. Indeed, if a wicked policy maker had decided to set up a failing enterprise, it would look a lot like ANDE. To begin with, the company's operations and most of its strategic decisions are ultimately a political call—by Paraguayan politicos. Presidential candidates campaign on a platform of cheap electricity and once they get to power use ANDE as a political tool to hire supporters and advance various political causes, such as subsidizing favored customers. Thanks to its monopoly on the generation, transmission, and distribution of electricity within Paraguay, ANDE tends to be profitable in the traditional sense. Private power generation is allowed, but on ANDE's conditions. So if you are a solar company, you are forced to sell your electricity only to ANDE at the price they set. In addition, ANDE's financial surplus must be transferred to the Ministry of Finance; in this sense, ANDE is only another item in the policy planning process and as such does not always get what it needs in terms of investments and reforms. According to its own estimates, ANDE has unmet investment needs amounting to more than $1 billion.[26] For example, the company loses around a quarter of all the electricity it produces due to theft and deficiencies in the distribution lines.[27] Just as frustrating, ANDE's customer service is notoriously lacking, featuring less empathy than a customer might find from a mafia boss. I once heard an ANDE president discourage Paraguayans from ironing clothes during siesta time, because otherwise they will overwhelm the neighborhoods' transformers. ANDE is also infamous for overcharging its customers without offering any recourse. Naturally, ANDE's constant outages and shutdowns are never well timed. One of the times famous American economist Jeffrey Sachs came to Asunción to speak about Paraguay's development needs, the power went off twice. Sachs is renowned in Paraguay for authoring a major report on the country's electricity challenges. Small businesses suffer the most, because they cannot afford pricey generators; a typical case is that of a small business owner who had to shut down its ice-cream parlor due to the constant power outages, which added up to nine outages in five days that on average lasted four hours each.[28] On top of everything, ANDE's problematic supply of electricity exacerbates environmental challenges by increasing the demand for petroleum-based fuels and wood. To cut ANDE some slack, the power outages also respond to Paraguayans' increased wealth, manifested in this case in more people able to afford air conditioning units.

Paraguay's untapped clean energy prowess comes from three hydroelectric dams: two are bi-national—the huge Itaipú jointly managed with Brazil and the medium-sized Yacyretá with Argentina—and one is the small Acaray, solely owned by Paraguay. In 2017, of the total energy generated by the three dams (measured in megawatt hours), Itaipú comprised 98.5 percent, Yacyretá 1.4 percent, and Acaray 0.1 percent.

Despite its role as the country's main clean energy engine, the Itaipú dam's origins and construction process are not as clean. It was all along a Brazilian idea; in the 1960s the country was in a confident mood with high economic growth, progressive social reforms, and the building from scratch of its modernist capital Brasilia. In 1964, the armed forces took power by force and brought a bravado to policymaking that, although unnecessary, was well timed. Only a few years after the coup d'etat, the so-called "Brazilian miracle" ushered in an era of double-digit growth rates between the late 1960s and the early 1970s that never again repeated itself.

In 1965, barely a year after overthrowing the civilian government, the Brazilian armed forces occupied and took possession of a large territory near the border with Paraguay. The move was directly in response to a flag-raising act by the Paraguayan government that had taken place a few months before, but it had also been brewing since the 1872 Loizaga–Cotegipe Treaty following the Triple Alliance War, which left open some questions about border limits.[29] The territory included the Saltos de Guairá falls, at the time the world's largest waterfall, and according to the Paraguayans that still remember visiting it, the country's most breathtaking natural wonder. The Stroessner regime was in no position to force the Brazilians to vacate their new possessions. It defaulted to diplomacy and begged Lyndon Johnson's Secretary of State Dean Rusk to mediate with the Brazilians. In those days of Cold War bipolar foreign policies, the Brazilian and Paraguayan military governments were on the anti-communist camp and thus earned the U.S. government's goodwill. While it is not completely clear how much U.S. mediation mattered, the end result was the Act of Iguazú of 1966, which established the removal of Brazilian troops from the Saltos de Guairá and the joint exploration of a dam project right in the conflictive area.

The "joint exploration" took a while, and only in 1973 with the signing of the Treaty of Itaipú did the two countries set the conditions for the dam's construction. For the Stroessner regime, Itaipú was both a political and economic victory that allowed it to strengthen its claim to power. The actual construction was a feast of corruption for Stroessner's cronies, with cost overruns and massive overpricing schemes, favoritism in the allocation of contracts, non-compliance with labor and environmental regulations, and a general leaching of resources for private benefit. It was at first estimated to cost under $5 billion, but ended up costing close to $20 billion. Paraguay's share of the cost was financed by loans from Brazil. When Itaipú was finished and began producing energy in 1984, it became the largest hydroelectric dam in the world until China's Three Gorges Dam took that title away in 2012. Even then, in 2016 Itaipú set the world record in annual electricity generation. Alas, the flooding and the higher water necessary to create Itaipú's reservoir basin wiped out the Saltos de Guairá falls together with countless Indigenous communities that had dwelled for centuries in the now flooded areas.

The overall solution to the border dispute was beneficial for Paraguay given that there were high chances of losing everything—waterfalls, dam, and border. Yet, the usufruct after decades of clean energy production largely favored Brazil. As a joint enterprise funded equally by both countries, the division of rents should have been a straight forward matter: 50–50 each and complete energy-usage autonomy. However, negotiators included language in both the Act of Iguazú and the Treaty of Itaipú that left sharing open to interpretation—mostly to Brazil's interpretation. For example, the Act of Iguazú's article IV established that "the electric energy […] will be divided in equal parts between the two countries." Clear enough, except that it added in the same article, "each party has the right of preference to acquire the energy at a fair price, which will be fixed by experts from both countries, of any quantity that is not utilized to supply the consumption needs of the other country." The Itaipú Treaty switched the "fair price" clause to a "compensation" clause, but the result has remained the same: Brazil still gets to use all the energy Paraguay does not utilize at a cost-based price. Any energy surplus can only be sold to the other country, and third party sales are prohibited. A careful investigation by Paraguayan-American researcher Miguel Carter estimated that Paraguay forewent billions in revenue for not charging market prices for the electricity it did not use and sold to Brazil. Specifically, Carter researched how much Brazilian electricity companies paid for energy within their domestic market and found Paraguay could have received an additional $75.4 billion corresponding to the 1985–2018 period if Brazil had paid market prices for the Itaipú energy instead of a cost-based price.[30] The foregone figure corresponds to more than double Paraguay's current GDP.

The Treaty of Itaipú's energy pricing and distribution agreements were set to last fifty years, ending in 2023. In that same year, Paraguay will have also paid off its debt from the dam's construction. While in 2009, Paraguay's president Fernando Lugo made progress by convincing his ideological fellow traveler, Brazil's president Lula da Silva, to pay more for the electricity, the potential gains for Paraguay of a successful negotiation in 2023 are even greater. Paraguay would like to dispose of its energy at will, selling it at market rates to Brazilian customers or to neighbors Argentina and Bolivia and potentially to other regional customers. The higher income would more than cover the major investments in infrastructure required to connect Itaipú to those potential markets. To what extent Brazilian negotiators will cede ground and let Paraguay reap more benefits is obviously far from certain. The zero-sum nature of the agreement means the most powerful party will likely impose its interests regardless of the small party's righteous demands. When I spoke to Brazilian experts who follow the Itaipú negotiations, the majority view was that Brazil will either keep the status quo or secure more benefits for itself.

Seen from the side of Brazil's energy consumption, it makes sense to keep prices low. Itaipú accounts for 15 percent of Brazil's total electricity consumption; the share is much higher for the industrial heartland located near Sao Paulo, Brazil's biggest city. Paraguay's annual share of electricity from Itaipú is almost equal to Sao Paulo's electricity consumption. To a great extent, Paraguay's unconsumed share from Itaipú has subsidized Sao Paulo and its metropolitan area's industrial growth for the past forty years, which means a price increase could have damaging consequences for the Brazilian economy as a whole. Another subsidy from Paraguayans to Brazilians resulted from Brazil forcing Itaipú to set prices below cost during the 1980s and 1990s, generating debts that had to be repaid in equal parts by both countries. Brazilians retort that without their credit guarantees, the dam would have never been built in the first place.

The scenario under which Paraguay gets higher rents is not necessarily encouraging either. There are two tradeoffs associated with Paraguay's potential energy bounty: first, large quantities of commodity rents tend to produce massive levels of corruption, something Paraguay has plenty of already. It is why a former Venezuelan minister of mines and hydrocarbons dubbed oil "the devil's excrement." Secondly, the influx of foreign currency can have damaging effects over the rest of the economy if the funds are not carefully managed. The latter is called "Dutch disease" and it is the effect that an influx of foreign currency has on the local currency. Because the foreign money appreciates the local currency (raises its value), the rest of the economy becomes more expensive, making exports less competitive vis-à-vis other markets.

Indeed, the way Paraguayans have administered Itaipú's operations and large existing rents is not reassuring, to say the least. Because Itaipú is a binational entity, both countries have autonomy to staff its ranks and distribute its royalties as they please. For Paraguayan politicians, Itaipú has been a low-hanging piñata, which they use to either appoint themselves or their followers with outrageous salaries, hire friends and family members, favor cronies with outsourced contracts, and shower constituencies with public projects. Itaipú royalties and taxes contribute to more than 10 percent of the Paraguay's fiscal intake, which is significant. However, this does not include the millions doled out every year to arbitrary projects—some necessary and some not so much, including bridges, school construction, hospital equipment, and roads, but also trips to Europe and the Caribbean, fancy lunches plus guards, consultants, and lawyers for Itaipú employees. The Supreme Court has ruled over the years that Itaipú should not be considered a government entity so it is not accountable to Congress or the comptroller general; likewise, its workers are not government workers thus have greater leeway to determine work hours and other benefits with their bosses. The company's board members receive a retirement package ("golden parachute" in Paraguayan parlance) averaging around $170,000 annually for life available after ten years of work.

Itaipú's smaller sister the Yacyretá dam is not much different when it comes to corruption in its construction and management. If Itaipú's corruption evokes a waterfall or a geyser depending on your perspective, Yacyretá grew to be what former Argentine president Carlos Menem (1989–1999) dubbed "a monument to corruption."[31] The idea and the construction of Yacyretá was largely Argentina's reaction to Brazil's construction of Itaipú. It was sped up in the 1970s energy crises when oil prices busted Latin American economies and forced them to search for alternative sources of energy. Thus, following some years of joint exploration efforts, in 1973 Argentina and Paraguay signed the Yacyretá Treaty establishing a binational enterprise located on their shared border by the Paraná River, with structure, pricing conditions, and corruption incentives almost identical to those of Itaipú. Just like Itaipú, Yacyretá's construction had huge overrun costs. Paraguayan journalist Andrés Colmán calculated the cost went from a budgeted $1.5 billion before construction to $10.5 billion when it was inaugurated, with an estimated $3.5 billion that was never accounted for.[32] And the construction of Yacyretá also paid lip service to environmental impact and the plight of the thousands of people that were displaced as a result of the flooding required to build the dam.

The use of Yacyretá's energy is equally skewed, with Argentina taking upwards of 90 percent of the total. Argentina does not always consume this share, but often resells some of it to Brazil. Andrew Nickson estimated that Argentina sells electricity to Brazil at $120 per MWh, but Paraguay only gets $8 per MWh for the same transaction.[33] It would help if Paraguay had the infrastructure to resell its Yacyretá energy, but it does not, and so it can only watch Argentina profit from afar. In a preview of what could happen during the Itaipú Treaty renegotiation, when the Yacyretá Treaty expired in 2014 and was partly renegotiated in 2017, Paraguay got almost nothing in terms of increased rents or better terms.

Riding the Environmental Kuznets Curve

Picture a scene in a bucolic park, where a family is placidly eating a picnic lunch. After they finish eating, the family proceeds to discard the remaining waste on the grass, while the father throws a beer can pitcher-style behind a tree. The scene did not happen in real life but in the second season of *Mad Men*,[34] a popular TV show set in the United States of the 1960s. Still, it portrayed what was then a completely acceptable practice that has become unimaginable in today's United States and rare in Paraguay. This evolution of environmental etiquette along the lines of our wealth is a phenomenon referred to as the "Environmental Kuznets Curve." Picture an inverted U with environmental degradation in the vertical axis and per capita income in the horizontal axis. Starting from the lower left corner, environmental degradation climbs up in tandem with per capita income until it reaches the curve's hump; thereafter it starts tapering down even as the economy continues to grow. Coincidentally, the U.S. per capita income during the 1960s was similar to modern Paraguay's per capita income (around $4,000 in current US$).[35] What drives movement along the environmental degradation curve is a mix of behavioral change and technology that result from growing incomes. If the *Mad Men* scene were to take place in modern Paraguay, the family would probably be ashamed to dispose of the picnic's waste on the grass (behavioral change). Furthermore, it is possible the Paraguayan dad would kick the beer can Lionel Messi–style behind a tree but the damage would be reduced thanks to modern cans' lower metal content (technology).

The behavioral change responds to growing wealth; the higher one's per capita income and the more one's basic needs that are fulfilled, the more people care about the environment. It is a tradeoff that has been repeated over and over in all developed economies. It existed when the United States and European economies were taking off in the Industrial Revolution, and it is still there as the Chinese and Indian economies move up to higher per capita incomes. In the case of Paraguay this tradeoff is visible across the board in the behavior of corporations, the public sector, and its people. In Paraguay there is no such thing as illegal fishing or poaching; fish and wildlife are mostly up for grabs as enforcement of deforestation laws is lax and most Paraguayans have limited environmental awareness.

Paraguay's biggest environmental threats are deforestation and water pollution. Unlike other developing countries, Paraguay does not have an air pollution problem thanks to low density of both population and manufacturing industries. Environmental damage has been the result of a simple story of slashing and burning forests in order to yield more cattle and soybeans. The amount of forested land has gone down in tandem with the rise of agriculture. Others factors specific to Paraguay, such as land tenure issues, weak governance and enforcement of law, lack of human and financial resources, and corruption, have also contributed to environmental damage. A weighty USAID "Forestry & Biodiversity Assessment" noted almost tongue-in-cheek that "Decisions regarding the use of forest resources and biodiversity are often made without sufficient scientific and technical data."[36] In this sense, a Paraguayan member of Congress once disclosed to me that environmental licenses go for $5,000.

In the twenty-five years from 1990 to 2015, Paraguay's forestland dropped from 52 million to 37 million acres. According to the 2015 Food and Agriculture Organization's Global Forest Resources Assessment—the gold standard for deforestation data—Paraguay had the world's sixth-highest annual net loss of forest area between 2010 and 2015.[37] With a forest cover of nearly 40 percent of the country's land area and the same economic fundamentals in place, the country is well positioned to reach the deforestation top ten again when a new Global Forest Resources Assessment comes out. Still, Paraguay is not being stingy with its forest protection regime. Protected wilderness territory covers nearly 15 percent of the country's total area, a percentage that is below the Latin America and the Caribbean average, almost the same as low and middle income countries, and higher than the United States.[38]

In Paraguay the challenge with deforestation is not so much the extent of the problem, but the speed. By the time the government passed a Zero Deforestation law in 2004, the Atlantic forest located to the east of the Paraguay River was almost gone; the World Bank estimated in 2018 that 94 percent of this forest had already been cut down.[39] The more accurate name of the law should have been "deforestation zero in the lands east of the Paraguay River" as the law allows forest clearing under some conditions in the Chaco region, west of the Paraguay River. The data shows that the deforestation ban in the eastern region had the effect of driving cattle ranchers west to the Chaco in search of land. While the situation in the Chaco region is not yet as expended, the pace of deforestation is rapid. The local environmental NGO Guyra has been using satellite images to determine the extent of forest loss in the Gran Chaco region—encompassing also Argentina, Brazil, and Bolivia—and for the 2012–2018 period, they reported the

Paraguayan Chaco lost an annual average of 619,000 acres of forest. The total for those six years was 3.7 million acres, a territory slightly bigger than Connecticut's total land mass.[40] With a rate of deforestation at this average, the whole Chaco forest cover would disappear by the year 2050.

As we have seen, the Paraguayan judicial system is ineffective in many ways and incapable of dealing with Paraguayans' knack for circumventing laws. The country already has thirty-five environmental laws, but none are fully enforced. And we have seen how politically connected individuals and corporations can sway the judicial sector to avoid penalties; the risk of going to jail for an environmental crime is close to zero. Judges in the interior of the country typically fail to convict polluting businesses either because they are in cahoots with the owners or because they fear the local politicians and the potential retaliation for driving out jobs from the area. The judicial system's ineffectiveness is transparent in the specific realm of environmental law. Take the 1973 Forestry Law. It mandates that 25 percent of all land over fifty acres must remain under forest cover. The law is laudable except for the Paraguayan catch: the remaining 25 percent that each landowner allocates for forest cover can be sold to another landowner, who is then allowed to chop down 75 percent of the protected parcel. And so it goes. In turn, forest fragmentation creates more environmental problems, as the remaining patchwork of trees does not really do it for the native fauna. These species need large swaths of native forest and biological corridors in between forests in order to survive. Even with the Zero Deforestation law in force, the level of deforestation in the Chaco between 2000 and 2015 exceeded what the Instituto Nacional Forestal (National Forestry Institute) permitted by approximately 750,000 acres,[41] an area slightly larger than Luxembourg. In spite of everything, there is hope in the Kuznets curve's prediction that higher income will lead to more environmental protection regardless of the existing legal framework.

Meanwhile, rapid population growth and the subsequent urbanization process have overwhelmed the country's capacity to safely manage human waste. Water in the Paraguay River has a dangerously high level of fecal coliform bacteria per liter. The Paraguayan water utility company ESSAP, short for Empresa de Servicios Sanitarios del Paraguay (Water & Sewer Company), estimates that only 2 percent of wastewater from homes receives decontamination treatment; only 11 percent of the country has sewage coverage. I have seen with my own eyes how sewage and street runoff flow straight into the Paraguay River. I cannot see, however, how Paraguay will reach the United Nation's target of halving the proportion of untreated wastewater by 2030. While the Paraguayan government has planned a $110 million investment to develop three new water treatment plants in Asunción for 2020, the larger investment needed to comply with UN goals could reach $6 billion. In one of Paraguay's most popular folk songs, "Recuerdos de Ypacaraí," a lover longs for his woman, singing, "Everything reminds me of you, my sweet love, by the blue water of Ypacaraí."[42] The song was composed in 1950 and I can attest its lyrics would have been different if written in present day Paraguay. On a visit to the lake, about an hour outside Asunción, its grayish water and stench of sewage overpowered my romantic senses. The general situation is not only bad for the human beings living in Paraguay, but also for the local and traveling wildlife. According to the World Wildlife Fund, the Paraguay River's contaminated waters are killing fish and the migratory birds that rely on them.

The Kuznets curve effects are not only channeled through the actions of corporations, but also through a population that does not always practice what it preaches. Notably, on some polls Paraguayans express concern about climate change and favor prioritizing environmental protection over economic growth. For example, according to a 2017 Latinobarómetro survey, 70 percent of Paraguayans support giving priority to the fight against climate change versus 7 percent prioritizing economic growth.[43] In addition, Paraguay signed the Paris Agreement on climate change at its inception in April 2016 and was one of the first countries to ratify it. In practice,

Lake Ypacaraí's waters, like many rivers and creeks, is contaminated with human and industrial waste (courtesy Alfonso Velázquez).

however, Paraguayans do not play the role of tree-huggers. Voters do not favor politicians with strong environmental credentials, nor support organizations that advocate for environmental causes. Political parties have yet to propose groundbreaking policies intended to take advantage of their clean electricity and stop the country's reliance on non-renewables energies, principally carbon-based fuels and biomass. In general, suboptimal trash collection and irresponsible trash disposal practices in both urban and rural areas do not seem to bother Paraguayans. The effect of Paraguayan neglect is clear to global surveys. The Environmental Performance Index (EPI)—a joint effort by the Yale Center for Environmental Law & Policy and Columbia University's Center for International Earth Science Information Network Report—has consistently ranked Paraguay in the table's lower third. The EPI measures countries' environmental health and ecosystem vitality across a number of variables, and in both macro measurements Paraguay has gotten an equally low score since EPI's first report in 2006.[44]

In order to top the Kuznets curve and start riding it down to where income does not constraint environmental protection, it is key for Paraguay to plug the economy into its hydroelectric energy bounty. The options available for Paraguay to become a clean-energy industry center are significant. The *Guardian's* Laurence Blair first reported on the growing cryptocurrency mining operations in Ciudad del Este in November 2018,[45] where there were eight crypto-mining facilities with some 20,000 processors (there were three million worldwide, two million in China alone) churning Bitcoin and Ethereum and growing. In that same month, the South Korea–based Commons Foundation announced plans to create the world's largest cryptocurrency mining center and global exchange in a 538,195 square foot plot provided by the Paraguayan government.[46] At around the same time, the Argentine bitcoin trader company Bitex opened an office in Asunción to broker local cryptocurrency transactions. In addition, some analysts have called attention to Paraguay's potential to become a datacenter hub for large companies such as Amazon, Apple, Tencent, or Alibaba.[47] Other analysts have noted the need to attract energy intensive industries, such as chemical and aluminum casting plants, and pulp and paper industries.[48] Similarly, electric cars should be the norm and not an expensive environmental-care signaling device for the wealthy.

A possible solution for limiting environmental damage before Paraguayans start moving down the Kuznets curve is to appeal to high-income countries' Kuznets-tested interest in protecting the environment. More specifically, environmental crusaders can start by leveraging the reputational risk of large foreign companies to put an environmental check on their Paraguayan providers. For example, a Paraguayan exporter of stevia

The sun sets in Paraguay's countryside (Katelyn Barone, Unsplash).

had to invest millions upgrading its processing plant after a U.S. Embassy official found out they were contaminating a river and brought the case to the company's main client, a large U.S. corporation. Because the cost of a public shaming campaign is so high for U.S. corporations that fail to protect the environment, the Paraguayan producer had to either adapt or else lose the business. Likewise, when the British NGO Earthsight uncovered the large extent of Paraguayan charcoal exports to the European Union that originated through reckless deforestation in the Chaco region, the giant French retailer Carrefour was forced to halt purchases. Other European buyers were put on the defensive and were compelled to investigate the case,[49] which goes to show that Paraguay's economic development depends increasingly on international relations and the effectiveness of the government's diplomacy, ready or not.

VII

Island Diplomacy

A country's diplomacy is largely the product of its unique circumstances, be they geographical, developmental, historical, or demographic. Its leaders and diplomats carry out foreign policy under the constraints that the international system imposes upon them. In the case of Paraguay, geographical and self-imposed isolation marked its diplomacy and lack thereof across different points in time. Augusto Roa Bastos's description of Paraguay as "an island surrounded by land," mentioned in Chapter V, was an attempt to explain his country's isolationism and the exceptionalism that stemmed from it. Exiled in Spain, Roa Bastos saw from a distance Paraguay's cultural idiosyncrasies, but in modern Paraguay every other talking head uses it to illustrate all kinds of social phenomena, from political cronyism to sub-par foreign direct investment. The metaphor helps to contextualize different aspects of Paraguay, even though it has obvious explanatory limits. In my judgment, it does a good job of making sense of the country's foreign policy; without the metaphor, Paraguay's international relations are hard to comprehend. How else does one explain some of Paraguay's unique diplomatic choices? For example, Paraguay is one of the few countries with diplomatic relations with Taiwan; for a while it was one of only three to have moved its Israeli Embassy to Jerusalem; and Paraguayan diplomats have no qualms about reaffirming their country's commitment to U.S. foreign policy goals and publicly shaking hands with the Iranian foreign affairs minister in the same day.

One can learn in a manual for Paraguayan diplomats, written by former minister of foreign affairs Leila Rachid, that the country's foreign policy rests on three pillars: (1) a commitment to the sanctity of borders and the principle of non-intervention; (2) free navigation of the rivers bordering its outer limits; and (3) the defense of democracy and human rights.[1] Yet, the foremost interest that has persisted across the ups and downs of history is the defense of the country's sovereignty, the combination of pillars (1) and (2). If history has taught Paraguay any lesson it is that

non-interference in the internal affairs of other states is a no-brainer. While
(3) is laudable and makes sense in the current regional context, it is not
what has kept Paraguayan sovereignty whole.

Regardless of the goals, the tools that Paraguayan diplomats have
employed have differed significantly, to say the least. For example, according to Diego Abente—one of Paraguay's leading international affairs
experts—the Stroessner regime's thirty-five-year-long foreign policy consisted of "life jacket" diplomacy,[2] thrown around to keep the regime afloat.
Unlike other countries, Paraguay has neither a tradition of non-partisan
diplomacy nor a coherent, long-term strategy. Rather, Paraguay's foreign
policies have been anchored to the president's office and based on his volatile instincts, and thus have tended towards the unpredictable. It is why a
2019 report from the *Financial Times* called Paraguay a "former foreign policy maverick,"[3] an accurate description, bar the adjective "former."

An island's geographic remoteness and absence of strategic rele-
vance naturally lowers its rulers' incentives to engage in active international diplomacy. Over time, they will develop isolationist habits, including
a sui generis understanding of how the external world works and how it
affects the country's interests. As Leila Rachid told me, "Geography leads
to introversion."[4] For Paraguay, the isolationist habits developed throughout its colonial period and were set in stone following independence when
its first leader, Rodríguez de Francia, adopted a turtle-like foreign policy of
retracting inside its shell. The isolationism was somehow vindicated when
decades later Francisco Solano López (FSL) made a reckless effort to leave
the shell with devastating results, bringing almost sixty years of forced diplomatic solitude. Furthermore, the Triple Alliance War seems to have left
Paraguayans forever afraid of the external world. Former senator and public intellectual Hugo Estigarribia compares Paraguay's isolationist tendencies to a caged rabbit afraid of leaving to face a world full of predators.[5] A
common fear I heard from Paraguayans of all stripes was that Brasiguayos
would trigger a Crimea-type intervention from Brazil if Paraguay stepped
out of its natural diplomatic boundaries.

In the dawn of democracy, Paraguayan international relations scholars
called upon the rabbit to leave the cage, urging it to end the country's "cultural landlocked nature." They further argued that "by becoming enclosed
among ourselves, it becomes almost impossible to understand the outside
world and its demanding rules of the game."[6] Then again, in different periods of time isolationism was conducive to protecting national interests.
Isolationism served Francia to avoid raising the issue of Paraguayan sovereignty with Argentina and Brazil, it kept foreigners at bay during the early
twentieth century's internal turmoil, it lessened pressure from the United
States to cut links with the Axis Powers during World War II, and it saved

the Stroessner regime from answering for its human rights violations. Even in modern Paraguay, there is still a reflex among some locals to run away from the world, close the country's doors, and avoid international entanglements. Yet, there is also an inclination to repeat the terrible mistakes of FSL and pursue foreign policy based on intangible principles or face-saving responses. When Mercosur suspended Paraguay over its hasty impeachment of President Fernando Lugo in 2012, an influential commentator argued the Paraguayan response should put "dignity" before economic costs.[7]

FSL's blunder points towards the metaphor's other key component, that of being "surrounded by land." Land borders have limited Paraguay's forced isolationism in a way akin to the fictional *Godfather's* regret: "Just when I thought I was out, they pull me back in." Sixty years after the Triple Alliance War, a conflict over boundaries with neighbor Bolivia brought back diplomacy and later war. Only in 1938, 127 years after declaring independence, was Paraguay able to sign border treaties with all its neighbors. Yet, land borders did not diminish Paraguay's sense of vulnerability and its tendency to fear the external world. Vulnerability and fear were aggravated by constant internal strife ever since the end of the Triple Alliance War through the years after the Chaco War with Bolivia. Civil wars, short-lived governments, and exile of thought leaders also had the consequence of limiting whatever blueprints existed for engaging with the world.

Many Paraguayans make the argument that foreign policy was an unaffordable luxury for a country that was barely able to keep the lights on. By the same token, foreign policy has always been key to the country's survival both as a political and economic entity given its two large neighbors. Thus, a more conscious investment in diplomacy could have gone a long way. In hindsight, we know Paraguay kept its national sovereignty and ended up with South America's second lowest per capita income. And while it is unclear how much diplomacy specifically mattered for either outcome, it has been at the common thread of Paraguay's birth, its almost disappearance, and its travails in striving to achieve greater economic growth.

For any country, the ultimate defense of sovereignty is obviously war, but that is not always a sufficient condition. Paraguay can attest to this, having fought major wars with each one of its neighbors. It lost the first one against the Triple Alliance countries and its claim to sovereignty became a moot point. What saved Paraguay's sovereignty was neither war nor diplomacy, but the deep distrust between victors Brazil and Argentina. The two countries did carve up chunks of Paraguayan territory, yet ultimately settled for the continuation of an independent Paraguay. Likewise, in the case of the Chaco War with Bolivia, Paraguay was the victor and kept intact its claims over a territory that to this day has higher strategic than productive value. Victory in war did not save Paraguay's sovereignty as an independent nation because it was never at stake. A loss against Bolivia would have kept Paraguay as a sovereign nation all the same.

Could a more active economic diplomacy have made Paraguay's per capita income higher? International trade in general is crucial for small countries,[8] but largely ineffective absent (1) basic physical infrastructure connecting the local economy to international markets; and (2) stable domestic institutions offering foreign investors and entrepreneurs a clear path to profits. Needless to say, neither of these two conditions existed in Paraguay until recently. As a result, for most of its history, Paraguayan economic diplomacy was a mendicant type that sought to milk international institutions and allies' resources, typically in order to advance interests linked to a specific government's survival than to Paraguay's economic wellbeing. Such a diplomacy got Taiwan to pay for Paraguay's Congress building and the South African apartheid regime to pay for the Paraguayan Supreme Court building. Similarly, when negotiating trade agreements, Paraguay has had a long-standing beggar-thy-neighbor diplomacy, which seeks to extract concessions, exemptions, and particular benefits from trading partners in order to protect politically connected local producers. As we saw in Chapter IV, Ciudad del Este's owes much of its economic life to Paraguay's exemptions to the Mercosur treaty.

A Pendulum, Chiang Kai-shek, and Apartheid

In general terms, the historic policy default among Paraguayan leaders has been a minimalist diplomacy aimed at pursuing a narrow set of factional interests. That is the case with Paraguay's historic pendulum swings of diplomacy between Argentina and Brazil. The pendulum moved based more on domestic partisan loyalties than on foreign policy considerations, and it left little room for other diplomatic engagements.

As we have seen, the years following independence were of extreme isolationism, so the pendulum was mostly dormant. It leaned ever so slightly towards Argentina, given their common colonial and cultural heritage. Those that opposed the early leaders' policies went into exile in Argentina. Similarly, the Argentine province of Corrientes served as the main conduit for Paraguay's fickle trade with the world. U.S. expert on Paraguay Melissa Birch noted that the main book on Paraguay's early diplomatic history period allocated eighteen pages to relations with Argentina and two pages to relations with Brazil when discussing the first part of the twentieth century.[9] In those post-independence years, Paraguayan sovereignty was reliant on Argentina and Brazil checking each other's expansionism; just like Uruguay under different conditions (mainly, wide and open access to the sea and no topographical barriers), Paraguay was nothing more than a buffer between the two competing neighbors. There is no doubt El Supremo Francia's policy of complete isolation had an impact on the preservation of Paraguay's independence. However, the degree of that impact does not compare with the much larger role played by Argentina and Brazil's opposing territorial aspirations. Carlos Antonio López, who succeeded Francia in 1844, put an end to the government's isolationism, while keeping good relations with its neighbors, and the result was peace and respect for Paraguay's independence. Only when FSL, in late 1864 and early 1865, managed to annoy both Argentina and Brazil at the same time did they band together to subjugate Paraguay. And even when Paraguay was a country in name only right at the Triple Alliance War's closing in 1870, the two big neighbors' distrust of each other was enough to keep Paraguay from becoming a borderland province. Not even the Paraguayan leader's "incompetence on a grand scale,"[10] as two American scholars described it, could bring the two large countries to compromise the full extent of Paraguayan independence. While fighting the war together was feasible, splitting up the country was beyond Brazil and Argentina's trust limits.

After the end of the Triple Alliance War, the pendulum of foreign influence moved for a while towards Brazil, whose troops were stationed in Paraguayan soil and remained the stick Brazilian diplomats wielded to push matters towards their country's interests. With the demise of the Colorados in 1904 and the advent of the Liberals, the pendulum moved back to Argentina and remained there through the early 1940s. At that time, Paraguay was an economic appendage to Argentina, even using the Argentine peso as the national currency until the guaraní was introduced in 1944. Argentine companies and investors owned the majority of land sold right after the Triple Alliance War, almost all of Paraguay's foreign trade ran through Argentina, and leaders of both countries sympathized in their politically liberal views and shared a fluent dialogue among them.

On the heels of the fight against the Axis powers during World War II, and in response to U.S. prodding, Brazil increased its influence in Paraguay until the end of the Stroessner regime in 1989. Getulio Vargas became the first Brazilian president to visit Paraguay in 1941 (for the Vargas family it was a return, as his father Manuel Vargas had fought in the Triple Alliance War), and later Brazil paid for the only bridge connecting Paraguay to Brazil. Brazil also trained many generations of Paraguayan soldiers, including one Alfredo Stroessner, who eventually died exiled in Brazil. To solidify matters, Stroessner gave political asylum to Argentine strongman Juan Domingo Perón in 1955, stifling the country's bilateral relationship with the Argentine government. It did not help that Argentina, in turn, gave asylum to the majority of Paraguayan anti–Stroessner conspirators and political exiles.

During the 1970s, with the establishments of military dictatorships in Argentina and Brazil, cooperation among the three countries blossomed, albeit towards evil ends and with tragic consequences. As we saw in Chapter II, acting through Plan Condor, the countries' military regimes set up an efficient system of diplomatic cooperation, information sharing, and logistical support to track down, imprison without trial, torture, and in many cases murder civilian opponents. Once democratic regimes returned to Argentina and Brazil, cooperation stopped, and Paraguay returned once again to its old diplomatic isolation until the Stroessner regime's downfall.

Before his demise, Stroessner cleverly anchored his "life jacket" diplomacy in the broad anti-communist group of countries, which in 1966 would form the World Anti-Communist League (WACL). The main force behind the league's founding and early efforts was Chiang Kai-shek (1887–1975), the Generalissimo who led the Republic of China from 1928 to 1949 from the mainland, and from Taiwan until 1975 following his defeat by Mao Zedong's communist forces. As military strongmen wedded to the anti-communist mantra and separated by more than 12,400 miles, Stroessner and Chiang Kai-shek were a perfect fit. And like many of Taiwan's former and current diplomatic allies, Paraguay was a low-maintenance partner that could be trusted with its votes at the United Nations and other relevant international fora. With or without communism, since 1957 when diplomatic relations were first established, the basic deal for Paraguay has been the same, whether or not there was a communist threat: I will accept your unconditioned funds in exchange for being a loyal diplomatic partner. For Stroessner, Taiwan's funds took the form of military gear and training and for the leaders that came after him the funds consisted of economic and social aid.

Paraguay's current value for Taiwan, and therefore Paraguay's bargaining power, has increased exponentially as more and more countries have switched allegiances to the People's Republic of China (PRC). As of 2021, Paraguay remains the largest of all the countries with diplomatic relations with Taiwan. This group's size average (excluding Paraguay) is smaller than Denmark's area and fills around 10 percent of the Paraguayan territory. Taiwanese largesse in Paraguay reflects this state of affairs. When President Mario Abdo Benítez took office in 2018, Taiwan's ambassador announced his country was giving a $150 million grant to the new administration, more than doubling their $70 million contribution to the previous president. Signs advertising Taiwanese aid projects dot both Asunción and the countryside. Taiwan is also providing $10 million for the construction of a modern technological university in the Paraguayan capital, featuring a twenty-five-acre campus and state of the art infrastructure. Cases of mismanagement and outright embezzlement of Taiwanese funds by Paraguayan officials do not seem to stop the flow. And unlike the efforts in Taipei to remove Chiang Kai-shek statues, the Generalissimo's own statue in Asunción remains standing.

For Paraguay, a simple cost-benefit analysis seems to counsel continuation of diplomatic relations with Taiwan. Paraguay has in practice quasi-normal relations with Beijing: China remains by far the largest market for imported goods. In spite of the PRC's prohibition on buying Paraguayan goods, exports reach China unbothered via Argentina, Brazil, Uruguay, and Hong Kong. Similarly, Chinese companies operate in Paraguay without any trouble. Some of the Chinese companies with local operations in Paraguay include telecom giant Huawei and car company Chery, among others; Chinese companies also regularly bid on public tender projects. For example, in 2018, the Paraguayan government awarded China's state-owned company Sinohydro a $61 million contract to upgrade Asunción's electrical grid and distribution network. Although some Paraguayan exporters complain that formal relations with China would allow them to negotiate higher prices for their products, the reality of trade negotiations with Chinese buyers is far more uncertain. Likewise, pro–China Paraguayans point out the potential for Chinese investment and access to credit, but here again the reality of Chinese promises dwarfs what it delivers, particularly in Latin America. Paraguayans already had a taste of unfulfilled Chinese promises in 2019 when Aceros del Paraguay Sociedad Anónima (ACEPAR), the Paraguayan state-owned steel company, was forced to break a contract with the Chinese company Henan Complant Mechanical and Electrical Company (HCME) following months of contract and payment disputes. HCME promised but never delivered multi-million dollar investments and jobs and left the country without much explanation. By sticking to Taiwan, Paraguay gets all of the above plus preferential access to Taiwan's markets, technological knowhow without hidden dangers, and the periodic largesse of Taiwanese funds, no questions asked. Needless to say, this cost-benefit analysis stands as long as the PRC decides to keep the status quo. Any small intervention either on the export or import side of the equation or on the Chinese companies' capacity to operate in Paraguay could change the computation significantly.

The other peculiar component of Stroessner's foreign policy was the relationship with South Africa's apartheid regime. A staunch anti-communist, but also shunned by the international community like Stroessner, the apartheid regime of South Africa found a reliable partner in Paraguay. Thus, in 1974, Stroessner became the first non–African head of state in twenty years to visit apartheid South Africa; the visit was repaid the following year when Prime Minister B.J. Vorster (1966–1978) came to Paraguay.[11] In addition to support at the United Nations, Stroessner helped the South Africans buy arms and munitions. For example, to sideline international sanctions, Paraguay would buy submarines and re-export them to South Africa. In turn, the South Africans gave Stroessner financial aid and military training.

Paraguay and the United States: Friends with Interests

An oft-repeated phrase among international relations' experts of the "realist" persuasion declares, "Countries do not have friends, only interests." Like many other international relations theories and principles, the "interests-only" theory does a good job of explaining reality, even if it has shortcomings. In the case of U.S.–Paraguay relations, the adverb "only" is too strong; both countries have shared a set of common values that can only be described as friendship. Thus, "friends with interests" comes closer to describing the full breath of U.S.–Paraguay relations since Edward A. Hopkins arrived in Asunción in 1845 as the first U.S. government representative in Paraguay.

The United States and Paraguay have never fought a war with each other, and only during one short period have they engaged in a belligerent act. It was in the mid–1850s, when the aforementioned Hopkins got himself in trouble with President Carlos Antonio López. As a result, the Paraguayan president expelled the young U.S. consul and canceled all the commercial deals he had completed. Months later, a Paraguayan river gunner fired on a U.S. naval vessel, *Water Witch*, that was trying to trespass maritime borders, killing one American and inflicting significant damage on the vessel. More than two years later, the U.S. government decided to retaliate by sending nineteen ships and 2,500 men to Paraguay. The move forced López to negotiate and finally pay $250,000 to the *Water Witch* victim's family.[12] But overall, diplomatic relations have remained cordial through the years. When in 1958 Vice President Richard Nixon landed in Asunción, days before his motorcade came under a mob attack in Venezuela, he praised Paraguay's reliability: "In the field of international affairs I do not know of any other nation which has risen more strongly against the threat of communism and this is one reason why I feel especially happy here."[13] You can substitute "against the threat of communism" with "for United States values and interests" and Nixon's statement turns into boilerplate text for any U.S. government visitor to Paraguay, now and then. Certainly, Paraguay's geographic location and lack of strategic relevance helped keep both countries in good terms throughout history. In the words of United States–Paraguay relations experts Mora and Cooney, Paraguay has remained largely "remote, small, and peripheral to U.S. policymakers,"[14] but, I would add, with short periods of intense interest.

To be sure, Paraguay and the United States have not always seen eye to eye, most notably during the Cold War years. During that time, the bilateral relationship can be encapsulated under what Seymour Martin Lipset called the "double-edged sword" of American power: sometimes enlightened, sometimes retrograde, and channeled into a foreign policy imbued by a "sense of moral absolutism."[15] It started with a light democratizing sword during the early years (1945–54), the sword then adopted a blunt anti-communist edge as the global confrontation was heating up (1957–1976), and finally it took the shape of a sharp human rights crusader in the latter years (1977–1989). On one side of the sword, the U.S. government funded an expert to train the Paraguayan police on torture techniques in 1956, creating a police unit responsible for large-scale human rights violations. On the other side, forty years later, it paid to digitize the Archives of Terror, documenting the abuses that U.S. government funds abetted.

The key element in the bilateral relation is its asymmetry: the United States is a lot more important to Paraguay than vice versa. Think about President Rutherford B. Hayes and Senator Huey P. Long's role in Paraguayan history. The reader must agree those two are not names typically associated with American greatness. One, an underachieving, largely forgotten president[16] and the other one, as described by H.L. Mencken, "[a] backwoods demagogue of the oldest and most familiar model—impudent, blackguardly, and infinitely prehensile."[17] Unless you are in Paraguay, that is. Both politicians have streets named after them, and additionally "Hayes" is the name of a city and its encompassing departamento. Hayes and Long earned Paraguay's appreciation by standing up for Paraguayan interests in the Chaco region: the former by awarding a disputed territory to Paraguay after the Triple Alliance War, and the latter by supporting Paraguayan claims during the Chaco War. Hayes and Long's deeds on behalf of Paraguay were of little note for American concerns, but were of enormous consequence for Paraguay.

U.S. engagement with Paraguay was almost non-existent before Franklin Delano Roosevelt started implementing his "Good Neighbor" policy in the 1930s. According to American historian Michael Grow, not only was trade minimal, but also just over thirty U.S. citizens lived in Paraguay circa 1939. Grow points out that by 1943 the U.S. Embassy in Asunción had grown so fast in personnel that the U.S. Ambassador Wesley Frost became concerned about negative "psychological repercussions" among the Paraguayans if more foreign service officers came to the Paraguayan capital.[18] It was in 1943, too, when President Higinio Morínigo became the first Paraguayan head of state to visit the United States on official travel. He met FDR, stayed at the president's guest house, and addressed the U.S. Congress. Conversely, no U.S. president has ever visited Paraguay. When Secretary of State Mike Pompeo came to Asunción for half a day in 2019, it was only the second time in the history a secretary of state had visited Paraguay. The previous time had happened in 1965, when Dean Rusk, Lyndon B. Johnson's secretary of state came to Paraguay to mediate a border conflict between Paraguay and Brazil.

Yet, the asymmetry has not translated into a one-sided relationship where the U.S. government dictates and Paraguay acquiesces. In this sense, U.S. foreign policy towards the Stroessner regime and its effects are a good example. Neither Stroessner nor democracy came about because of U.S. wishes. Both regimes fitted American interests at different historical times and were encouraged accordingly. Stroessner saw the opening and took up the anti-communist cause with gusto; he sent troops to the Dominican Republic in 1965 to aid U.S. forces and went as far as offering Paraguayan troops to support U.S. war efforts in Vietnam in 1968.[19] Relations with Taiwan and apartheid South Africa followed. But Letelier's assassination (recounted in Chapter I) a short distance away from the White House, made it clear the U.S. government was getting a raw (Condor) deal; Henry Kissinger's State Department had given a consenting nod to a group of murderous individuals willing to strike terror even in the heart of American power. It also tore to pieces the idea, common among many Latin American leaders, of an all-knowing, all-powerful U.S. intelligence regime able to control facts on the ground. From the Jimmy Carter presidency (1977–1981) when human rights rose to the top of priorities, until 1989, several U.S. efforts tried to nudge Stroessner toward political liberalization without success, and the relationship soured. In 1985, President Ronald Reagan, who shared Stroessner's anti-communist fervor, gave a speech in which he called Stroessner's Paraguay a dictatorship in the same league with bad boys Augusto Pinochet's Chile, Fidel Castro's Cuba, and Daniel Ortega's Nicaragua.[20] When the Cold War ended and Latin American military dictatorships started falling like dominoes, the Stroessner regime's position vis-à-vis the U.S. government became even more untenable. Yet, U.S. government pressure could only get Stroessner to release political prisoners and let some exiles return without altering the regime's permanence.

Even if half-hearted and wavering, U.S. support for the Stroessner regime will forever remain a stain in the bilateral relations. However, it is important to recall the context under which American leaders and diplomats acted. A State Department official in 1959, 1965, or 1976 who looked at Paraguay's illiberal history of coups, revolutions, and deadly foreign wars would have been foolish in recommending a democracy-or-else policy. That foreign service officer would have been rightly afraid of pushing the country towards unchartered (democratic) ground. We now know the threat of communism in Paraguay was grossly exaggerated, but it was not obvious back then. U.S. diplomats did press Stroessner to become more democratic and to treat his fellow citizens more justly, albeit inconsistently. The U.S. policy of "yes (to anti-communism) but (protect human rights)" in Paraguay as in other Latin American countries was, in the words of author John Dinges, "grasped as a single, muddled endorsement of the brutal tactics in which (U.S.) unsubtle allies were already engaged."[21]

Regardless of the past, in the first decade after Stroessner's departure, the U.S. Embassy became a partner and counselor of choice for Paraguayan government authorities, from the president down the totem pole, but also for the opposition. On the fateful night of April 22, 1996, when General Lino Oviedo threatened a coup d'état, President Wasmosy went so far as spending the night at the U.S. Embassy's compound and consulted with Ambassador Robert Service about what to do next. Today, with more than $10 million in annual U.S. government assistance to Paraguay,[22] no other country comes close in putting dollars where the diplomatic mouth is. A new, $250 million embassy compound set to open in 2021 signals Uncle Sam will be around for a little while longer. Certainly, in Paraguay, the U.S. comes close to former Secretary of State Madeleine Albright's definition of being "the indispensable nation," funding major efforts against drug interdiction, money laundering, and in support of public administration reform and sustainable economic growth. Publications consistently place the American ambassador as one of Paraguay's most influential people, in spite of ambassadors' efforts to stay under the radar. In turn, when political crises happen, Paraguayan politicians and opinion makers watch U.S. Embassy's public statements and tweets to see which way the wind is blowing, even if in most instances American diplomats have neither levers to pull nor obvious national interests to pursue. One of the ambassadors I worked with often expressed (in private) a displeasure for having to carry out proconsul-type of actions on behalf of Paraguayans. In this sense, public and politicians alike consistently overestimate the influence of la embajada on domestic affairs, something that at *1776 Avenida Mariscal Francisco Solano López* everyone is keen to let stand.

Still an Island After All These Years

Speaking of island diplomacy, two foreign policy scholars from Iceland, Sverrir Steinsson and Baldur Thorhallsson, in their comprehensive

2017 academic paper "Small State Foreign Policy," listed a number of must-haves for successful small-country diplomacy. One is that "small states have successfully employed the strategies of coalition-building and image-building,"[23] an area where Paraguay has had mixed results. Under Stroessner, Paraguay joined and actively nurtured the anti-communist coalition, with positive results in terms of the regime's survival. However, the strategy had long-lasting negative effects on the country's image. In particular, the result of so many years of isolationism, ostracism, and life-jacket diplomacy earned Paraguay the mistrust of the international community. For instance, Paraguay has never been able to place a senior diplomat in one of the leading international organizations. No Paraguayan has served as secretary general of the Organization of American States (OAS) or as its assistant secretary. Same for the IADB presidency or the top positions for Latin America at the World Bank and the IMF. Similarly, no Paraguayan has ever served in the Inter-American Court of Human Rights. The Paraguayan diplomat who reached the highest rank in an international organization was Luis María Ramírez Boettner, who was the United Nations representative in Brazil from 1972 to 1980. It says a lot about Paraguayan diplomacy that unlike other senior authorities in international bodies, Ramírez Boettner moved up the ranks without official support from his home country. It does not help either that the other high-ranked Paraguayan "diplomat" was the former head of the South American Football Confederation (CONMEBOL) Nicolás Leoz (1986–2013). When he died in 2019, Leoz was under house arrest in Asunción and fighting extradition to the United States following his indictment on bribery, money laundering, and wire fraud charges linked to broadcasting and sponsorship rights for soccer competitions.

Steinsson and Thorhallsson also note that small countries have the advantage of small bureaucracies that can make decisions rapidly; because of its size, they add, "decision-making often occurs informally."[24] Here the authors assume away that the small bureaucracy is competent. In Paraguay there is a tiny foreign policy intelligentsia and thus little discussion or multi-party agreement over Paraguay's international relations "grand strategy." Congress is not involved in diplomacy except to participate in toothless international organizations or to travel to eccentric locales with family members. The Ministry of Foreign Affairs spends under $100 million annually, or around 2 percent of the annual national budget; it hires on average ten new foreign service officers per year via an exam established in 2007 in which typically 200 applicants take part. The senior MFA leadership still includes chain-smoking diplomats working in cluttered offices with stacks of papers and surrounded by administrative personnel of little use but to push papers and fetch coffee. In 2019, the MFA's union complained in the following terms: "There is no sense of justice but improvisation, disorder and sloppiness, with the logical result of little institutional achievements of value, with a civil service frustrated and without incentives to work, and with authorities absolutely isolated from reality."[25]

Paraguayan diplomacy does indeed feature informal decision-making. In this sense, Stroessner's diplomatic relations with South Africa were in line with Paraguay's long-standing tradition of one-off diplomatic moves. More recently, in 2018, President Cartes decided to move the Paraguayan Embassy in Israel from Tel Aviv to Jerusalem. He did so with three months left in his five-year term and seemingly with little consultation other than among his inner circle. Almost as soon as the new President Mario Abdo Benítez was inaugurated, his foreign affairs minister announced the re-relocation of the embassy back to Tel Aviv. In turn, the Israeli government recalled its ambassador and shut down the embassy in Asunción. But Abdo Benítez was no stranger to casual foreign policy. As a senator, he presided over a special senate session in 2015 that passed a resolution acknowledging the Armenian genocide. The senate's resolution identified "the Turkish-Ottoman Empire" as the genocide's perpetrator. The same Abdo Benítez would four years later during his presidency open a Paraguayan Embassy in Ankara and host Turkish President Recep Erdoğan in Asunción.

Thankfully for Paraguay, Steinsson and Thorhallsson note that "it has never been as easy being small as it is in the current international system with its unprecedented degree of peace, economic openness, and institutionalization."[26] For Paraguay in particular, this benign international system has been helpful in protecting its democracy and enhancing its economic opportunities. The post–Stroessner foreign policymakers took consistent steps to obtain international protections for their young democracy. General Rodríguez's first legal change was to join the American Convention on Human Rights, a region-wide pact established in 1969 to protect and uphold the basic rights most Paraguayan governments across history failed to honor. In addition, in 1998 Paraguay was a founding signatory of the Ushuaia Protocol, which instituted Mercosur's "Democratic Clause." The clause allows parties to suspend membership based on the interruption of democracy. In fact, Paraguay has already been suspended once after the impeachment of President Fernando Lugo in 2012. Finally, Paraguay was also a supporter of the OAS's Inter-American Democratic Charter, adopted on the fateful morning of September 11, 2001. What all these documents have in common is that they bind Paraguay to a democratic order, constraining institutional breaks, and raising the costs of prolonging such breaks.

Meanwhile, the post–Stroessner economic diplomacy can be

described as a slow but steady process of putting on what American author Thomas Friedman called the "Golden Straitjacket," the set of policies endorsed by multilateral organizations that locks a country's policies in market-economy mode and constraint its politics.[27] Paraguay's stellar macroeconomic management, with low inflation rate, price stability, balanced budget, and openness to foreign investment fit the "Golden Straitjacket" like a glove. Paraguay also joined international bodies like the OECD's Development Centre, and signed the OECD's Multilateral Convention on Mutual Administrative Assistance in Tax Matters, an international mechanism to combat cross-border tax evasion.

For Steinsson and Thorhallsson, small countries' degree of success under a benign international system is "contingent on the time, effort, and resources that small states put into diplomacy."[28] Alas, because the Paraguayan government does not allocate enough human and financial resources to support a more proactive diplomacy, foreign policy tends to be overwhelmed by external circumstances. Foreign policy expert Lucas Arce called it "reactive" foreign policy.[29] It is how Paraguay joined Mercosur, more as one would board a departing train than as the result of a conscious plan to boost regional trade. Since the early 1980s Argentina and Brazil had been actively enhancing bilateral trade through both trade liberalization measures and the signing of legal commitments. By the time the Mercosur treaty was signed in 1991, Argentina and Brazil had already worked up the deal and gave Paraguay and Uruguay the option to join or stay behind. Likewise, when in 2019 Brazil slapped a tariff on Paraguayan auto parts that almost wiped clean the whole local industry, the MFA looked like a deer in the headlights. Worse still, once the decision was made public members of the administration and the previous administration chose to blame each other instead of joining forces.

The Mercosur case indicates that it makes sense to pull the appropriate resources, but the estimation is not clear-cut enough to garner the required political will. Even when the case for allocating more resources is evident to all, Paraguay still dithers. For example, with thirty soldiers, Paraguay's contribution to the United Nations Peacekeeping Operations ("blue helmets") is puny. Uruguay with almost 1,000 soldiers wearing blue helmets, puts Paraguay to shame. And it is not a "contribution" since each blue helmet soldier gets paid $16,920 per year (U.S. taxpayers pick up a third of the bill), a figure that is almost triple the Paraguayan per capita income. There is also the added value of learning from different cultures, new technologies, and foreign languages. Furthermore, there is the additional benefit of having potential troublemakers with military rank gainfully employed in far-away lands.

Absent adequate resources for diplomacy, Paraguayan presidents also engage in a sort of buddy-diplomacy in which leaders conduct foreign policy by making friends with other countries' presidents. Paraguay's negotiations with Brazil over the Itaipú dam at two points in history are a case in point. First Stroessner and later Lugo convinced Brazil to support Paraguay's demands with a leader-to-leader approach based on the leaders' respective world views. In the case of Stroessner, the commonality with Brazil was a military-led fight against communism, while in Lugo's case it was his rapport with President Lula da Silva and their similar leftist political agenda. The agreements to build the dam and improve Paraguay's terms were more Brazilian indulgences to Paraguayan leaders with a common worldview than ideology-free realpolitik pursuits of national interest.

Steinsson and Thorhallsson argue that influential small states are those "able to develop issue-specific power to make up for what they lack in aggregate structural power."[30] By accident of its geography, Paraguay has been able to accrue power thanks to the two dams it shares with Argentina and Brazil. Without the dams, Paraguay's capacity to advance other national interests vis-à-vis its two large neighbors would be much diminished. Yet, due to the lack of an effective foreign policy bureaucracy and the presidency's informality towards diplomacy described above, Paraguay's "issue-specific power" is weaker than it should be. Moreover, Paraguay lacks what American international relations scholar Joseph Nye called "soft power,"[31] the capacity to shape international policies and attract other countries based on economic and cultural factors as opposed to using raw coercive power. Paraguay has most clearly the potential of using its green energy as soft power to pursue foreign policy goals, but so far Paraguayan diplomats have not taken this path. It does not help Paraguay's soft power that its diplomats have consistently voted against lesbian, gay, bisexual, and transgender (LGBT) and abortion rights in international fora, two issues that have widespread support among its most important diplomatic partners such as the Mercosur countries and the United States. The railing against these two issues is compounded by some of Latin America's most restrictive laws against abortion and constant harassment against members of the LGBT community.

Such lack of international self-awareness is at the core of the Paraguayan diplomacy's identity problem. Since the reestablishment of democracy in 1989, the different presidents and respective foreign affairs ministries have struggled to define what it is that Paraguay stands for. The reason for this failure goes back to its long-standing isolationism, but also has to do with the quality of its democracy. Being a young democracy, Paraguay has not yet developed a foreign policy ethos anchored on issues that most Paraguayans favor. Other than the defense of sovereignty, no other issue has percolated from the greater participation of citizens in the policy making process. By the same token, the diplomatic heritage and the various still unresolved problems from the Stroessner period limit the extent of Paraguay's "soft power" possibilities. Many of Paraguay's senior career diplomats entered the foreign service when Stroessner was still in power and so their professional growth was stunted. They missed the early years in the diplomatic career when global contacts are made and international networks are formed. Thus, when international diplomacy calls for senior leadership, nobody can find Paraguay on the map. Island diplomacy indeed.

VIII

Epilogue

*Modern Paraguay
and Its Challenges*

I started researching and writing this book after witnessing the events of March 31, 2017, the day demonstrators torched the Paraguayan Congress. I wanted to understand not only the unfolding ordeal, but also its origins, causes, and consequences. In short, I wanted to understand modern Paraguay. Now, after more than three years living and working in Paraguay, I have learned the following key lessons about the country:

1. Paraguay's democracy is still developing; the sets of institutions that govern the country remain open-ended and in trial-and-error mode. The Tocquevillian "ceaseless agitation" is vigorous, but political parties are not trusted to mediate society's problems. If politics is the art of the possible, in Paraguay, the range of possibilities still includes violent means.
2. Paraguay is not yet a country fully ruled by laws. Although it has a constitution and legal framework in line with international standards, the political and cultural underpinnings needed for the rule of law are still lacking. Paraguayans have a problematic relationship with the law as evidenced by a large informal economy and high levels of corruption.
3. Like any thoughtful economist would tell you, economic growth will fluctuate. Will it fluctuate at a positive rate long enough to achieve widespread prosperity? Highly possible. But if you have read this far, you know Paraguayans have shown they are capable of shooting themselves in the foot and causing long-term misery.
4. Paraguay's young population is a double-edged sword; like in other countries with similar demographics, political violence and radical changes are as likely as higher economic growth and easier public

finances. The biggest challenge is to plug its growing young urban
population into the formal economy.

5. Plentiful clean, renewable energy is a tremendous asset for
   Paraguay's development, with a potential to transform the economy.
   But this advantage remains largely untapped. To what extent the
   country can harness the necessary human capital and investments
   required for success is still unclear.

6. Paraguay's diplomacy still clings to its old isolationist tendencies,
   with an overly parochial approach to global engagements. In spite
   of the existential consequences that diplomacy mistakes have had
   on Paraguay, the country's policy makers continue to neglect the
   resources necessary to conduct a more consequential diplomacy.

If I were to tweet a 140-character summary it would say: "Modern Paraguay
comprises a young democracy, a dynamic economy, and a social fabric in
turmoil. Green energy doesn't trump low human capital."

In This Bright Future You Can't Forget Your Past

February 3, 2019, was the thirtieth anniversary of the fall of the
Stroessner regime and the establishment of democracy. The government set
up major commemorations, remembering the long struggle for democracy,
honoring the victims, and educating the new generations on the value of
political freedom, a free press, and clean elections. The president invited all
political parties, civil society groups, and the diplomatic corps to attend the
day's main ceremony, which included a prime-time speech by the president
available in all media platforms. In his speech, the president encouraged
all Paraguayans to remember the past and its travails, to treasure democracy, and to continue working every day to make Paraguay's democracy
stronger and more prosperous. Alas, none of that happened. Instead, President Mario Abdo Benítez, a Stroessner-regime princeling, traveled to Ciudad del Este and only mentioned the thirty-year anniversary half-jokingly
when pressed by journalists. The non-event commemoration illustrates
both Paraguayan state failure to confront its past misdeeds, and the lack
of a civil society strong enough to bring the state to bear accountability for
those misdeeds. It is also a signal that the country's democratic institutions
and the citizenship that sustain them have some work in store. Progress
on soul-searching by itself is not going to make Paraguay a high-income
country, but it will be a sign of broader changes typically correlated with
prosperity.

Indeed, Paraguay's past can be depressing. In *The Last Dictator*, a 1970
documentary about Paraguay, director Alan Whicker called the country "a

medieval backwater." Pick any time in history, and the assessment would be equally gloomy. As recent as 2003, Paraguay had defaulted on its sovereign debt, only seventeen years after its previous default in 1986, and the economic perspectives were as glum as ever. In contrast, the present and the future both look significantly better. Today, Paraguayans experience on average longer lives, higher incomes, more years of formal education, and have more political freedoms than at any point in their history. Furthermore, there is every reason—theoretical or derived from empirical evidence—to believe Paraguay will grow at high rates and converge with richer countries in the coming decades. During colonial times, Paraguay's income was probably similar to the world's per capita income of around $3 a day; by 2016, the average Paraguayan earned $26 a day, more than doubling the 1990 income of $11 a day.[1] It constitutes a tremendous improvement for all Paraguayans, even with its skewed income distribution. In 2002 almost three out of five Paraguayans lived in poverty; by 2019 the number had fallen to one out of four. Paraguay is slightly above the Latin American average when it comes to achieving the United Nations Sustainable Development Goals. The country's score is not worsening in any of the seventeen goals, and it is set to conquer Goal #1 (No poverty) by 2030.

Notwithstanding Paraguay's own efforts at chasing prosperity, the global growth rate that is vanquishing poverty, disease, and illiteracy at the fastest rate in the history of humankind will catch up with Paraguay sooner rather than later. Already, the world per capita income increased on average by more than $1,900 every ten years since 1965.[2]

That is the half-full glass. The half-empty version indicates the average per capita income of its neighbors Argentina, Bolivia, and Brazil for 2016 was $13 a day higher than Paraguay. Furthermore, Paraguay's growth rate in 1990–2016 was lower than each one of its three neighbors. It shows Paraguay not only remains below average but also has not grown as fast as economic theory would indicate. In turn, social indicators remain problematic. In 2019, according to the Labor Ministry, one in four children aged ten to seventeen were employed, and seven out ten teenagers quit school in order to work. Likewise, the World Bank's Governance Indicators paint a problematic picture. Paraguay has made some progress in areas of political stability and regulatory quality, but either stagnated or regressed in other areas, particularly on corruption control and rule of law. What's more, it remains below the Latin American average in all areas.

The views of those that in the past offered Paraguay a path forward must serve to manage present expectations. For example, a 1945 U.S. government video set the scene for today's opportunities: "Paraguay has today the opportunity to achieve that success which has so stubbornly eluded her during the past. Her children and her people are strong of body and have shown a willingness and an ability to learn. And the land they live in has been blessed by nature with a mild climate and productive soil. A good start has already been made in education and health, in agriculture and industry."[3] More recently, in 1991, in the understatement of a lifetime authors Roett and Sacks counseled, "With competent leadership, Paraguay's economic prospects are good."[4]

In the past, forceful political change came to Paraguay when new generations of leaders formed coalitions to bring regime change. Many times, changes involved the use of violence as incumbent political elites refused to change.[5] In modern Paraguay, regime change is not in the cards, but generational change still remains the best hope for the country. German physicist Max Planck quipped that science advances one funeral at a time. Paraguay too will advance one funeral at a time. Indeed, so much of the current low confidence in the Paraguayan political class originates in the lack of a break with the dictatorial past and its corresponding slow gliding towards democracy. Likewise, a great many of Paraguay's successful businesses have roots in the Stroessner era. In the not so distant future, new millionaires and businesses will rise (and fall) without being tainted by Stronismo.

Positive change is happening. In the three and a half years I lived in Paraguay, significant changes took place that were unimaginable before. For example, in October 2019, the Supreme Court upheld the conviction of former senator Víctor Bogado on corruption charges. Bogado became the first Paraguayan legislator to be convicted for crimes committed during his congressional tenure. His crime was as typical as it was petty: he used senate representation funds to pay for his household's nanny. In the not-too-distant past, Bogado's crime would have gone unpunished; the Supreme Court ruled two days before the statute of limitations was set to expire. Just as notable, the Senate had impeached Bogado for corruption three months before his conviction.

Remarkably, the two examples of corruption in the political system mentioned in Chapter II have faced legal action, even if the practices in which they engaged have not disappeared. First, in 2018, prosecutors arrested senator Oscar González Daher (OGD) on corruption charges. OGD had been impeached twice from the senate so by the time a judge approved his arrest he was sent to jail together with his son, who was also involved in the family business. Secondly, in 2019, the Paraguayan Congress impeached Sandra McLeod, and prosecutors filed preliminary corruption charges against both her and her spouse, Zacarías Clan boss Senator Javier Zacarías Irún.

The Supreme Court's new activism against corruption is directly connected to having new judges who were selected through a transparent process and came to the job without political connections or suspicious legal past. A similar cleansing process is taking place at the Prosecutor's Office, where in the bad old days judicial corruption ran wild. Remarkably, the judicial sector's progress is being pushed by civil society groups. I had the chance of getting to know civil society's most active leaders; their drive to end impunity and stamina to resist challenges, threats, and everything the system will throw at them give me hope for a better Paraguay.

Winds of change are blowing in all areas. Circa 2019, the three biggest cities—Asunción, Ciudad del Este, Encarnación—where a third of the population lives, elected mayors from non-traditional parties for the first time in history. After years of neglect, successive governments have poured asphalt into Paraguayan roads like never before; some forecasts expect paved roads will reach 40 percent of the total by 2030. The construction of two additional bridges connecting Paraguay to Brazil are underway, and a highway connecting the heart of the Chaco region to the border with Brazil is also under construction.

Similarly, there are encouraging prospects in many areas. When other countries around the world are rioting over the high cost of energy, in Paraguay the cost of electricity is expected to fall 50 percent once all the country's debts for the construction of the Itaipú dam are paid off in 2023. Meanwhile, greater urbanization is expected to increase tolerance towards other religions, sexual orientation, and ethnicity, as it has happened in most other countries. Likewise, greater urbanization together with higher per capita incomes will inevitably raise environmental standards. In recent years, it has become common to see volunteer crews cleaning up trash from riversides and demanding accountability for those that pollute the waters. Young Paraguayans have gathered in downtown Asunción to demonstrate against deforestation and indiscriminate logging in the Paraguayan Chaco.

From Paraguay to Denmark

As I was getting off a morning meeting in downtown Asunción in 2019, I stepped out into the streets and suddenly remembered the line from Francis Ford Coppola's 1979 film *Apocalypse Now* when Lieutenant Colonel Bill Kilgore brags, "I love the smell of napalm in the morning." Except the smell was of tear gas coming from nearby streets, where around 2,000 protestors were marching to Congress to pressure legislators to pass an electoral reform bill. The civic protests followed growing public outrage about the traditional ways of Paraguayan politicians. The protests were another proof that Paraguay's Tocquevillian "ceaseless agitation" was still going strong.

Unfortunately, "ceaseless agitation" is not enough to achieve the widespread prosperity observed in developed countries. Which brings us to Denmark. I started my journey searching for Paraguay's long and winding road to development-nation status, what international development experts Lant Pritchett and Michael Woolcock described as becoming Denmark-like. More specifically, noted Pritchett and Woolcock, the long-term goal for a country like Paraguay is "to ensure that the provision of key services such as clean water, education, sanitation, policing, safety/sanitary regulation, roads, and public health is assured by effective, rules-based, meritocratic, and politically accountable public agencies."[6]

In other words, becoming more like Denmark means pursuing a concrete non-utopian path to prosperity. It is another way of avoiding the catastrophes and the tremendous pain that ideological crusades bring about to the average citizen. As American political commentator Will Wilkinson argues, the fact that governance and competitiveness rankings across the political spectrum place Denmark at the top counsel pragmatism about what societies can achieve in practical terms, regardless of ideal theoretical goals. Wilkinson notes that the differences in public policies among those in the top ten of all rankings (regardless of their ideological orientation) are small compared to the large differences between the top ten and the low-ranked countries.[7] For countries like Paraguay positioned not far from the mean scores, the road to Denmark involves a Lockean approach to reform of tweaking at the margin. This is in contrast to the more Rousseauian approach traditionally favored in Latin America of burning down the house before building a new one.

In this sense, in *The Origins of Political Order*, American political scientist Francis Fukuyama delineated a trinity-in-unity formula, based on solid historical evidence, required to get to the paradigmatic Denmark. In Fukuyama's 600-page explanation, successful political orders cannot go without political accountability, an effective state, and rule of law. But not so fast Paraguay; Fukuyama, like Pritchett and Woolcock, wisely cautions that getting to Denmark is not simply about mimicking the Danes. The formula is the destination, not the map.

How can Paraguay reach Denmark then? At its most basic, John Parish Robertson, the British explorer quoted in Chapter VI, already laid out what is necessary in Paraguay. What every town and province of South America wants, Robertson said, "[are] men of real political integrity, and some moderate knowledge of the business of life, as conducted in more civilized countries, to give impulse and direction to public affairs."[8] Robertson's simplicity echoes Adam Smith's 1775 recipe for countries such as Paraguay: "Little else is requisite to carry a state to the highest degree of opulence from the lowest barbarism, but peace, easy taxes, and a tolerable administration of justice; all the rest being brought about by the natural course of things."[9] In Adam Smith's road-to-wealth scorecard, Paraguay tallies two out of three (peace and easy taxes).

Paraguayan progress could use some new ideas, but mostly it requires what Confucian philosopher Mencius called "the unceasing correction of his errors."[10] Paraguayans already understand their past errors as most problems are long-standing. In his 1931 book *Paraguay's Woes*, Teodosio González denounced problems such as contraband, corruption, misuse of public funds, abuse of pre-trial detention, and court backlogs, which remain current in modern times.[11] At the opening of the 1991 Constitutional Assembly, the president of the assembly Oscar Facundo Ynsfrán described Paraguay's unceasing errors with flowery candor:

> The clash or discord between what the rule mandates and what reality does not comply with, is a constant that has undermined the public spirit that, not infrequently, has despaired of its laws and of the men who corrupt it, vitiating its conception and its designs. Our political order, wanting to conform to law, has been, however, and almost always, in conflict with the ethical principles that should have served as justification. That divorce or disagreement between legality and ethics, may have been the root of our institutional ills. Many of our rulers have felt the unstoppable desire to accumulate positions and dignities and have been fond of the harmful practice of manipulating the political organs of the State that have held externally at least the halo of national representation. The tendency—almost inertia—to want to perpetuate themselves in public office, especially in those of greater hierarchy, clearly speaks to us that, although we proclaim as blazon our egalitarian sense of life and our rights, we harbor personal ambitions that by definition denounce our attachment to privilege, to employment that requires little effort but is highly profitable, and to providentialism. These habits of political irrationality have cost us all kinds of misfortunes that we have tried to temper with the nimbus of our martial glories, as if martyrology were the only way to deserve the consideration of the planet's civilized nations. The civil society, depositary par excellence of the people's concerns has suffered the restrictions that mean the absence of the essential citizen guarantees for the exercise of their political rights and the harmonious development of culture and science.[12]

Although development experts have little certainty about how to bring the type of inclusive growth that forever changes a country (aka "Denmark"), we all understand what big-time evils should be avoided. Or as Charlie Munger—billionaire Warren Buffett's longtime business partner—calls the "inversion" approach to problem solving, expressed in the following maxim: "All I want to know is where I am going to die so I do not go there."[13] In other words, avoiding the things Paraguay *should not* do can be the key to success more than doing what it (supposedly) *should* do. A logical corollary of this maxim is what Greek historian Polybius counseled: "The most instructive, indeed the only method of learning to bear with dignity the vicissitude of fortune, is to recall the catastrophes of others."[14] As a country arriving late to economic development, Paraguay has something that a lot of countries lacked: Monday's newspaper. Price controls, protectionism, industrial policies, military or civilian authoritarianism, botched monetary policy, cultural autarchy, restrictions to freedom of speech, crony capitalism—these are some of the catastrophes that Latin American governments have generated, and that Paraguayans need to recall.

In a similar vein, recalling the catastrophes of others also means not trying to re-invent the wheel. Helio Vera, the lawyer cum distiller of Paraguayaness, titled one of his books *In Search of the Missing Bone*.[15] According to Vera's telling, El Supremo José Gaspar Rodríguez de Francia ordered an expert to perform an autopsy on a Paraguayan to see whether the corpse showed an extra bone. The irritated Francia wanted to know if the extra bone explained why Paraguayans never raised their heads when speaking to another person. In many ways, the search for solutions in developing countries resembles the search for the missing bone; they become outlandish policies with no discernible rationale.

What makes Denmark a metaphor for development success has a lot to do with the Danes' way of doing things. That is, there is something about them—high labor productivity, civic culture, bourgeois values, and even high suicide rates—that turns political and socio-economic variables into gold. It reminds me of air-guitar competitions when they score performances based on "airness." What is "airness"? Hard to describe it in words, but when you watch Air Guitar World Champs Craig "Hot Lixx Hulahan" Billmeier or Rob "The Marquis" Messel you immediately realize they have "airness." The Danes, they have development airness.

For Paraguay, it means that at the end of the day, no specific law or change in regulations will have a substantial effect on the political system or corruption levels without their own version of airness. Corruption is a case in point. There is no way of controlling every little step that every government official takes. Ditto for private contractors; no government agency can check every public work. At some point, public conscientiousness needs to evolve towards doing the right thing for the right thing's sake. It is not clear what is the fastest path to such conscientiousness; higher per capita income correlates well with public conscientiousness, but it raises the question of causality. Maybe public conscientiousness causes higher per capita income.

The good news for Paraguay is that those countries that reached Denmark's station started off from a baseline that did not include enlightened politicians or well-informed citizens. Furthermore, even after reaching Denmark, the development software remains glitchy. Jean-Claude Juncker, the former president of the European Commission (2014–2019) and a national from Luxembourg, one of the world's wealthiest countries, channeled Paraguayan resignation when he mused, "We all know what to do, we just don't know how to get re-elected after we've done it."[16]

Whatever road to Denmark Paraguay chooses, it cannot go without fuel for economic growth. Without it, Fukuyama's trinity is unattainable; rule of law and functioning state agencies that serve all citizens equally require a pretty penny. Paraguay needs a steady economic growth not only to lift most boats, but also to produce the resources to help those who stay behind, foster a more tolerant citizenship, and build the foundations for future prosperity. Regardless, 85 percent of Paraguayans make a living by earning labor income; among those in the lower income brackets, less than 10 percent of their incomes derive from government transfers.[17] It means that in modern Paraguay, economic growth is doing the heavy lifting of living standards. Similarly, as we have seen, the only path for Paraguay to get over the Kuznets curve's hump and stop environmental degradation is to increase its per capita income, a feat made impossible without sustained economic growth. When incomes are tight across the land, other priorities take precedence over Mother Nature.

Nonetheless, Paraguay should not bet on its natural bounty alone to achieve economic growth. It is common for news articles to describe a developing country's troubles and finish off with the admonition "in spite of having large natural resources." A typical example is Venezuela; read any news reports about it and the author will quickly remind the reader that Venezuela has one of the world's largest reserves of oil. I have heard the same conceit about Paraguay: the story normally goes "Paraguay only needs to get serious, look at all the natural resources they have!" To repeat the point made by U.S. economist Julian Simon, the ultimate resource is the human mind. Or as another American economist Deirdre McCloskey succinctly put it, what matters for economic prosperity is "[what you have] between your ears."[18]

The good news for Paraguay is that a lot can be achieved in terms of innovation and productivity without high average human capital. Consider Paraguayan soccer. By any measure, soccer is an area where Paraguayans punch above their weight. Paraguayan soccer players strive in the most competitive markets, its club teams and national team have won all Fédération Internationale de Football Association's (FIFA) top tournaments except for the World Cup (only nine countries in the whole world have won it). The CONMEBOL is headquartered in Paraguay and is currently led by the Paraguayan Alejandro Domínguez; the longest serving president was also a Paraguayan, Nicolás Leoz (1986–2013). The country's soccer infrastructure (stadiums, practice fields, etc.) is of good quality, and the local league pays lucrative salaries and employs foreign players and coaches. If only the rest of the economy looked more like the soccer industry, Paraguay would be an upper middle-income economy. Paraguayan soccer's development shows the usual constraints of a more prosperous economy and higher per capita income—low productivity and human capital, social inequalities, geographic location—can be overcome. Visit the smallest of Paraguay's rural communities and you will find a basic infrastructure nucleus consisting of scattered houses, a two-classroom school, a Catholic chapel, a general store, and a soccer field. These communities have experienced significant hardships throughout history but produced top-quality soccer players. No doubt, Paraguay's corruption and lax judicial system were a match made in heaven for international soccer executives and corporations. But it raises an obvious question: why didn't other Paraguayan economic industries thrive as well? They all face the same incentives and constraints.

Still, to reach Danish prosperity and keep it Paraguay needs to eventually break free from the current vicious circle in which companies and high earning individuals refuse to pay taxes because they do not receive public services in return. The country's road infrastructure and the educational attainment of Paraguayans cannot improve without appropriate funding. However, there is a fatal inconsistency among those in the know who chastise the Paraguayan government for its inability to deliver basic services at the same time they ask that same government to do more. Thus, committing the Paraguayan government to do the developmental heavy lifting must be confronted with the inescapable reality of a political system that has neither been capable nor effective in establishing Francis Fukuyama's trinity of political accountability, an effective state, and the rule of law. For instance, if you were to pick a worst overseer for Paraguayan education, it would be none other than the Ministry of Education.

Civil society and the non-government sector in general could play a critical role in advancing Paraguay's own development airness. For instance, the problem of poverty in Paraguay is also a problem of unstable families due to broken relationships. Keeping more of the Paraguayan demographic dividend within a stable, two-income household would be a boon for long-term prosperity. The challenge is unshackling Paraguayan legislation from the discriminatory clauses that prevent a greater number of people, principally lesbian, gay, bisexual, and transgender couples, from marrying and adopting children. By the same token, secular NGOs need to frown upon with religious vigor those social vices, such as alcohol abuse, smoking, drug use, and domestic violence, that undermine adult relationships and their offspring. In this sense, the demographic dividend has a greater chance of having a positive impact if the under thirty-five-year-old cohort can grow up avoiding family disruptions. Although data does not exist for Paraguay, in most countries, single parent households tend to yield children with worse health, educational outcomes, and propensity to engage in criminal activities than two-parent households. Furthermore, civil society advocacy can help unshackle women from housework and family care and empower them to serve a more influential role in government and corporations. Moving women to more productive economic activities has shown consistent positive effects over a country's average income, but also in terms of basic gender equality. Just as critically, the Paraguayan super wealthy need to step up and follow the example of Andrew Carnegie, John D. Rockefeller, and Bill Gates. That means using their vast fortunes to feed those in need, build schools, libraries, and hospitals, fund scholarships, and encourage all Paraguayans to build a better country without solely relying on their problematic government.

Immigrants are another source of matchless economic and cultural dynamism that requires little in terms of a functioning government. The achievements of Mennonites, Brasiguayos, and other immigrant groups in Paraguay such as the Japanese and Koreans indicate that economic development is about people and not geographical location. Paraguay has shown the world that any group of people can thrive under difficult conditions when armed with the right mix of human capital and self-initiative. Few policies provide the type of innovation, technology transfer, and cultural dynamism that Paraguay sorely needs than welcoming immigration laws. Certainly, modern Paraguay's cultural traditions are about immigrant traditions. The polka, Paraguay's national dance, was introduced by central Europeans; the country's national instrument, the Paraguayan harp, evolved from the Celtic harp. There are both positive and negative large-effects to immigration, but by definition they carry a small probability. For instance, on the negative tail-end, the son of an immigrant may turn into a dictator and derail the country's development. In fact, Paraguay already incurred that risk in the form of Alfredo Stroessner, so statistically speaking the country is in a favorable position.

Above all, Paraguay's path to prosperity will take time. The larger sweep of history reveals that more years passed between the foundation of Asunción and Paraguay's independence declaration than between independence and modern times. By the time those time periods coincide in the year 2085, it is safe to assume the average Paraguayan will enjoy a much higher income and access to goods and services unseen in the history of humankind. Whether the human and environmental costs are significant or not and whether they were worth the outcome will fall on future Paraguayans to appraise.

Chapter Notes

Introduction

1. Nickson, Andrew R. 2015. *Historical Dictionary of Paraguay*. Maryland: Rowman and Littlefield, p. ix.

2. After I moved to Paraguay, I learned that in March 1937, the Paraguayan government changed the immigration law by decree and established arbitrary guidelines to either limit or ban certain nationalities from entering the country. While Jews were the decree's unnamed target, foreign affairs minister Juan Stefanich went one step further and specifically instructed consular officers to avoid giving visas to Jewish people. My family might have been aware of this policy by the time they arrived in Montevideo in December 1938. See Seiferheld, Alfredo. 2016. *Nazismo y Fascismo en el Paraguay. Los años de la guerra 1936–1945*. Asunción: ServiLibro, p. 129.

3. Mercosur is the Spanish acronym for "Mercado Común del Sur" (Southern Common Market). It is a trade pact established by the 1991 Treaty of Asunción; its members are Argentina, Brazil, Paraguay, and Uruguay.

4. Steward, Julian H. Foreword to Service, Elman R., and Service Helen S. 1954. *Tobatí: Paraguayan Town*. Chicago: the University of Chicago Press, p. v.

5. McDonald, Ronald H. 1981. "The Emerging New Politics in Paraguay." *Inter-American Economic Affairs*, 35(1), p. 25–44.

6. https://www.youtube.com/watch?v=UKhHsx6ffKs.

7. Hilton, Isabel. 1990. "The General." *Granta 31*. Spring 1990. Granta Publications, p. 13.

8. Macintyre, Ben. 2004. "You Don't Want to Live There." *New York Times*, February 29, 2004. http://www.nytimes.com/2004/02/29/books/you-don-t-want-to-live-there.html.

9. *The Simpsons* episode "Homer's Triple Bypass," written by Gary Apple and directed by David Silverman and Michael Carrington. It originally aired on December 17, 1992.

10. CNN. *Anthony Bourdain: Parts Unknown*. Season 4, episode 3 titled "Paraguay." Episode aired October 12, 2014.

11. Colmán Gutiérrez, Andrés. 2018. *Mengele en Paraguay*. Con la colaboración de Desirée Esquivel y Narciso Meza Martínez. Asunción: ServiLibro.

12. Macintyre Ben. *Forgotten Fatherland: The Search for Elisabeth Nietzsche*.

13. Seiferheld, Alfredo. 2016. *Nazismo y Fascismo en el Paraguay. Los años de la guerra 1936–1945*. Asunción: ServiLibro, p. 397.

14. Macintyre, Ben. 1992. *Forgotten Fatherland. The Search for Elisabeth Nietzsche*. New York: Farrar Straus Giroux, p. 205.

15. Hall, Allan. 2012. "Secret files reveal 9,000 Nazi war criminals fled to South America after WWII." *Daily Mail*. Published 19 March 2012. http://www.dailymail.co.uk/news/article-2117093/Secret-files-reveal-9-000-Nazi-war-criminals-fled-South-America-WWII.html.

16. Klein, Christopher. 2017. "The 7 Most Notorious Nazis Who Escaped to South America." *History Stories*. Published December 27, 2017. https://www.history.com/news/the-7-most-notorious-nazis-who-escaped-to-south-america.

Chapter I

1. Quote appears in Lambert, Peter and Nickson, Andrew (editors). 2013. *The Paraguay Reader: History, Culture, Politics (The Latin America readers)*. Durham, NC: Duke University Press. Kindle Edition, p. 256.

2. Chipa is Paraguay's national snack. It is made of cassava or corn starch and usually shaped like a doughnut.

3. Lamenza, G. N., and Plischuk, M. 2015. "Avances en bioarqueología del Chaco boreal." *Arqueología Iberoamericana* 28, pp. 75–80. http://laiesken.net/arqueologia/archivo/2015/28/11.

4. Named after the English cleric and scholar Thomas Malthus, the Malthusian trap describes the pre-industrial revolution's demographic cycle. It takes place when the population grows faster than the agricultural production, making food supply inadequate for feeding the population. In turn, slower population growth due to famine allows the food supply to match the existing population until the cycle repeats itself.

5. Monte de López Moreira, Mary. 2011. *Historia del Paraguay*. Asunción: Editorial Servilibro. http://www.portalguarani.com/672_mary_monte_de_lopez_moreira/16504_historia_del_paraguay__por_mary_monte_de_lopez_moreira.html.

6. Durán Estragó, Margarita. "Conquista y Colonización (1537–1680)" in Telesca, Ignacio (coordinator). 2014. *Historia del Paraguay*. Asunción: Taurus, pp. 64–65.

7. If you really want to know, the capital's full name is "La Muy Noble y Leal Ciudad de Nuestra Señora Santa María de la Asunción" (The Very Noble and Loyal City of Our Lady Saint Mary of the Assumption).

8. The founder of Asunción, Juan de Salazar, described the place circa 1545 as "a town of 500 inhabitants and more than 500,000 tribulations." Melià, Bartomeu. "Historia de la lengua guaraní." in Telesca, Ignacio (coordinator). 2014. *Historia del Paraguay*. Asunción: Taurus, p. 425.

9. Lambert, Peter and Nickson, Andrew (editors). 2013. *The Paraguay Reader: History, Culture, Politics (The Latin America readers)*. Durham, NC: Duke University Press. Kindle Edition, p. 11.

10. Telesca, Ignacio. "La colonia desde 1680 a 1780" in Telesca, Ignacio (coordinator). 2014. *Historia del Paraguay*. Asunción: Taurus, p. 95.

11. Lambert, Peter and Nickson, Andrew (editors). 2013. *The Paraguay Reader: History, Culture, Politics (The Latin America readers)*. Durham, NC: Duke University Press. Kindle Edition, p. 28.

12. Velázquez, Rafael Eladio. 2018. *Una Periodización de la Historia Paraguaya*. Asunción: El Lector, p. 28.

13. *Bragueta* means "zipper fly" and braguetazo is the act of marrying for money or other particular interests. Vera, Helio. 2011. *En busca del hueso perdido (Tratado de paraguayología)*. Edición Homenaje. Asunción: ServiLibros, p. 149.

14. James Eston Hay surveyed the literature and concluded that "each Spaniard kept an average of ten Indian 'wives.'" Hay, James Eston. 1993. "Tobatí: Tradition and change in a Paraguayan Town." Ph.D. dissertation. Department of Sociology, University of Florida, Gainesville, p. 80. http://ufdcimages.uflib.ufl.edu/UF/00/09/89/05/00001/tobatitradizionc00hayj.pdf.

15. Hay, James Eston. 1993. "Tobatí: Tradition and change in a Paraguayan Town." Ph.D. dissertation. Department of Sociology, University of Florida, Gainesville, p. 178. https://archive.org/stream/tobatitraditionc00hayj/tobatitraditionc00hayj_djvu.txt.

16. Telesca, Ignacio. "Afrodescendientes: esclavos y libres." in Telesca, Ignacio (coordinator). 2014. *Historia del Paraguay*. Asunción: Taurus, p. 339.

17. La Nación. 2019. "Asunción tuvo casi el 50 percent de población negra antes de la Independencia." Published May 19, 2019. https://www.lanacion.com.py/gran-diario-domingo/2019/05/19/asuncion-tuvo-casi-el-50-de-poblacion-negra-antes-de-la-independencia.

18. Hay, James Eston. 1993. "Tobatí: Tradition and change in a Paraguayan Town." Ph.D. dissertation. Department of Sociology, University of Florida, Gainesville, pp. 156–58. https://archive.org/stream/tobatitraditionc00hayj/tobatitraditionc00hayj_djvu.txt.

19. Maeder, Ernesto J. A. "Las misiones jesuíticas" in Telesca, Ignacio (coordinator). 2014. *Historia del Paraguay*. Asunción: Taurus, pp. 117–18.

20. The Spanish term is *reducciones*

and originally meant to reduce into settlements.

21. Livi-Bacci, Massimo, and Maeder, Ernesto J. 2004. "The Missions of Paraguay: The Demography of an Experiment." *Journal of Interdisciplinary History*, xxxv:2 (Autumn, 2004), p. 190. http://www.latinamericanstudies.org/paraguay/paraguay-missions.pdf.

22. *Ibid.*

23. Roett, Riordan and Sacks, Richard Scott. 1991. *Paraguay. The Personalist Legacy*. Boulder: Westview Press, p. 16.

24. Rivarola, Milda. 2018. "Políticas fiscales y desigualdad en Paraguay." *Novapolis*. No. 13–Junio 2018, p. 46.

25. Fukuyama, Francis. 2011. *The Origins of Political Order: From Prehuman Times to the French Revolution*. New York: Farrar, Straus and Giroux.

26. The United Nations Educational, Scientific and Cultural Organization (UNESCO) declared the Jesuit Missions of La Santísima Trinidad de Paraná and Jesús de Tavarangue as World Heritage Sites in 1993.

27. Caballero Campos, Herib. "El virreinato del Río de la Plata (1776–1810)." in Telesca, Ignacio (coordinator). 2014. *Historia del Paraguay*. Asunción: Taurus, pp. 135–36.

28. Cantero, José. 2016. *Paraguay: An Economic History*. Kindle Edition, p. 13.

29. *Ibid.*, p. 46.

30. A similar point was made by F. A. Hayek in 1944. See Caldwell, Bruce (editor). 2009. *The Road to Serfdom: Text and Documents—The Definitive Edition (The Collected Works of F. A. Hayek, Volume 2)*. Chicago: University of Chicago Press, pp. 157–170.

31. Hay, James Eston. 1993. "Tobatí: Tradition and change in a Paraguayan Town." Ph.D. dissertation. Department of Sociology, University of Florida, Gainesville, p. 189. http://ufdcimages.uflib.ufl.edu/UF/00/09/89/05/00001/tobatitraditionc00hayj.pdf.

32. According to TripAdvisor. https://www.tripadvisor.com/Attractions-g294080-Activities-Asuncion.html#ATTRACTION_SORT_WRAPPER.

33. Abente, Diego. 1987. "The War of the Triple Alliance: Three Explanatory Models." *Latin American Research Review*, p. 60. http://www.latinamericanstudies.org/paraguay/triple.pdf.

34. Thucydides. 431 BC. *History of the Peloponnesian War*. https://www.mtholyoke.edu/acad/intrel/melian.htm.

35. The casualty rates are confounded by imperfect census data before and after the war. In addition, the final number of casualties fallen in battle is confounded by lower population numbers due to non-violent causes such as disease, starvation, and immigration.

36. Brezzo, Liliana M. "Reconstrucción, poder político y revoluciones (1870–1920)." in Telesca, Ignacio (coordinator). 2014. *Historia del Paraguay*. Asunción: Taurus, pp. 206–7.

37. Nye, Eric W. 2017. *Pounds Sterling to Dollars: Historical Conversion of Currency*. http://www.uwyo.edu/numimage/currency.htm.

38. Brezzo, Liliana M. "Reconstrucción, poder político y revoluciones (1870–1920)." in Telesca, Ignacio (coordinator). 2014. *Historia del Paraguay*. Asunción: Taurus, p. 208.

39. Lewis, Paul H. 1993. *Political Parties and Generations in Paraguay's Liberal Era, 1869–1940*. Chapel Hill: The University of North Carolina Press, pp. 19–20.

40. Some of them actually fought with the foreign troops and were labeled "legionaries." To this day the term is used in politics to disparage individuals with alleged foreign proclivities.

41. Hay, James Eston. 1993. "Tobatí: Tradition and change in a Paraguayan Town." Ph.D. dissertation. Department of Sociology, University of Florida, Gainesville, p. 124. http://ufdcimages.uflib.ufl.edu/UF/00/09/89/05/00001/tobatitraditionc00hayj.pdf.

42. Filártiga Callizo, Camilo. 2016. "La estabilidad del sistema de partidos políticos de Paraguay, 1989–2014." Published in Academia.edu. https://www.academia.edu/30297540/La_estabilidad_del_sistema_de_partidos_de_Paraguay_1989-2014.

43. Lewis, Paul H. 1993. *Political Parties and Generations in Paraguay's Liberal Era, 1869–1940*. Chapel Hill: The University of North Carolina Press, p. 52.

44. Brezzo, Liliana M. "Reconstrucción, poder político y revoluciones (1870–1920)." in Telesca, Ignacio (coordinator). 2014. *Historia del Paraguay*. Asunción: Taurus, p. 218.

45. Cantero, José. 2016. *Paraguay: An Economic History*. Kindle Edition, p. 105.

46. Author interview, August 7 & 8, 2017.

47. Roett, Riordan and Sacks, Richard Scott. 1991. *Paraguay. The Personalist Legacy*. Boulder: Westview Press, p. 43.

48. Schurz, William L. "The Chaco Dispute Between Bolivia and Paraguay." *Foreign Affairs Magazine*. July 1929 Issue. https://www.foreignaffairs.com/articles/bolivia/1929-07-01/chaco-dispute-between-bolivia-and-paraguay.

49. Velandia, Karenina. 2017. "El general ruso que ayudó a Paraguay a ganar una guerra y se convirtió en héroe." *BBC Mundo*, Published November 3, 2017. http://www.bbc.com/mundo/resources/idt-sh/General_Ruso_Spanish.

50. Lambert, Peter and Nickson, Andrew (editors). 2013. *The Paraguay Reader: History, Culture, Politics (The Latin America readers)*. Durham, NC: Duke University Press. Kindle Edition, pp. 203–4.

51. Roett, Riordan and Sacks, Richard Scott. 1991. *Paraguay. The Personalist Legacy*. Boulder: Westview Press, p. 47.

52. Lewis, Paul H. 1993. *Political Parties and Generations in Paraguay's Liberal Era, 1869–1940*. Chapel Hill: The University of North Carolina Press, p. 183.

53. Gómez Florentín, Carlos. 2011. *Higinio Morínigo, el soldado dictador*. Asunción: Editorial El Lector. http://www.portalguarani.com/1266_carlos_gomez_florentin/14601_higinio_morinigo_el_soldado_dictador_2011__por_carlos_gomez_florentin.html.

54. Scavone Yegros, Ricardo. "Guerra internacional y confrontaciones políticas (1920–1954)." in Telesca, Ignacio (coordinator). 2014. *Historia del Paraguay*. Asunción: Taurus, p. 258.

55. Borda, Dionisio, and Masi, Fernando (editors). 2010. *Estado y Economía en Paraguay. 1870–2010*. Asunción: CADEP, p. 95. The authors based their estimate using the Geary–Khamis dollar and the Angus Maddison series.

56. Lewis, Paul H. 1980. *Paraguay Under Stroessner*. Chapel Hill: The University of North Carolina Press, p. 70.

57. Paraguayans use two terms to refer to the Stroessner years: "Stronato" and "Stronismo."

58. Riquelme, Marcial. 1994. "Toward a Weberian Characterization of the Stroessner Regime in Paraguay (1954–1989)." *Revista Europea De Estudios Latinoamericanos Y Del Caribe / European Review of Latin American and Caribbean Studies* (57), 29–51. Retrieved from http://www.jstor.org/stable/25675638.

59. Weber, Max. 1978. *Economy and Society*. Berkeley: University of California Press. https://archive.org/stream/MaxWeberEconomyAndSociety/MaxWeberEconomyAndSociety_djvu.txt.

60. I have heard these stories from several sources. The Paraguayan newspaper *Última Hora* has documented how Stroessner maintained a "harem" of adolescent women at an Asunción house with the sole purpose of sexually abusing them. See Última Hora. 2016. "A Stroessner le traían las nenas para ser violadas." Tuesday, May 31, 2016. http://www.ultimahora.com/a-stroessner-le-traian-las-nenas-ser-violadas-n995744.html. Martín Almada also described how the recruitment and exploitation of adolescent women took place. See Creigh, Emily; Almada, Martín. 2016. *Journey to the Heart of the Condor: Love, Loss, and Survival in a South American Dictatorship*. Peace Corps Writers / Casa Satori. Kindle Edition, pp. 36–37.

61. Boccia Paz, Alfredo; González, Myrian; and Palau, Rosa. 2006. *Es mi informe. Los archivos secretos de la policía de Stroessner*. Asunción: Centro de Documentación y Estudios & Servilibro.

62. Fukuyama, Francis. 2011. *The Origins of Political Order: From Prehuman Times to the French Revolution*. New York: Farrar, Straus and Giroux, p. 17.

63. "Rent-seeking" is a concept first developed by U.S. economist Gordon Tullock and later expanded by another U.S. economist, Anne Krueger. According to the Concise Encyclopedia of Economics, "rent-seeking" occurs when individuals, *"obtain benefits for themselves through the political arena. They typically do so by getting a subsidy for a good they produce or for being in a particular class of people, by getting a tariff on a good they produce, or by getting a special regulation that hampers their competitors."* Henderson, David R. 2008. "Rent Seeking." *The Concise Encyclopedia of Economics. Library of Economics and Liberty*. http://www.econlib.org/library/Enc/RentSeeking.html.

64. Nickson, Andrew. "El régimen de Stroessner (1954–1989)." in Telesca, Ignacio (coordinator). 2014. *Historia del Paraguay*. Asunción: Taurus, p. 286.

65. Última Hora. 2011. "Una inmensa fortuna que jamás fue justificada." January 26, 2011. http://www.ultimahora.com/una-inmensa-fortuna-que-jamas-fue-justificada-n397988.html. ABC Color. 2009. "Llamativamente, ahora juez se aferra a expediente de Gustavo Stroessner." March 15, 2009. http://www.abc.com.py/edicion-impresa/policiales/llamativamente-ahora-juez-se-aferra-a-expediente-de-gustavo-stroessner-1155289.html.

66. ABC Color. 2002. "Disputa por réplica de la Casa Blanca lleva más de seis años." December 15, 2002. http://www.abc.com.py/edicion-impresa/policiales/disputa-por-replica-de-la-casa-blanca-lleva-mas-de-seis-anos-676892.html.

67. Nickson, Andrew. "El régimen de Stroessner (1954–1989)." in Telesca, Ignacio (coordinator). 2014. *Historia del Paraguay*. Asunción: Taurus, p. 267.

68. Abente, D. 1988. "Constraints and Opportunities: Prospects for Democratization in Paraguay." *Journal of Interamerican Studies and World Affairs*, 30(1), p. 84.

69. Mora, F. 1998. "The Forgotten Relationship: United States-Paraguay Relations, 1937–89." *Journal of Contemporary History*, 33(3). P. 467–8. Retrieved from. http://www.jstor.org/stable/261125.

70. Nickson, Andrew. "El régimen de Stroessner (1954–1989)." in Telesca, Ignacio (coordinator). 2014. *Historia del Paraguay*. Asunción: Taurus, p. 272.

71. Lapacho (*Handroanthus impetiginosus*) is the national tree of Paraguay.

72. Comisión de Verdad y Justicia. 2008. *Informe Final, Capítulo Conclusiones y Recomendaciones, p.* 29. http://www.derechoshumanos.net/lesahumanidad/informes/paraguay/Informe_Comision_Verdad_y_Justicia_Paraguay_Conclusiones_y_Recomendaciones.pdf.

73. Creigh, Emily; Almada, Martín. *Journey to the Heart of the Condor: Love, Loss, and Survival in a South American Dictatorship*. Peace Corps Writers / Casa Satori. Kindle Edition, pp. 9–10.

74. BBC. 2002. "Paraguay's Archive of Terror." http://news.bbc.co.uk/1/hi/world/americas/1866517.stm.

75. Boccia Paz, Alfredo; González, Myrian; and Palau, Rosa. 2006. *Es mi informe. Los archivos secretos de la policía de Stroessner*. Asunción: Centro de Documentación y Estudios & Servilibro.

76. Dinges, John. 2012. *The Condor Years: How Pinochet And His Allies Brought Terrorism To Three Continents*. The New Press. Kindle Edition, p. 7–8.

77. Drexler was inspired to write the song "El pianista del ghetto de Varsovia" from the story of Polish Holocaust survivor and author Wladyslaw Szpilman.

78. Huntington, Samuel P. 1993. *The Third Wave: Democratization in the Late Twentieth Century*. Norman: University of Oklahoma Press.

79. Hilton, Isabel. 1990. "The General." *Granta* 31, Spring 1990. Granta Publications, p. 78.

80. Lambert, Peter. "¿Una ruptura con el pasado? Los primeros dos años del gobierno de Nicanor Duarte Frutos en el contexto de la transición a la democracia." in Diego Abente y Fernando Masi (editors). 2005. *Estado, Economía y Sociedad. Una Mirada Internacional a la Democracia Paraguaya*. Asunción: Centro de Análisis y Difusión de la Economía Paraguaya, p. 141.

81. Other key elements include the rule of law, accountability, responsiveness, and functioning checks and balances among government branches. See Diamond, Larry, and Morlino, Leonardo. 2004. "The Quality of Democracy: An Overview." *Journal of Democracy*, October 2004 Volume 15, Issue 4, pp. 20–31.

82. Diego Abente Brun noted the 1989 election utilized the Stroessner-era electoral registry with its bulge of 900,000 untraceable voters. See Abente Brun, Diego. "Después de la dictadura." in Telesca, Ignacio (coordinator). 2014. *Historia del Paraguay*. Asunción: Taurus, p. 297.

83. Vinocur, John. 1984. "A Republic of Fear." *New York Times*, September 23, 1984. https://www.nytimes.com/1984/09/23/magazine/a-republic-of-fear.html.

84. Abente Brun, Diego. "Después de la dictadura." in Telesca, Ignacio (coordinator). 2014. *Historia del Paraguay*. Asunción: Taurus, p. 297.

85. The dialogue is available at https://www.youtube.com/watch?v=SlURCSjlmIY.

86. Borda, Dionisio. 2007. "Paraguay: resultados de las reformas (2003–2005) y sus perspectivas." *Comisión Económica para América Latina y el Caribe (CEPAL)*. Serie Informes y estudios especiales, No 18, p. 13.

87. *Ibid.*

88. Abente Brun, Diego. "Después de la dictadura." in Telesca, Ignacio (coordinator).

2014. *Historia del Paraguay.* Asunción: Taurus, p. 303.

89. The case remains open to this day. With its traditional ineffectiveness the Paraguayan justice never got to the bottom of it.

90. Abente Brun, Diego. "Después de la dictadura." in Telesca, Ignacio (coordinator). 2014. *Historia del Paraguay.* Asunción: Taurus, p. 307.

91. González Delvalle, Alcibíades. *El gobierno de Nicanor Duartes Frutos. El difícil camino hacia la transición.* La Historia del Paraguay, ABC Color. Fascículo No. 43, Capítulo 23. http://www.portalguarani. com/440_alcibiades_gonzalez_ delvalle/20223_el_gobierno_de_nicanor_ duarte_frutos__por_alcibiades_gonzalez_ delvalle.html.

92. Smith, Tony. 2003. "Paraguay's Voters Appear to Extend Party's 5-Decade Rule." *New York Times.* April 28, 2003. http://www. nytimes.com/2003/04/28/world/paraguay-s-voters-appear-to-extend-party-s-5-decade-rule.html.

93. Borda, Dionisio. 2007. "Paraguay: resultados de las reformas (2003–2005) y sus perspectivas." *Comisión Económica para América Latina y el Caribe (CEPAL).* Serie Informes y estudios especiales, No 18, p. 37.

94. Lachi, Marcelo. 2004. "Gobernabilidad democrática al 'estilo' paraguayo." *Revista de Estudios Políticos Contemporáneos.* Edición 7, Mayo 2004. http:// www.portalguarani.com/660_marcello_ lachi/15079_gobernabilidad_democratica_ al_estilo_paraguayo_marcello_lachi_.html.

95. Data from the Organisation for Economic Co-operation and Development (OECD) http://stats.oecd.org.

96. Liberation theology is a twentieth century and mostly Latin American interpretation of Catholic doctrine focused on fighting poverty and social inequality. The name was coined by the Peruvian priest Gustavo Gutiérrez in his book *A Theology of Liberation* (1971). Its supporters espouse practical biblical interpretation and liturgical practice among the poor. Liberation theology's momentum in the 1950s and 1960s was fueled by a period of rapid social and economic changes in Latin America, with young people being active advocates of political change.

97. ABC Color. 2010. "Morales declara a Lugo 'padre de los paraguayos.'" August 16, 2010. http://www.abc.com.py/ nacionales/morales-declara-a-lugo-padre-de-los-paraguayos-147418.html.

98. Lewis, Paul H. 1993. *Political Parties and Generations in Paraguay's Liberal Era, 1869–1940.* Chapel Hill: The University of North Carolina Press, p. 27.

99. Marsteintredet, Leiv; Llanos, Mariana, and Nolte, Detlef. 2013. "Paraguay and the Politics of Impeachment." *Journal of Democracy,* October 2013, Number 4, p. 121

100. Author interview, July 24, 2017.

101. Última Hora. 2012. "Federico Franco incrementó 7 veces su patrimonio en los últimos 4 años." October 14, 2012. http:// www.ultimahora.com/federico-franco-incremento-7-veces-su-patrimonio-los-ultimos-4-anos-n568882.html.

102. Source: "Informe de las finanzas públicas de la República del Paraguay, 2018." p. 9. http://www.hacienda.gov.py.

Chapter II

1. Tocqueville, Alexis De. 2007. *Democracy in America.* Volume I and II. Kindle Edition, p. 141.

2. For example, the 2017 Latin American Congress of Political Science's theme was "Democracies in recession?" See also Diamond, Larry. 2015. "Facing Up to the Democratic Recession." *Journal of Democracy* January 2015. Volume 26, Issue 1, pp. 141–155.

3. Vinocur, John. 1984. "A Republic of Fear." *New York Times,* September 23, 1984. https://www.nytimes.com/1984/09/23/ magazine/a-republic-of-fear.html.

4. Tocqueville, Alexis De. 2007. *Democracy in America.* Volume I and II. Kindle Edition, p. 142.

5. Latinobarómetro data obtained from http://www.latinobarometro.org.

6. Boidi, María Fernanda, and Zechmeister, Elizabeth J. 2018 "Cultura política de la democracia en Paraguay y en las Américas, 2016/17: Un estudio comparado sobre democracia y gobernabilidad." *Vanderbilt University, Latin American Public Opinion Project (LAPOP),* pp. 5–6. https:// www.vanderbilt.edu/lapop/paraguay/ AB2016-17_Paraguay_Country_Report_ V3_05.03.18_W.pdf.

7. Transparency International. 2017. "People and Corruption: Latin America and the Caribbean." Global Corruption

Barometer, p. 6. https://www.transparency. org/_view/publication/7983.

8. Dahl, Robert. 1971. *Polyarchy: Participation and Opposition.* Yale University Press.

9. Pritchett, Lant, and Woolcock, Michael. 2004. "Solutions When the Solution is the Problem: Arraying the Disarray in Development." *World Development.* Vol. 32, No. 2, pp. 191–212. http://www.kysq. org/docs/Pritchett_Woolcock.pdf.

10. According to Latinobarómetro data obtained from http://www. latinobarometro.org, when Latin Americans were asked, "In general, would you say you are very satisfied, just satisfied, not very satisfied or not satisfied with the way democracy works in your country?" between 2000 and 2013, Venezuelans consistently posted one of the highest rates for the response "very satisfied."

11. Latinobarómetro data obtained from http://www.latinobarometro.org. The average figure comes from twenty annual surveys carried out between 1995 and 2017; Latinobarómetro did not conduct surveys in 1999 and 2012.

12. Latinobarómetro data obtained from http://www.latinobarometro.org.

13. Universidad de Buenos Aires Grupo de Estudios Sociales sobre Paraguay.

14. Duarte Recalde, Liliana Rocío. 2015. "La política comparada en Paraguay como materia pendiente." *Geary, M., Lucca, J. B. y Pinillos, C. (editors) Política latinoamericana comparada.* Rosario: UNR Editora, pp. 166–170. https://www.academia.edu/20860699/ La_pol%C3%ADtica_comparada_en_Paraguay_como_materia_pendiente.

15. Vera, Helio. Prologue to Boccia Paz, Alfredo. 2004. *Diccionario usual del Stronismo.* Asunción: Editorial Servilibro. http://www.portalguarani.com/748_roberto_goiriz/7050_diccionario_usual_del_stronismo__diseno_de_tapa_roberto_goiriz.html.

16. Andrews, Matt; Pritchett, Lant, and Woolcock, Michael. 2017. *Building State Capability. Evidence, Analysis, Action*, p. 10.

17. *Ibid.*

18. Izquierdo, Alejandro, Pessino, Carola, and Vuletin, Guillermo (editores). 2018. "Mejor gasto para mejores vidas: cómo América Latina y el Caribe puede hacer más con menos." *Banco Interamericano de Desarrollo*, pp. 159 & 171. https://publications.iadb.org/publications/ spanish/document/Mejor-gasto-para-mejores-vidas-C%C3%B3mo-Am%C3%A9rica-Latina-y-el-Caribe-puede-hacer-m%C3%A1s-con-menos.pdf.

19. Setrini, Gustavo. 2011. "Twenty Years of Paraguayan Electoral Democracy: from Monopolistic to Pluralistic Clientelism." *Tinker Foundation Incorporated and CADEP.* Working Paper No. 3, p. 22. http://209.177.156.169/libreria_cm/ archivos/pdf_1014.pdf.

20. Source: IMF Data. http://data.imf. org.

21. Source: The World Bank. 2016. "Size of the Public Sector: Government Wage Bill and Employment.: February 17, 2016. http://www.worldbank.org/en/topic/ governance/brief/size-of-the-public-sector-government-wage-bill-and-employment.

22. Source: "Informe de las finanzas públicas de la República del Paraguay, 2018." pp. 8–9. http://www.hacienda.gov. py/web-presupuesto/archivo.php?a=86868 98f9a93999498548e8b955755565d5395898 b86025&x=cdcd06c&y=9999038.

23. International Monetary Fund. 2017. "Paraguay: 2017 Article IV Consultation—Press Release and Staff Report." IMF Country Report No. 17/233, p. 12. http:// www.imf.org/~/media/Files/Publications/ CR/2017/cr17233.ashx.

24. Franks, Jeffrey, Mercer-Blackman, Valerie, Sab, Randa, and Benellip, Roberto. 2005. "Paraguay: Corruption, Reform, and the Financial System." *International Monetary Fund*, p. xi. https://www.imf.org/ external/pubs/nft/2005/paraguay/reform. pdf.

25. Chong, Alberto, Rafael LaPorta, Florencio Lopez-de-Silanes, and Andrei Shleifer. 2014. "Letter Grading Government Efficiency." *Journal of European Economic Association* 12 (2): 277–299.

26. *The Sopranos* episode "No Show," written by David Chase and Terrence Winter and directed by John Patterson. It originally aired on September 22, 2002.

27. United Nations Development Programme. 2016. Paraguay Human Development Report 2016. Human Development for Everyone, p. 2. http://hdr.undp.org/ sites/all/themes/hdr_theme/country-notes/ PRY.pdf.

28. Lewis, Paul H. 1993. *Political Parties and Generations in Paraguay's Liberal*

Era, 1869–1940. Chapel Hill: The University of North Carolina Press, p. 41.

29. Nichols, Byron A. 1969. *The Role and Function of Political Parties in Paraguay*. A dissertation submitted to Johns Hopkins University in conformity with the requirements for the degree of Doctor of Philosophy. Baltimore, Maryland. University Microfilms, Inc., Ann Arbor, Michigan.

30. *Carai* or *Karai* is a guaraní word whose meaning has evolved across time. It used to mean a revered shaman, then evolved to the meaning Nichols utilizes as a larger-than-life leader, and nowadays simply means "mister" or "sir."

31. Nichols, Byron A. 1969. *The Role and Function of Political Parties in Paraguay*. A dissertation submitted to Johns Hopkins University in conformity with the requirements for the degree of Doctor of Philosophy. Baltimore, Maryland. University Microfilms, Inc., Ann Arbor, Michigan, p. 32.

32. Hicks, Frederic. 1971. "Interpersonal Relationships and Caudillismo in Paraguay." *Journal of Inter-American Studies and World Affairs*, 13(1), p. 107.

33. ABC Color. 2019. "Quería cambiar puerta de IPS por un pezón." June 4, 2019. http://www.abc.com.py/edicion-impresa/politica/queria-cambiar-puerta-de-ips-por-un-pezon-1820541.html.

34. Service, Elman R., and Service Helen S. 1954. *Tobatí: Paraguayan Town*. Chicago: the University of Chicago Press, p. 129.

35. Ayala, Eligio. 1989. *Migraciones paraguayas. Algunas de sus causas*. Asunción: Archivo del Liberalismo. http://www.portalguarani.com/318_eligio_ayala/20724_migraciones_paraguayas_1915__por_eligio_ayala.html.

36. Krouwel, André. 2003. "Otto Kirchheimer and the catch-all party." *West European Politics*. Volume 26, 2003, Issue 2.

37. I owe this idea to José Tomás Sánchez, a Paraguayan Political Science PhD candidate at Cornell University. http://www.anr.org.py.

38. http://www.plra.org.py.

39. Commonly attributed to the late American comedian Groucho Marx, the quote actually appeared before he was born. See Quote Investigator's entry https://quoteinvestigator.com/2010/05/09/groucho-principles.

40. Line taken from Swann's 1973 classic "Yo no me arrastro."

41. Sánchez, José Tomás. "Todo lo puedo en 'mis debilidades' que me fortalecen. El Partido Colorado y la fuerza de su inestabilidad interna." *Tereré Cómplice*. Published on June, 14 2018. https://tererecomplice.com/2018/06/14/todo-lo-puedo-en-mis-debilidades-que-me-fortalecen-el-partido-colorado-y-la-fuerza-de-su-inestabilidad-interna.

42. Thompson, Hunter S. "Paraguay to the polls: It's a Dictatorship, but Few Seem to Care Enough to Stay and Fight." *The National Observer*. January 28, 1963. https://ia601504.us.archive.org/1/items/ItsADictatorshipBut/January%2028%201963%20Paraguay.pdf.

43. Author interview, May 11, 2017.

44. Lewis, Paul H. 1982. *Socialism, Liberalism, and Dictatorship in Paraguay*. Stanford: Hoover Institution Press, p. 125.

45. This is an oft-repeated phrase among Paraguay's journalists and political analysts whose source is unknown. Another version states, "The Colorado Party will always win, even if the candidate is Donald Duck."

46. La Nación. 2018. "Ovelar, duro con Petta: 'Cree que esto es el Encuentro Nacional y esto es el Partido Colorado.'" May 4, 2018. https://www.lanacion.com.py/politica/2018/05/04/ovelar-duro-con-petta-cree-que-esto-es-el-encuentro-nacional-y-esto-es-el-partido-colorado.

47. See for example, ABC Color. 2017. "La actividad política no entusiasma a votantes." July 9, 2017. http://www.abc.com.py/edicion-impresa/politica/la-actividad-politica-no-entusiasma-a-votantes-1611300.html.

48. Sources: Tribunal Superior de Justicia Electoral. https://tsje.gov.py. International IDEA, https://www.idea.int/data-tools/country-view/249/40.

49. Cabello, Cesar, and Vázquez Aranda, Víctor. 2016. "Preferencias Electorales en Paraguay: Segmentos y Patrones de comportamiento." *Investigación para el Desarrollo*, p. 58. http://desarrollo.org.py/admin/app/webroot/pdf/publicati ons/29-12-2017-08-40-59-505877970.pdf. See also Boidi, María Fernanda, and Zechmeister, Elizabeth J. 2018. "Cultura política de la democracia en Paraguay y en las Américas, 2016/17: Un estudio comparado sobre democracia y gobernabilidad."

Vanderbilt University, Latin American Public Opinion Project (LAPOP), pp. 26–27.

50. *Psilocybe cubensis*, popularly known as "cucumelo" in Argentina, Paraguay, and Uruguay, is a psychedelic mushroom that grows in some areas of Paraguay, among other locations across the world.

51. Duarte-Recalde, Liliana Rocío. 2017. "Democracy and Representation in Paraguay." *Open Journal of Sociopolitical Studies*, Issue 10(1) 2017, p. 83. https://www.researchgate.net/profile/Liliana_Duarte_Recalde/publication/316641683_Democracy_and_Representation_in_Paraguay/links/59092dc6a6fdcc496167fc7d/Democracy-and-Representation-in-Paraguay.pdf.

52. Potthast, Barbara. "La mujer en la historia del Paraguay" in Telesca, Ignacio (coordinator). 2014. *Historia del Paraguay*. Asunción: Taurus, pp. 325–6.

53. Friedman, Benjamin M. 2006. *The Moral Consequences of Economic Growth*. New York: Vintage.

54. Based on 2008 and 2013 average results, men's turnout is rate is 67.7 percent and women's 65.7 percent. See Cabello, Cesar, and Vázquez Aranda, Víctor. 2016. "Preferencias Electorales en Paraguay: Segmentos y Patrones de comportamiento." *Investigación para el Desarrollo*. http://desarrollo.org.py/admin/app/webroot/pdf/publications/29-12-2017-08-40-59-505877970.pdf.

55. Soto, Lilian. 2015. "Partidos políticos y participación política de las mujeres en Paraguay." Asunción: Centro de Documentación y Estudios (CDE), p. 21. http://www.cde.org.py/wp-content/uploads/2015/01/Partidos-pol%C3%ADticos-y-participaci%C3%B3n-pol%C3%ADtica-de-las-mujeres-en-Paraguay-Elementos-para-el-debate-CDE-2014.pdf.

56. *Ibid, p.* 24.

57. ARD, Inc. 2009. *Paraguay Democracy and Governance Assessment.* Prepared for the United States Agency for International Development. http://pdf.usaid.gov/pdf_docs/pbaah431.pdf.

58. Semillas para la Democracia. 2018. "Síntesis de informe de observación electoral. Elecciones generales. Año 2018."

59. The factual source of the phrase is unknown, even though it is widely repeated among Paraguayan experts and printed in news stories.

60. Diamond, Larry. 1999. *Developing Democracy: Toward Consolidation.* Baltimore: Johns Hopkins University Press.

61. Freedom House. *Freedom in the World Report.* www.freedomhouse.org.

62. The Economist Intelligence Unit is a sister company of the British magazine *The Economist.* The Economist Intelligence Unit. 2018. "Democracy Index 2017. Free speech under attack." https://www.eiu.com/topic/democracy-index.

63. Abente Brun, Diego. 2007. "The Quality of Democracy in Small South American Countries: The Case of Paraguay." Working Paper #343, November 2007, p. 32. http://citeseerx.ist.psu.edu/viewdoc/download?doi=10.1.1.124.4578&rep=rep1&type=pdf.

64. Author interview, August 9, 2017.

65. Garbarino Acosta, Alberto. 2017. "Un nuevo absurdo." *Última Hora.* September 17, 2017. http://www.ultimahora.com/un-nuevo-absurdo-n1108279.html.

66. Hayek, F.A. 1973. *Law, Legislation and Liberty, Volume 1.* Chicago: The University of Chicago Press.

67. See for example, Abente Brun, Diego. 2007. "The Quality of Democracy in Small South American Countries: The Case of Paraguay." Working Paper #343, November 2007, p. 28. http://citeseerx.ist.psu.edu/viewdoc/download?doi=10.1.1.124.4578&rep=rep1&type=pdf.

68. Martínez-Escobar, Fernando. 2016. "¿Políticos delirantes?" *Tereré Cómplice,* published on December 29, 2016. https://tererecomplice.com/2016/12/29/politicos-delirantes.

69. Benítez González, Victor Raúl. 2018. "Quién vencerá las elecciones del 2018." *5 días,* January 2, 2018. https://www.5dias.com.py/quien-vencera-las-elecciones-del-2018.

70. Nichols, Byron A. 1969. *The Role and Function of Political Parties in Paraguay.* A dissertation submitted to Johns Hopkins University in conformity with the requirements for the degree of Doctor of Philosophy. Baltimore, Maryland. University Microfilms, Inc., Ann Arbor, Michigan, p. 48.

71. Última Hora. September 14, 2018. "Los Zacarías Irún copan cargos en todos los poderes del Estado." https://www.ultimahora.com/los-zacarias-irun-copan-cargos-todos-los-poderes-del-estado-n2707251.html.

72. Gustavo Setrini describes it as "pluralistic clientelism." Setrini, Gustavo.

2011. "Twenty Years of Paraguayan Electoral Democracy: from Monopolistic to Pluralistic Clientelism." *Tinker Foundation Incorporated and CADEP.* Working Paper No. 3. http://209.177.156.169/libreria_cm/archivos/pdf_1014.pdf.

73. Última Hora. July 10, 2017. "Oviedo Matto viola ley contra nepotismo al llenar de parientes el Congreso" http://www.ultimahora.com/oviedo-matto-viola-ley-contra-nepotismo-al-llenar-parientes-el-congreso-n1095609.html.

74. Lachi, Marcello, and Rojas Sheffer, Raquel. 2018. *Correligionarios. Actitudes y prácticas políticas del electorado paraguayo.* Asunción: Centro de Estudios y Educación Popular Germinal y Arandura Editorial.

75. Morínigo, José Nicolás. 2008. "Clientelismo y padrinazgo en las prácticas patrimonialistas de gobierno en el Paraguay." *Revista de Estudios Políticos Contemporáneos NOVAPOLIS,* No. 3 (13), Abril 2008, p. 17. http://www.portalguarani.com/660_marcello_lachi/17500_el_clientelismo_electoral_en_el_sistema_politico_paraguayo__coordinador_editorial_marcello_lachi.html.

76. Lachi, Marcello, and Rojas Sheffer, Raquel. 2018. *Correligionarios. Actitudes y prácticas políticas del electorado paraguayo.* Asunción: Centro de Estudios y Educación Popular Germinal y Arandura Editorial, p. 41.

77. Vera, Helio. 2017. *El país de la sopa dura. Tratado de paraguayología II.* 5a Edición. Asunción: ServiLibro, p. 105.

78. Miranda, Carlos R. 1990. *Paraguay y la Era de Stroessner.* Asunción: RP Ediciones. http://www.portalguarani.com/2436_carlos_r_miranda/6395_paraguay_y_la_era_de_stroessner__por_carlos_r_miranda.html.

79. Lachi, Marcello. 2013. "Capital político, pertenencia y lealtad partidaria en el electorado del Departamento de Ñeembucú." *Centro de Estudios y Educación Popular Germinal.* No 19, Diciembre 2013, pp. 8–9. http://www.portalguarani.com/660_marcello_lachi/26287_capital_politico_pertenencia_y_lealtad_partidaria_en_el_electorado_del_departamento_de_neembucu__germinal__documentos_de_trabajo_n_19_diciembre_2013.html.

80. *Ibid.*

81. Achen, Christopher H., and Bartels, Larry M. 2016. *Democracy for Realists: Why Elections Do Not Produce Responsive*

Government. Princeton: Princeton University Press. Kindle Edition. Kindle location 256–258.

82. *Ibid.* Kindle location 295–296.

83. See also Caplan, Bryan. 2007. *The Myth of the Rational Voter: Why Democracies Choose Bad Policies.* Kindle Edition. Princeton: Princeton University Press. Somin, Ilya. 2013. *Democracy and Political Ignorance: Why Smaller Government Is Smarter.* Stanford: Stanford University Press. Kindle Edition.

84. The AmericasBarometer by the Latin American Public Opinion Project (LAPOP), www.LapopSurveys.org. According to the 1996 survey, 59 percent of Paraguayan respondents agreed with the statement, "Stroessner helped the poor."

85. According to Setrini, by 1989 there were 1.7 million members. However, Nickson alleges the number is exagerated as the country's 1988 electoral registry had just 1.4 million voters. Setrini, Gustavo. 2011. "Twenty Years of Paraguayan Electoral Democracy: from Monopolistic to Pluralistic Clientelism." *Tinker Foundation Incorporated and CADEP.* Working Paper No. 3, p. 20. http://209.177.156.169/libreria_cm/archivos/pdf_1014.pdf. Nickson, Andrew. "El régimen de Stroessner (1954–1989)." in Telesca, Ignacio (coordinator). 2014. *Historia del Paraguay.* Asunción: Taurus, p. 278.

86. Nickson, Andrew. *Ibid.*

87. Morínigo, José Nicolás. 2008. "Clientelismo y padrinazgo en las prácticas patrimonialistas de gobierno en el Paraguay." *Revista de Estudios Políticos Contemporáneos NOVAPOLIS,* No. 3 (13), Abril 2008, p. 19. http://www.portalguarani.com/660_marcello_lachi/17500_el_clientelismo_electoral_en_el_sistema_politico_paraguayo__coordinador_editorial_marcello_lachi.html.

88. Bergen, Ernst. 2008. *Jumping Into Empty Space: A Reluctant Mennonite Businessman Serves In Paraguay's Presidential Cabinet.* Good Books. Kindle Edition. Kindle locations 1214–1215.

89. Última Hora. 2018. "Auto familiar: Gobierno lanza nuevos modelos." April 16, 2018. https://www.ultimahora.com/auto-familiar-gobierno-lanza-nuevos-modelos-n1143155.html.

90. ABC Color. 2017. "Incluir fallecidos es parte de nuestra cultura, según Almirón." January 25, 2017. http://www.abc.com.py/edicion-impresa/

politica/incluir-fallecidos-es-parte-de-nuestra-cultura-segun-almiron-1558836.html.

91. Public choice is the theory that explains how political decision-making results from the aggregate decisions of self-interested agents. The set of incentives and institutions to gain and retain political power is crucial to understand the way politicians operate.

92. *Última Hora*. 2018. "La jubilación vip se suma a jugosos privilegios, como dieta y combustible." June 23, 2018. https://www.ultimahora.com/la-jubilacion-vip-se-suma-jugosos-privilegios-como-dieta-y-combustible-n1301677.html.

93. Ayala, Eligio. 1989. *Migraciones paraguayas. Algunas de sus causas.* Asunción: Archivo del Liberalismo. http://www.portalguarani.com/318_eligio_ayala/20724_migraciones_paraguayas_1915__por_eligio_ayala.html.

94. Abente Brun, Diego. 2007. "The Quality of Democracy in Small South American Countries: The Case of Paraguay." Working Paper #343, November 2007, p. 27. http://citeseerx.ist.psu.edu/viewdoc/download?doi=10.1.1.124.4578&rep=rep1&type=pdf.

95. Przeworski, A., Alvarez, M., Cheibub, J. A. and Limongi, F. 2000. *Democracy and Development: Political Institutions and Well-Being in the World, 1950–1990.* Cambridge: Cambridge University Press, p. 54.

96. Filártiga Callizo, Camilo. 2016. "La estabilidad del sistema de partidos políticos de Paraguay, 1989–2014." Published in Academia.edu. https://www.academia.edu/30297540/La_estabilidad_del_sistema_de_partidos_de_Paraguay_1989-2014.

97. Ferreira, Amílcar. 2017. "Los cinco motores del futuro económico del Paraguay." In Benítez González, Victor Raúl (editor). 2017. *La historia del futuro. El Paraguay a partir del 2018.* Asunción: Editorial Libre, p. 49.

98. O'Rourke, P.J. 1992. *Give War a Chance: Eyewitness Accounts of Mankind's Struggle Against Tyranny, Injustice, and Alcohol-Free Beer.* New York: Grove Press, p. 39.

Chapter III

1. Borda, Dionisio, and Masi, Fernando (editors). 2010. *Estado y Economía en Paraguay. 1870–2010.* Asunción: CADEP, p. 7.

2. Cantero, José. 2016. *Paraguay: An Economic History.* Kindle Edition, p. 136.

3. *Ibid, p.* 111.

4. Triffin, Robert. 1946. *Monetary and Banking Reform in Paraguay.* Washington: Board of governors of the Federal Reserve System, p. 17.

5. Faruqee, Hamid and David, Antonio C. 2017. "Why 2018 Is a Pivotal Year for Paraguay." *International Monetary Fund Blog Diálogo a Fondo.* Published December 5, 2017. http://www.imf.org/external/np/blog/dialogo/120517.pdf.

6. ABC Digital. 2018. "Paraguay: el gran paso de ser pocos, pobres, rurales y aislados a ser muchos, ricos, urbanos e integrados." June 17, 2018. http://www.abc.com.py/edicion-impresa/suplementos/economico/paraguay-el-gran-paso-de-ser-pocos-pobres-rurales-y-aislados-a-ser-muchos-ricos-urbanos-e-integrados-1713003.html.

7. Almeida, Eduardo, Bastos, Fabiano, Quijada, Alejandro, Acevedo, Maria Cecilia. 2018. "Paraguay: Rutas para el Desarrollo." *Banco Interamericano de Desarrollo.* p. 34. https://publications.iadb.org/bitstream/handle/11319/8853/Paraguay-Rutas-para-el-desarrollo.pdf?sequence=1&isAllowed=y).

8. Quoted by Acosta Garbarino, Alberto. 2010. "Paraguay, ¿un país balsa? No se hunde ni levanta vuelo." *Última Hora*, June 27, 2010. http://www.ultimahora.com/paraguay-un-pais-balsa-no-se-hunde-ni-levanta-vuelo-n334395.html.

9. *The Economist.* 2017. "Defining emerging markets." October 7, 2017, U.S. Edition. Kindle location 1162–1165.

10. *Ibid.* Kindle location 1160–1162.

11. https://data.worldbank.org.

12. La Nación. 2019. "Negocio bursátil: Mercado que crece a "contracorriente." September 11, 2019. https://www.lanacion.com.py/mitad-de-semana/destacado/2019/09/11/negocio-bursatil-mercado-que-crece-a-contracorriente.

13. All numbers taken from World Bank. https://data.worldbank.org.

14. *Ibid.*

15. Paraguay's score went from 3.25 in 1994 to 3.76 in 2014 (the higher the number, the less diversified). Export Diversification and Quality selected indicators:

Paraguay. *International Monetary Fund.* http://data.imf.org.

16. Colmán, Humberto. 2017. "El Desacoplamiento del Crecimiento ¿Vamos por diferentes caminos?" *Ministerio de Hacienda*, Subsecretaría de Estado de Economía. Blog Económico, Jueves 19 de enero de 2017. http://www.economia.gov.py/index.php/blog-econ%C3%B3mico/el-desacoplamiento-del-crecimiento#sthash.lhmRQ7Ej.dpbs.

17. Almeida, Eduardo, Bastos, Fabiano, Quijada, Alejandro, Acevedo, Maria Cecilia. 2018. "Paraguay: Rutas para el Desarrollo." *Banco Interamericano de Desarrollo.* https://publications.iadb.org/bitstream/handle/11319/8853/Paraguay-Rutas-para-el-desarrollo.pdf?sequence=1&isAllowed=y).

18. Azevedo, Gabriel. 2018. "Paraguai investe em portos e estradas para transportar safra brasileira." *Gazeta do Povo.* Published April 15, 2018. https://www.gazetadopovo.com.br/agronegocio/expedicoes/expedicao-safra/2017-2018/paraguai-investe-em-portos-e-estradas-para-transportar-safra-brasileira-clqiddd7c78a0qt5ho3rcspgm.

19. Data from the Encuesta Permanente de Hogares. http://www.dgeec.gov.py.

20. World Development Indicators, The World Bank. https://data.worldbank.org.

21. Beliz, Gustavo, and Chelala, Santiago. 2016. "El ADN de la integración regional. La voz de los latinoamericanos por una convergencia de calidad: innovación, equidad y cuidado ambiental." *Instituto para la Integración de América Latina y el Caribe (INTAL).* Nota Técnica IDB-TN-1120, p. 112. https://publications.iadb.org/bitstream/handle/11319/7896/El-ADN-de-la-integracion-regional-La-voz-de-los-latinoamericanos-por-una-convergencia-de-calidad-innovacion-equidad-y-cuidado-ambiental.pdf?sequence=4&isAllowed=y.

22. WeChat is known as "China's App for Everything," offering users a large platform for all kind of services, from basic text messaging to digital money. Its number of monthly active users is estimated at nearly 1 billion.

23. http://descubre.iadb.org/es/digilac.

24. Data from the Encuesta Permanente de Hogares. http://www.dgeec.gov.py.

25. Data from the Ministry of Public Works and Communications. http://www.mopc.gov.py/la-red-vial-del-paraguay-tiene-87200-km-n3620.

26. World Economic Forum. 2017. The Global Competitiveness Report 2016–2017. http://www3.weforum.org/docs/GCR2016-2017/05FullReport/TheGlobalCompetitivenessReport2016-2017_FINAL.pdf.

27. Asociacion Latinoamericana de Integracion. 2016. "El costo de la mediterraneidad: los casos de Bolivia y Paraguay. ALADI/SEC/Estudio 216, 5 de agosto de 2016. http://www.aladi.org/biblioteca/Publicaciones/ALADI/Secretaria_General/SEC_Estudios/216.pdf.

28. Aquino, Jesús. 2015. "Estimación de la Productividad Total de Factores de Paraguay: mediciones alternativas." *Ministerio de Hacienda*, Subsecretaría de Estado de Economía Dirección de Estudios Económicos, Setiembre 2015. http://www.economia.gov.py/application/files/6314/6591/0634/Documento_PTF_Final_092015.pdf.

29. Organisation for Economic Co-operation and Development and Inter-American Development Bank. 2016. "Boosting Productivity and Inclusive Growth in Latin America." http://www.oecd.org/latin-america/Boosting_Productivity_Inclusive_Growth.pdf.

30. Organisation for Economic Co-operation and Development and Inter-American Development Bank. 2016. "Boosting Productivity and Inclusive Growth in Latin America." p. 124. http://www.oecd.org/latin-america/Boosting_Productivity_Inclusive_Growth.pdf.

31. See Deirdre McCloskey's trilogy *Bourgeois Virtues, Bourgeois Dignity*, and *Bourgeois Equality* all published by University of Chicago Press.

32. Enterprise Surveys, The World Bank. http://www.enterprisesurveys.org.

33. *Ibid.*

34. Almeida, Eduardo, Bastos, Fabiano, Quijada, Alejandro, Acevedo, Maria Cecilia. 2018. "Paraguay: Rutas para el Desarrollo." *Banco Interamericano de Desarrollo*, pp. 24–26. https://publications.iadb.org/bitstream/handle/11319/8853/Paraguay-Rutas-para-el-desarrollo.pdf?sequence=1&isAllowed=y.

35. Bosch, Mariano, Pagés, Carmen, and Ripani, Laura. 2018. "The future of work in Latin America and the Caribbean. A great opportunity for the region?

Inter-American Development Bank, p. 13. https://publications.iadb.org/publications/english/document/the-future-of-work-in-latin-america-and-the-caribbean-pr.pdf.

36. In constant 2010 U.S.$. https://data.worldbank.org.

37. Scartascini, Carlos; Spiller, Pablo; Stein, Ernesto; Tommasi, Mariano (editores). 2011. "El juego político en América Latina: ¿Cómo se deciden las políticas públicas?" *Banco Interamericano de Desarrollo*, p. 349. https://webimages.iadb.org/publications/spanish/document/El-juego-pol%C3%ADtico-en-Am%C3%A9rica-Latina%C2%BFC%C3%B3mo-se-deciden-las-pol%C3%ADticas-p%C3%BAblicas.pdf.

38. Barro, Robert J., et al. "Convergence Across States and Regions." *Brookings Papers on Economic Activity*, vol. 1991, no. 1, 1991, pp. 107–182. JSTOR, www.jstor.org/stable/2534639.

39. Using the variable GDP per capita (constant 2010 U.S.$). https://data.worldbank.org.

40. Comisión Económica para América Latina y el Caribe (CEPAL). 2018. "Panorama Fiscal de América Latina y el Caribe 2018. Los desafíos de las políticas públicas en el marco de la Agenda 2030," p. 60 http://repositorio.cepal.org/bitstream/handle/11362/43405/1/S1800082_es.pdf.

41. Pisani, Michael J. and Ovandoy, Fernando G. 2018. "Brief Report: Measuring the Informal Sector in Paraguay." Centro de Análisis y Difusión de la Economía Paraguaya (CADEP). February, 2019, p. 4. https://bit.ly/2DwUkaH.

42. Peña, Santiago. 2017. "Hacia un Impuesto a la Renta Personal más justo." *Blog Económico, Ministerio de Hacienda.* Published February 2, 2017. https://www.economia.gov.py/index.php/blog-econ%C3%B3mico/hacia-un-impuesto-la-renta-personal-mas-justo

43. Enterprise Surveys, The World Bank. http://www.enterprisesurveys.org.

44. Desantis, Daniela. 2017. "'Made in Paraguay': a cheaper label for some Brazilian manufacturers." *Reuters*, February 24, 2017. https://www.reuters.com/article/us-paraguay-brazil/made-in-paraguay-a-cheaper-label-for-some-brazilian-manufacturers-idUSKBN163256.

45. Almeida, Eduardo, Bastos, Fabiano, Quijada, Alejandro, Acevedo, Maria Cecilia. 2018. "Paraguay: Rutas para el Desarrollo." *Banco Interamericano de Desarrollo*, p. 49. https://publications.iadb.org/bitstream/handle/11319/8853/Paraguay-Rutas-para-el-desarrollo.pdf?sequence=1&isAllowed=y.

46. Bergen, Ernst. 2008. *Jumping Into Empty Space: A Reluctant Mennonite Businessman Serves In Paraguay's Presidential Cabinet.* Good Books. Kindle Edition. Kindle locations 419–420.

47. Administración Nacional de Electricidad (ANDE), Compañía Paraguaya de Comunicaciones (Copaco), Empresa de Servicios Sanitarios del Paraguay (ESSAP), Industria Nacional de Cemento (INC), Petropar, Puertos, Dirección Nacional de Aeronáutica Civil (DINAC), Cañas Paraguayas SA (CAPASA), and Ferrocarriles del Paraguay SA (FEPASA).

48. Federación Interamericana del Cemento. 2018. *Informe Estadístico.* http://ficem.org/dev/wp-content/uploads/2018/09/CIFRAS-DE-LA-INDUSTRIA-CEMENTERA-MUNDIAL.pdf.

49. Service, Elman R., and Service Helen S. 1954. *Tobatí: Paraguayan Town.* Chicago: the University of Chicago Press, p. 21.

50. Nichols, Byron A. 1969. *The Role and Function of Political Parties in Paraguay.* A dissertation submitted to Johns Hopkins University in conformity with the requirements for the degree of Doctor of Philosophy. Baltimore, Maryland. University Microfilms, Inc., Ann Arbor, Michigan. Preface.

51. Thompson, Hunter S. "Paraguay to the polls: It's a Dictatorship, but Few Seem to Care Enough to Stay and Fight." *The National Observer.* January 28, 1963. https://ia601504.us.archive.org/1/items/ItsADictatorshipBut/January%2028%201963%20Paraguay.pdf.

52. Almeida, Eduardo, Bastos, Fabiano, Quijada, Alejandro, Acevedo, Maria Cecilia. 2018. "Paraguay: Rutas para el Desarrollo." *Banco Interamericano de Desarrollo*, p. 79.

53. Benítez González, Victor Raúl (editor). 2017. *La historia del futuro. El Paraguay a partir del 2018.* Asunción: Editorial Libre, p. 147.

54. According to 2017 data from the government's statistics office, the Dirección General de Estadísticas, Encuestas y Censos (DGEEC), the poverty rate was 26.4 percent.

55. Farfán Bertrán, María Gabriela. 2018. "Poverty & Equity Brief. Latin America & the Caribbean. Paraguay. October 2018." *World Bank Group.* https://databank.worldbank.org/data/download/poverty/33EF03BB-9722-4AE2-ABC7-AA2972D68AFE/Global_POVEQ_PRY.pdf.

56. Banco Mundial. 2018. "Paraguay. Invertir en capital humano: una revisión del gasto público y de la gestión en los sectores sociales." © World Bank, p. 8. http://documentos.bancomundial.org/curated/es/933691542659029507/pdf/132203-WP-P164146-SPANISH-v5-16-11-2018-13-37-58-PYInvertirenCapitalHumanofinalImagebank.pdf.

57. Nikolajczuk, Mónica. 2018. "Élites económicas, poder político y medios de comunicación en Paraguay." *Novapolis.* N° 13—Junio 2018, p. 101.

58. Corporación Latinobarómetro. 2018. *Informe 2018.* www.latinobarometro.org.

59. Boidi, María Fernanda, and Zechmeister, Elizabeth J. 2018. "Cultura política de la democracia en Paraguay y en las Américas, 2016/17: Un estudio comparado sobre democracia y gobernabilidad." *Vanderbilt University, Latin American Public Opinion Project (LAPOP),* p. 55.

60. Author's calculation based on Gallup News Global Emotions Reports 2012–18. http://news.gallup.com.

61. Harari, Yuval Noah. 2015. *Sapiens: A Brief History of Humankind.* New York: Harper. Kindle location 5845–5847.

62. Unless indicated otherwise, all current data come from the 2012 national census.

63. Service, Elman R., and Service Helen S. 1954. *Tobatí: Paraguayan Town.* Chicago: the University of Chicago Press, p. 6.

64. Hay, James Eston. 1993. "Tobatí: Tradition and change in a Paraguayan Town." Ph.D. dissertation. Department of Sociology, University of Florida, Gainesville, p. 210. http://ufdcimages.uflib.ufl.edu/UF/00/09/89/05/00001/tobatitraditionc00hayj.pdf.

65. Smith, Adam. *An Inquiry Into the Nature and Causes of the Wealth of Nations.* Public Domain Books. Kindle Edition. Kindle Location 309.

66. Service, p. 85.

67. *Ibid,* p. xix.

68. La Nación. 2018. "OK a pedido de oleros de Tobatí." December 15, 2018 https://www.lanacion.com.py/politica_edicion_impresa/2018/12/15/ok-a-pedido-de-oleros-de-tobati.

69. Service, p. 258.

70. *Ibid,* p. 265.

71. *Ibid,* p. 11.

72. *Ibid,* p. xxiii.

73. Lewis, Paul H. 1980. *Paraguay Under Stroessner.* Chapel Hill: The University of North Carolina Press, p. 163.

74. Service, p. 297.

75. Hay, p. 407.

Chapter IV

1. Although called a "soup," sopa paraguaya is a corn bread. Legend has it that one of the early president's cooks started cooking a regular soup but because of a mistake with the ingredients found herself with a solid "soup." The president liked the final product and called it "sopa paraguaya."

2. Evans, Peter B. 1989. *Predatory, Developmental, and Other Apparatuses: A Comparative Political Economy Perspective on the Third World State.* Sociological Forum, 4, 561–587.

3. Acemoglu, Daron, and James A Robinson. 2012. *Why Nations Fail: The Origins of Power, Prosperity and Poverty.* 1st ed. New York: Crown.

4. Krueger, A. 1974. *The Political Economy of the Rent-Seeking Society.* The American Economic Review, 64(3), 291–303. Retrieved from http://www.jstor.org/stable/1808883.

5. Smith, Adam. *An Inquiry Into the Nature and Causes of the Wealth of Nations.* Public Domain Books. Kindle Edition. Kindle Locations 244–245.

6. Kirzner, Israel M. 2015. *Competition and Entrepreneurship.* University of Chicago Press.

7. Ruiz Diaz, Francisco. 2012. "Mythbusters. Explorando el Comercio Exterior Paraguayo." Informe del Observatorio de Economía Internacional y del Centro de Análisis y Difusión de la Economía Paraguaya. http://www.cadep.org.py/uploads/2012/06/Mythbusters.pdf.

8. Neuwirth, Robert. 2011. *Stealth of Nations: The Global Rise of the Informal Economy.* Knopf Doubleday Publishing Group. Kindle Edition, p. 114.

9. PRO Desarrollo Paraguay. 2016.

Economía Subterránea: el Caso Paraguayo. 4ª. Edición, p. 44. http://www.pro.org.py/wp-content/uploads/2016/11/ECONOMIA_SUBTERRANEA_2016.pdf.

10. Financial Times. April 7, 2017. "Former 'contraband capital' gets down to business." On-line edition. https://www.ft.com/content/f1833fc6-1a1d-11e7-bcac-6d03d067f81f.

11. World Bank. 2017. *Doing Business 2017: Equal Opportunity for All.* Washington, DC: World Bank, p. 182. http://www.doingbusiness.org/~/media/WBG/DoingBusiness/Documents/Annual-Reports/English/DB17-Report.pdf.

12. Albisu Ardigó, Iñaki. 2016. "Paraguay: Overview of Corruption and Anti-Corruption." *Transparency International.* www.transparency.org/files/content/corruptionqas/Country_profile_Paraguay_2016.pdf.

13. Fisman, Ray. 2017. Corruption: What Everyone Needs to Know? Oxford University Press. Kindle Edition, p. 1.

14. *Ibid,* p. 4. According to Fisman, "Corruption happens as a result of interactions among individuals in which, given the choices others make, no one person can make herself better off by choosing any other course of action."

15. Douglas C. North Nobel Prize Lecture. http://www.nobelprize.org/nobel_prizes/economic-sciences/laureates/1993/north-lecture.html.

16. Bergen, Ernst. 2008. *Jumping Into Empty Space: A Reluctant Mennonite Businessman Serves In Paraguay's Presidential Cabinet.* Good Books. Kindle Edition. Kindle Location 360.

17. Auriol, Emmanuelle, Straub, Stephane and Flochel, Thomas. 2015. "Public Procurement and Rent-Seeking: The Case of Paraguay." p. 4. http://www.tse-fr.eu/sites/default/files/TSE/documents/doc/by/auriol/rent_seeking_sep_2015.pdf.

18. Fisman Raymond and Miguel, Edward. 2006. "Cultures of Corruption: Evidence From Diplomatic Parking Tickets." *The National Bureau of Economic Research.* NBER Working Paper No. 12312. http://www.nber.org/papers/w12312.pdf.

19. *Ibid.*

20. The article's author, Aldo Benítez, traces the source of the joke to the comedy duo "Los Compadres." La Nación. 2016. "Atyrá: El otro país dentro de Paraguay." July 19, 2016. http://www.lanacion.com.py/2016/07/19/atyra-el-otro-pais-dentro-de-paraguay.

21. Transparency International. 2017. "People and Corruption: Latin America and the Caribbean." Global Corruption Barometer, p. 15. https://www.transparency.org/_view/publication/7983.

22. Hicks, F. 1971. "Interpersonal Relationships and Caudillismo in Paraguay." *Journal of Interamerican Studies and World Affairs,* 13(1), p. 98.

23. Since 2014, Brazilian judges have investigated corruption at the state-controlled oil company Petrobras. While the trial began with allegations that executives received bribes for inflated contracts, it grew to become a rebuke of Brazil's political class and its shady trafficking of favors.

24. PRO Desarrollo Paraguay. 2016. Economía Subterránea: el Caso Paraguayo. 4ª. Edición, p. 48. http://www.pro.org.py/wp-content/uploads/2016/11/ECONOMIA_SUBTERRANEA_2016.pdf.

25. Pisani, Michael J. and Ovandoy, Fernando G. 2018. "Brief Report: Measuring the Informal Sector in Paraguay." *Centro de Análisis y Difusión de la Economía Paraguaya (CADEP).* February 2019, p. 4. https://bit.ly/2DwUkaH.

26. Medina, Leandro, and Schneider, Friedrich. 2018. "Shadow Economies Around the World: What Did We Learn Over the Last 20 Years?" *International Monetary Fund,* IMF Working Paper, WP/18/17, p. 53. https://www.imf.org/~/media/Files/Publications/WP/2018/wp1817.ashx.

27. Dirección General de Estadística, Encuestas y Censos. 2018. "Ocupación Informal: Encuesta de Hogares EPH 2012–2017." http://www.dgeec.gov.py.

28. According to Banco Mundial. 2017. Diagnóstico del empleo en Paraguay: La transformación dinámica del empleo en Paraguay. Cuadernillo del "Resumen." Banco Mundial, Washington DC. Licencia: Creative Commons de Reconocimiento CC BY 3.0 IGO, p. iii.

29. Vargas, Jose P Mauricio. 2015. "Informality in Paraguay: Macro-Micro Evidence and Policy Implications." *International Monetary Fund,* Working Paper WP/15/245, p. 12. https://www.imf.org/external/pubs/ft/wp/2015/wp15245.pdf.

30. Doing Business, The World Bank. http://www.doingbusiness.org.

31. Titelman, Daniel (coordinator). 2018. "Panorama Fiscal de América

Latina y el Caribe Los desafíos de las políticas públicas en el marco de la Agenda 2030." *Comisión Económica para América Latina y el Caribe (CEPAL)*, p. 49. http://repositorio.cepal.org/bitstream/handle/11362/43405/1/S1800082_es.pdf.

32. Borda, Dionisio. 2007. "Paraguay: resultados de las reformas (2003–2005) y sus perspectivas." *Comisión Económica para América Latina y el Caribe (CEPAL)*. Serie Informes y estudios especiales, No 18, p. 30.

33. Salomon, Matthew. 2019. "Illicit Financial Flows to and from 148 Developing Countries: 2006–2015." *Global Financial Integrity*, p. 31. https://www.gfintegrity.org/wp-content/uploads/2019/01/GFI-2019-IFF-Update-Report-1.29.18.pdf.

34. http://www.abc.com.py/temas/de-donde-saco-la-plata-3343.html.

35. World Bank. 2018. *Doing Business 2019: Training for Reform—Paraguay (English)*. Doing Business 2019. Washington, D.C.: World Bank Group. http://documents.worldbank.org/curated/en/925711541163825870/Doing-Business-2019-Training-for-Reform-Paraguay.

36. Basabé-Serrano, Santiago. 2015. "Informal Institutions and Judicial Independence in Paraguay, 1954–2011." *Law & Policy*, Volume 37, Issue 4, October 2015, pp. 350–378.

37. Ríos-Figueroa, Julio, and Staton, Jeffrey K. 2014. "An Evaluation of Cross-National Measure of Judicial Independence." *Journal of Law, Economics and Organization*. Volume 30, Issue 1, pp. 104–37.

38. *The Economist*. 2010. "Viktor Chernomyrdin." Published November 4, 2010. http://www.economist.com/node/17414237.

39. ABC Digital. September 11, 2017. "Jueces ni siquiera cumplen el manual antichicanas que implementó la Corte." http://www.abc.com.py/edicion-impresa/judiciales-y-policiales/jueces-ni-siquiera-cumplen-el-manual-antichicanas-que-implemento-la-corte-1630709.html.

40. United States Department of State. 2016. Paraguay Country Report on Human Rights Practices for 2016, p. 15. https://www.state.gov/documents/organization/265818.pdf.

41. For example, the main source of global data on rule of law—the World Justice Project's Rule of Law Index—does not have statistics on Paraguay.

42. Miller, Terry, and Kim, Anthony B. 2017. "Index of Economic Freedom." *Institute for Economic Freedom, Heritage Foundation*. Washington, D.C.: Heritage Foundation, p. 83. http://www.heritage.org/index/pdf/2017/book/index_2017.pdf

43. The report aggregates data from fifteen different reports, including the Heritage Foundation's.

44. Kaufmann D., A. Kraay, and M. Mastruzzi. 2010. The Worldwide Governance Indicators: Methodology and Analytical Issues. The Worldwide Governance Indicators are available at: www.govindicators.org.

45. Vera, Helio. 2017. *El país de la sopa dura. Tratado de paraguayología II*. 5a Edición. Asunción: ServiLibro, p. 15.

46. Centro de Estudios de Justicia de las Americas. 2017. Índice de Accesibilidad a la Información Judicial en Internet 2017. http://www.cejamericas.org/en/areas-de-trabajo/tecnologia-de-la-informacion-y-transparencia/transparencia-rendicion-de-cuentas-y-acceso-a-la-informacion-judicial/indice-de-accesibilidad-a-la-informacion-judicial-en-internet-2017#-resultados-globales-iacc.

47. *Ibid.* http://biblioteca.cejamericas.org/bitstream/handle/2015/4656/ceja-indice-accesibilidad3.pdf?sequence=1&isAllowed=y.

48. Latinobarometro data obtained from http://www.latinobarometro.org.

49. Le Clerq Ortega, Juan Antonio and Rodríguez Sánchez Lara, Gerardo (Coordinators). 2017. *Global Impunity Index 2017*. Puebla: Fundación Universidad de las Américas. https://www.udlap.mx/cesij/files/IGI-2017_eng.pdf.

50. Coordinadora de Derechos Humanos del Paraguay. 2018. *Informe Anual Sobre La Situación de los Derechos Humanos en Paraguay 2018*, p. 308. http://codehupy.org.py/wp-content/uploads/2018/12/DDHH_2018_web.pdf.

51. ARD, Inc. 2009. *Paraguay Democracy and Governance Assessment*. Prepared for the United States Agency for International Development, p. 10–11 http://pdf.usaid.gov/pdf_docs/pbaah431.pdf.

52. Jaitman, Laura (editor). 2017. *The Costs of Crime and Violence, New Evidence and Insights in Latin America and the Caribbean*. Inter-American Development Bank, p. 30. https://publications.iadb.org/bitstream/handle/11319/8133/The-Costs-of-Crime-

and-Violence-New-Evidence-and-Insights-in-Latin-America-and-the-Caribbean.pdf?sequence=7&isAllowed=y.

53. Murphy, Kevin, Andrei Shleifer, and Robert W. Vishny. 1991. "The Allocation of Talent: Implications for Growth." *Quarterly Journal of Economics*, pp. 503–530.

54. Its three members are also members of the Supreme Court; they are selected by the other SC members based on a Council of Magistrates recommendation.

55. The 1803 case was the first time the U.S. Supreme Court established its supremacy with regard to "judicial review." The case is relevant because the court acted unilaterally based on separation of power principles.

56. *Tereré* is the most popular drink among Paraguayans. It is an infusion of yerba mate prepared with iced water and aromatic herbs.

57. Garat, Guillermo. 2016. "Paraguay: la tierra escondida. Examen del mayor productor de cannabis de América del Sur." Bogotá: Friedrich-Ebert-Stiftung (FES). https://library.fes.de/pdf-files/bueros/la-seguridad/12809.pdf.

58. Londoño, Ernesto. 2019. "A Defiant Interview in a Jail Cell, Soon to Turn Into a Murder Scene." *New York Times*. January 3, 2019. https://www.nytimes.com/2019/01/03/world/americas/marcelo-pinheiro-veiga-prison-killing-paraguay.html.

59. United Nations Office on Drugs and Crime. 2018. *World Drug Report. Booklet 1, p.* 1. https://www.unodc.org/wdr2018/prelaunch/WDR18_Booklet_1_EXSUM.pdf.

60. United Nations Office on Drugs and Crime. 2018. *World Drug Report. Booklet 2,* p. 7. https://www.unodc.org/wdr2018/prelaunch/WDR18_Booklet_2_GLOBAL.pdf.

61. United States Department of State, Bureau for International Narcotics and Law Enforcement Affairs. 2018. "Paraguay International Narcotics Control Strategy Report Volume II. Money Laundering and Financial Crimes." https://py.usembassy.gov/wp-content/uploads/sites/274/vol-2-English.pdf

62. ABC Color. 2018. "Roban 42 fusiles de la Policía." August 24, 2018. http://www.abc.com.py/nacionales/roban-42-fusiles-de-la-policia-1734419.html.

Chapter V

1. Hirschman, Albert O. 1970. *Exit, Voice, and Loyalty: Responses to Decline in Firms, Organizations, and States.* Cambridge: Harvard University Press.

2. World Bank, http://data.worldbank.org/indicator/SP.URB.TOTL.IN.ZS.

3. Data from United Nations Population Division. World Urbanization Prospects: 2018 Revision.

4. Última Hora. 2018. "En el Abasto, hay 400 menores en calle y alrededor de 90 fuman crac." April 5, 2018. http://www.ultimahora.com/en-el-abasto-hay-400-menores-calle-y-alrededor-90-fuman-crac-n1141292.html.

5. United Nations. 2018. "Report of the Special Rapporteur on contemporary forms of slavery, including its causes and consequences, on her mission to Paraguay." p. 10. https://undocs.org/pdf?symbol=fr/A/HRC/39/52/ADD.1.

6. United States Department of Labor. 2018. "2018 Findings on the Worst Forms of Child Labor: Paraguay." https://www.dol.gov/agencies/ilab/resources/reports/child-labor/paraguay.

7. Banco Mundial. 2017. "Diagnóstico del empleo en Paraguay: La transformación dinámica del empleo en Paraguay. Cuadernillo del 'Resumen.'" Banco Mundial, Washington DC. Licencia: Creative Commons de Reconocimiento CC BY 3.0 IGO, p. 1.

8. http://www.nationmaster.com/country-info/stats/Agriculture/Farm-workers#2008.

9. Food and Agriculture Organization of the United Nations. 1998. FAOSTAT statistics database. http://www.fao.org/faostat/en/#data.

10. World Economic Forum. 2017. The Global Competitiveness Report 2017–2018. http://www3.weforum.org/docs/GCR2017-2018/05FullReport/TheGlobalCompetitivenessReport2017%E2%80%932018.pdf.

11. Pisani, Michael J., Rojas, Gustavo, and Ovando, Fernando G. 2019. "Gender and Own-Account Employment in Paraguay—Findings from the Encuesta Permanente de Hogares, 2017 and 2018: A Research Note." Centro de Análisis y Difusión de la Economía Paraguaya (CADEP). June 2019. https://mega.nz/#!1TwiVAiT!feBhRoy8pp_m3fYbbWLdTO8DSGdgi2vqQtAIdT7d5OQ.

12. World Health Organization. 2018.

Global Status Report on Road Safety 2018. Geneva: World Health Organization.https://apps.who.int/iris/bitstream/handle/10665/276462/9789241565684-eng.pdf?ua=1.

13. Dirección General de Estadística, Encuestas y Censos. 2016. *Anuario 2016 Paraguay.* http://www.dgeec.gov.py/Publicaciones/Biblioteca/anuario2016/Anuario%20Estadistico%20del%20Paraguay%202016.pdf.

14. The actual incident took place on a property called "Marina Kue" that used to house a Navy base but it is commonly termed "Curuguaty" after the nearby town.

15. Mecanismo Nacional de Prevención de la Tortura. 2018. *Personas privadas de libertad en Paraguay–Marzo 2019.* Asunción: Mecanismo Nacional de Prevención de la Tortura. http://mnp.gov.py/index.php/investigacion-social/2015-08-23-04-10-39/func-startdown/222.

16. Mecanismo Nacional de Prevención de la Tortura. 2018. *Pabellón la bronca. Índice de ocupación de instituciones de privación de libertad de la República del Paraguay.* Asunción: Mecanismo Nacional de Prevención de la Tortura, p. 14. http://mnp.gov.py/index.php/investigacion-social/2015-08-23-04-09-46/func-download/192/chk,6b9112ff93bae0c9f91f981915a8999c/no_html,1.

17. Serafini, Verónica and Egas, María Isabel. 2018. *Empleo femenino en Paraguay. Tendencias y políticas públicas.* Asunción: Centro de Análisis y Difusión de la Economía Paraguaya, p. 59.

18. Serafini, Verónica and Egas, María Isabel. 2018. *Empleo femenino en Paraguay. Tendencias y políticas públicas.* Asunción: Centro de Análisis y Difusión de la Economía Paraguaya, p. 59, pp. 30–32.

19. Organisation for Economic Co-operation and Development. 2019. "Social Institutions & Gender Index. Paraguay Country Profile." https://www.genderindex.org/wp content/uploads/files/datasheets/2019/PY.pdf.

20. Economist Intelligence Unit. 2013. "Women's Entrepreneurial Venture Scope." p. 72. http://www.gbaforwomen.org/download/womens-entrepreneurial-venture-scope/?wpdmdl=3541.

21. Spectator Index. 2019. https://www.instagram.com/spectatorindex/p/Bt_ux-Bg4e0.

22. This is a catch-all term used to rail against sexual education at schools, reproductive rights, lesbian, gay, bisexual, and transgender (LGBT) rights and in support of "traditional" gender norms.

23. United Nations, Department of Economic and Social Affairs, Population Division (2015). World Population Prospects: The 2015 Revision, custom data acquired via website.

24. Banco Mundial. 2018. *Paraguay: Diagnóstico Sistemático de País,* p. 15.

25. Gandelman, Néstor. 2017. "Do the rich save more in Latin America?" *The Journal of Economic Inequality.* Volume 15, Number 1, p. 82.

26. World Development Indicators, The World Bank.

27. Banco Mundial. 2018. *Paraguay: Diagnóstico Sistemático de País,* p. 62.

28. Última Hora. 2018. "La solución no pasa por dar más clases de matemática o de lengua." November 17, 2018. https://www.ultimahora.com/la-solucion-no-pasa-dar-mas-clases-matematica-o-lengua-n2779855.html

29. World Bank. 2018. The Human Capital Project. World Bank, Washington, DC. © World Bank. https://openknowledge.worldbank.org/handle/10986/30498 License: CC BY 3.0 IGO.

30. Novella, Rafael; Repetto, Andrea; Robino, Carolina; Rucci, Graciana (editores). 2018. "Millennials en América Latina y el Caribe: ¿trabajar o estudiar?" *Banco Interamericano de Desarrollo,* pp. 345-\-381. https://publications.iadb.org/bitstream/handle/11319/9289/Millennials-en-America-Latina-y-el-Caribe-trabajar-o-estudiar.pdf?sequence=1&isAllowed=y.

31. ABC Digital. 2018. "Una historia de superacion." Published December 11, 2018. http://www.abc.com.py/edicion-impresa/locales/una-historia-de-superacion-1767775.html.

32. *The Economist.* 2018. "China sounds the alarm over its stressed-out schoolchildren." Published August 18, 2018. https://www.economist.com/china/2018/08/18/china-sounds-the-alarm-over-its-stressed-out-schoolchildren.

33. Pizarro, Mar Langa. "Historia de la literatura." in Telesca, Ignacio (coordinator). 2014. *Historia del Paraguay.* Asunción: Taurus, p. 408.

34. Banco Mundial. 2018. "Paraguay. Invertir en capital humano: una revisión del gasto público y de la gestión en los

sectores sociales." © World Bank. http://documentos.bancomundial.org/curated/es/933691542659029507/pdf/132203-WP-P164146-SPANISH-v5-16-11-2018-13-37-58-PYInvertirenCapitalHumanofinalImagebank.pdf.

35. World Bank. 2018. World Development Report 2018: Learning to Realize Education's Promise. Washington, DC: World Bank, p. 189. https://openknowledge.worldbank.org/bitstream/handle/10986/28340/9781464810961.pdf.

36. reAcción Paraguay. 2018. "Informe del Monitoreo de Ejecución Física del FONACIDE Ciudad del Este 2018. Proyecto ParaguaYOite." https://drive.google.com/file/d/103LTnFAKKMFiC4-rLZ21eflNpToua0_d/view.

37. Altinok, Nadir; Angrist, Noam; Patrinos, Harry Anthony. 2018. *Global data set on education quality (1965–2015) (English).* Policy Research working paper; no. WPS 8314. Washington, D.C.: World Bank Group, p. 44. http://documents.worldbank.org/curated/en/706141516721172989/Global-data-set-on-education-quality-1965-2015.

38. Pritchet, Lant. 2013. *The Rebirth of Education: Schooling Ain't Learning.* Washington DC: Center for Global Development.

39. Borda, Dionisio (editor), González, Cynthia, García, Diana. 2015. *Inserción de los Jóvenes en el Mercado del Trabajo.* Asunción: CADEP, p. 39.

40. U.S. Census Bureau. 2016. *American Community Survey 1-Year Estimates.* Retrieved from https://factfinder.census.gov.

41. U.S. Department of Homeland Security. 2015. *Yearbook of Immigration Statistics.* https://www.dhs.gov/immigration-statistics.

42. U.S. Census Bureau. 2000. *Census 2000 Special Tabulations (STP-159).* Retrieved from https://factfinder.census.gov.

43. Lambert, Peter and Nickson, Andrew (editors). 2013. *The Paraguay Reader: History, Culture, Politics (The Latin America readers).* Durham, NC: Duke University Press. Kindle Edition, p. 169.

44. Associated Press. 2010. "En Paraguay, menonitas transformaron el desierto en polo industrial." El Universo, July 12, 2010. https://www.eluniverso.com/2010/07/12/1/1382/paraguay-menonitas-transformaron-desierto-polo-industrial.html.

45. Scavone Yegros, Ricardo. "Guerra internacional y confrontaciones políticas (1920–1954)." in Telesca, Ignacio (coordinator). 2014. *Historia del Paraguay.* Asunción: Taurus, p. 261.

46. Nickson, Andrew. 2017. *Diccionario histórico de Paraguay.* Asunción: Intercontinental Editora, p. 695.

47. The Guardian. 2018. "Forced labour in Paraguay: the darkness at the bottom of the global supply chain." Published September 18, 2018. https://www.theguardian.com/environment/2018/sep/18/forced-labour-in-paraguay-the-darkness-at-the-bottom-of-the-global-supply-chain.

48. Wagner, Carlos. 1990. *Brasiguaios: homens sem pátria.* 1º Ed. Petrópolis: Vozes.

49. Nickson, R. Andrew. 1981. "Brazilian Colonization of the Eastern Border Region of Paraguay." *Journal of Latin American Studies,* No. 13, p. 120.

50. Franca Marques, Denise Helena; Rodrigues, Roberto Nascimento; Fazito de Almeida Rezende, Dimitri; Soares, Weber; and Vélez, José María. 2013. "La circularidad de los 'brasiguayos' en las fronteras de Paraguay y Brasil." *Estudios Sociológicos.* Vol. 31, No. 93 (septiembre-diciembre, 2013), pp. 865–898. Published by: El Colegio de Mexico.

51. Albuquerque, José L. C. 2005. "Campesinos paraguayos y 'brasiguayo' en la frontera este del Paraguay." in Fogel, Ramón, and Riquelme, Marcial. 2005. *Enclave sojero, merma de soberanía y pobreza.* Asunción: centro de estudios rurales interdisciplinarios (ceri), p. 177.

52. Dirección General de Estadística, Encuestas y Censos. "Censo de Comunidades de los Pueblos Indígenas. Resultados Finales 2012." *III Censo Nacional de Población y Viviendas para Pueblos Indígenas.* http://www.dgeec.gov.py/Publicaciones/Biblioteca/comunidad%20indigena/Censo%20de%20Comunidades%20de%20los%20Publos%20ndigenas%20Resultados%20Finales%202012.pdf.

53. ABC Color. 2018. "Presentan el perfil genético del paraguayo." December 5, 2018. http://www.abc.com.py/nacionales/realizan-el-perfil-genetico-del-paraguayo-1766053.html.

54. Melià, Bartomeu. 2011. *Mundo Guaraní.* Segunda edición, editada por Adriana Almada. Asunción: Banco Inter-Americano de Desarrollo, p. 92.

55. Neufeld, Alfred. 2004. *Contra la Sagrada Resignación. Cristianismo y Cosmovisiones Fatalistas en el Paraguay. Un Análisis Histórico, Teológico y Contextual.* Asunción: El Lector.

56. Author interview, July 12, 2019.

57. Romero Sanabria, Aníbal. 2016. *Más paraguayo que la mandioca.* Asunción: Self-published, pp. 32–35

58. DGEEC. 2018. Encuesta Permanente de Hogares, 2017. http://www.dgeec.gov.py/Publicaciones/Biblioteca/Resultados%20EPH/PRINCIPALES%20RESULTADOS%20EPH%202017.pdf.

59. United Nations. 2015. "Report of the Special Rapporteur on the rights of Indigenous peoples, Victoria Tauli-Corpuz, regarding the situation of Indigenous peoples in Paraguay." Presented to the Human Rights Council, Thirtieth session, August 13, 2015, p. 1. http://unsr.vtaulicorpuz.org/site/images/docs/country/2015-paraguay-a-hrc-30-41-add-1-en.pdf.

Chapter VI

1. Robertson, J. P. and J. P. and W. P. Robertson, W. P. 1839. *Letters on Paraguay: comprising an account of a four years' residence in that Republic, under the Government of the Dictator Francia.* v.1. 1792–1843, pp. 260–261. https://hdl.handle.net/2027/hvd.32044011020047.

2. Carlyle, Thomas. 1900. *Critical and Miscellaneous Essays. Volume IV.* New York: Charles Scribner's Sons, p. 288. https://ia600202.us.archive.org/22/items/criticalmiscella04carl/criticalmiscella04carl.pdf.

3. Vietnam has an area of 127,880 square miles and Paraguay an area of 157,047 square miles.

4. Simon, Julian L. 1996. *The Ultimate Resource 2.* Princeton: Princeton University Press.

5. Service, Elman R., and Service Helen S. 1954. *Tobatí: Paraguayan Town.* Chicago: the University of Chicago Press, p. 61.

6. Food and Agriculture Organization of the United Nations. 1998. FAOSTAT statistics database. http://www.fao.org/faostat/en/#data.

7. It is 26,338.5 percent. Data from Food and Agriculture Organization of the United Nations. 1998. FAOSTAT statistics database. http://www.fao.org/faostat/en/#data.

8. International Monetary Fund. 2017. "Paraguay: 2017 Article IV Consultation—Press Release and Staff Report." IMF Country Report No. 17/233, p. 24.

9. Food and Agriculture Organization of the United Nations. 1998. FAOSTAT statistics database. http://www.fao.org/faostat/en/#data.

10. Nickson, Andrew. 2017. *Diccionario Histórico de Paraguay.* Asunción: Intercontinental Editora S.A, p. 837.

11. See for example Studwell, Joe. 2013. *How Asia Works: Success and Failure in the World's Most Dynamic Region.* New York: Grove Press.

12. World Bank Group, International Bank of Reconstruction and Development. 2018. "Country Partnership Framework for the Republic of Paraguay for the Period FY19-FY23, Report No 131046PY. http://documents.worldbank.org/curated/en/891841547849263157/text/131046-Corrigendum-PUBLIC-after-1-22-Final-R2018-0269-1.txt.

13. Guereña, Arantxa and Villagra, Luis Rojas. 2016. "Yvy Jára. Los dueños de la tierra en Paraguay." *Oxfam*, p. 10. https://www-cdn.oxfam.org/s3fs-public/file_attachments/yvy_jara_informe_oxfamenparaguay.pdf.

14. Banco Mundial. 2018. *Paraguay: Diagnóstico Sistemático de País*, p. 37.

15. Birbaumer, Georg. 2017. *La degradación de la agricultura familiar en el Paraguay. ¿Sobrevivencia o desaparición? Nuevas estrategias para el desarrollo rural.* Asunción: Editorial El Lector, pp. 74–5.

16. Data from the World Bank Group, http://www.doingbusiness.org/data/exploreeconomies/paraguay#getting-electricity.

17. CERES. 2016. "Análisis comparativo de las tarifas eléctricas en Argentina y América Del Sur. Buenos Aires: Universidad de Belgrano. http://v.ub.edu.ar/centros_de_estudio/ceres/ceres_marzo2016.pdf.

18. https://www.youtube.com/watch?v=UKhHsx6ffKs.

19. Measured as kilowatt-hours per person per year as of 2014. Source: World Bank, http://data.worldbank.org.

20. World Economic Forum. 2017. "The Global Competitiveness Report 2016-2017." http://www3.weforum.org/

docs/GCR2017-2018/05FullReport/ TheGlobalCompetitivenessReport201 7%E2%80%932018.pdf.

21. Vice Ministerio de Minas y Energía. 2018. *Balance Energético Nacional 2017.* https://www.ssme.gov.py/vmme/pdf/ balance2017/BEN2017.pdf.

22. Canese, Ricardo. 1987. *La biomasa como alternativa energética en el Paraguay.* Asunción: BASE.

23. Source: World Bank, http://data. worldbank.org (2014 data).

24. This indicator is called "energy intensity." Source: World Bank, http://data. worldbank.org (2014 data).

25. The index aggregates social and environmental indicators that capture three dimensions of social progress: Basic Human Needs, Foundations of Wellbeing, and Opportunity. https://www.socialprogressindex. com/?tab=2&code=PRY.

26. ABC Color. 2018. "La ANDE soporta fuerte escasez de recursos para encarar sus proyectos." September 27, 2018. http://www.abc.com.py/edicion-impresa/ economia/la-ande-soporta-fuerte-escasez-de-recursos-para-encarar-sus-proyectos-1744378.html.

27. ABC Color. 2018. "ANDE pierde unos U.S.$ 12 millones al mes." October 16, 2018. http://www.abc.com.py/nacionales/ ande-millones-en-perdidas-1750248.html.

28. Última Hora. 2019. "Sueño truncado: Cerró su heladería por los continuos cortes de la ANDE." January 29, 2019. https://www.ultimahora.com/ sueno-truncado-cerro-su-heladeria-los-continuos-cortes-la-ande-n2794487.html.

29. Blanc, Jacob. 2018. "Itaipu's Forgotten History: The 1965 Brazil–Paraguay Border Crisis and the New Geopolitics of the Southern Cone." *Journal of Latin American Studies*, Volume 50, Issue 2 May 2018, pp. 383–409.

30. Carter, Miguel. 2019. "Itaipú, la riqueza energética perdida del Paraguay." Conference delivered at the Centro Cultural Paraguayo Americano on April 8, 2019.

31. Gasulla, Luis. 2017. *El negocio político de la obra pública: De la patria contratista a Menem. De los noventa a Kirchner. De CFK a Macri.* Buenos Aires: Penguin Random House Grupo Editorial Argentina.

32. Colmán Gutiérrez, Andrés. 2018. *Mengele en Paraguay.* Con la colaboración de Desirée Esquivel y Narciso Meza Martínez. Asunción: ServiLibro, p. 142.

33. Nickson, Andrew. 2019. "Reassessment of the Itaipú Treaty and 'Brasiguayo' Political Power Could Reshape Paraguay's Relationship with Brazil." *LSE Latin American and the Caribbean Centre.* https://blogs. lse.ac.uk/latamcaribbean/2019/03/18/ reassessment-of-the-itaipu-treaty-and-brasiguayo-political-power-could-reshape-paraguays-relationship-with-brazil.

34. *Mad Men* episode "The Gold Violin." Written by Jane Anderson, Andre Jacquemetton, Maria Jacquemetton, and Matthew Weiner. Directed by Andrew Bernstein. It first aired on September 7, 2008.

35. https://data.worldbank.org.

36. United States Agency for International Development. 2017. USAID/Paraguay Tropical Forestry & Biodiversity Assessment. USAID Global Environmental Management Support (GEMS), December 2017, p. 39.

37. Food and Agriculture Organization of the United Nations. 2016. "Global Forest Resources Assessment 2015. How are the world's forests changing?" Second edition, p. 17. http://www.fao.org/3/a-i4793e.pdf.

38. Measured as "Terrestrial protected areas (percent of total land area)." https:// data.worldbank.org.

39. Banco Mundial. 2018. *Paraguay: Diagnóstico Sistemático de País*, p. 20.

40. Guyra Paraguay. 2018. "Monitoreo Mensual del Cambio de Uso y Cobertura de la Tierra, Incendios y Variación de la Cubierta de Aguas en el Gran Chaco Americano. Junio 2018." http://guyra.org.py/wp-content/uploads/2018/01/JUNIO-2018.zip.

41. United States Agency for International Development. 2017. USAID/Paraguay Tropical Forestry & Biodiversity Assessment. USAID Global Environmental Management Support (GEMS), December 2017, p. 11. http://www.usaidgems.org/ Documents/FAA&Regs/FAA118119LAC/ USAID_GEMS_%20118119%20Paraguay_ FINAL_Dec2017_PUBLIC.pdf.

42. Ypacaraí is a lake located about thirty-one miles (fifty kilometers) east of Asunción.

43. Latinobarómetro data available at http://www.latinobarometro.org.

44. EPI data available at https://epi.yale. edu.

45. The *Guardian.* 2018. "Should Paraguay invest its energy wealth in bitcoin

'mining' or fighting poverty?" November 5, 2018. https://www.theguardian.com/global-development/2018/nov/05/should-paraguay-invest-its-energy-wealth-in-bitcoin-mining-or-fighting-poverty.

46. Commons Foundation. 2018. "Commons Foundation Signs Contract for Blockchain Business Backed by the Paraguay Government." Press Release. Published November 18, 2018. https://www.prnewswire.com/news-releases/commons-foundation-signs-contract-for-blockchain-business-backed-by-the-paraguay-government-300751948.html.

47. Davenport, Emily, Folch, Christine, and Vasu, Connor. 2018. "Itaipú Dam: Paraguay's Growth Potential." *Itaipú Post-2023.* https://itaipupost2023.com/2018/06/19/new-white-paper-paraguays-growth-potential.

48. Toledano, Perrine and Maennling, Nicolas. 2013. "Leveraging Paraguay's Hydropower for Sustainable Economic Development." *Columbia Center on Sustainable Investment*, p. 40. http://ccsi.columbia.edu/files/2014/01/Leveraging-Paraguays-Hydropower-for-Economic-Development-Final-CCSI.pdf.

49. The Guardian. 2017. "Will European supermarkets act over Paraguay forest destruction?" September 1, 2017. https://www.theguardian.com/environment/andes-to-the-amazon/2017/sep/01/will-european-supermarkets-act-over-paraguay-forest-destruction.

Chapter VII

1. Rachid, L., and Ramirez, R. 2008. *Política exterior de la República del Paraguay: herramienta para el desarrollo en un mundo globalizado.* Memoria de Gestion: 2003, 8a ed.). Asunción: AGR Servicios Gráficos.

2. Abente, Diego (editor), Masi, Fernando, Gomez Florentín, Carlos. 2017. *Política Exterior Brasileña. Oportunidades y obstáculos para el Paraguay.* Asunción: CADEP, p. 184.

3. Financial Times. 2019. "Former foreign policy maverick Paraguay emerges from obscurity." Special Report Investing in Paraguay. June 10, 2019. https://www.ft.com/content/a01323ee-59eb-11e9-840c-530737425559

4. Author interview, October 9, 2019.

5. Author interview, August 29, 2019.

6. Simón, José Luis G. (editor). 1990. *Política Exterior y Relaciones Exteriores del Paraguay Contemporáneo.* Asunción: Centro Paraguayo de Estudios Sociológicos, p. 15.

7. Acosta Garbarino, Alberto. 2012. "La dignidad no tiene precio." *Última Hora.* July 1, 2012. https://www.ultimahora.com/la-dignidad-no-tiene-precio-n541638.html.

8. Alesina, Alberto, Spolaore, Enrico, and Wacziarg, Romain. 2005. "Trade, Growth and the Size of Countries." Handbook of Economic Growth, in: Philippe Aghion, and Steven Durlauf (ed.), *Handbook of Economic Growth*, edition 1, volume 1, chapter 23. Elsevier, pp. 1499–1542.

9. Birch, Melissa H. 1990. "La Política Pendular: Política de Desarrollo del Paraguay en la Post Guerra." In Simón, José Luis G. (editor). 1990. *Política Exterior y Relaciones Exteriores del Paraguay Contemporáneo.* Asunción: Centro Paraguayo de Estudios Sociológicos, p. 163.

10. Roett, Riordan and Sacks, Richard Scott. 1991. *Paraguay. The Personalist Legacy.* Boulder: Westview Press, p. 31.

11. Cabral López, María Antonella. 2014. "Cooperación bilateral con el Paraguay: una breve reseña de su desarrollo entre 1954 y 1989." *Población y Desarrollo*, v. 39 p. 103. http://revistascientificas.una.py/index.php/RE/article/view/829/pdf_129.

12. See Roett, Riordan and Sacks, Richard Scott. 1991. *Paraguay. The Personalist Legacy.* Boulder: Westview Press, p. 145. And Mora, F. Cooney, J. 2007. *Paraguay and the United States: Distant Allies.* Athens: University of Georgia Press, pp. 14–21.

13. Mora, F., and Cooney, J. 2007. *Paraguay and the United States: Distant Allies.* Athens: University of Georgia Press, p. 140.

14. *Ibid, p.* 122.

15. Lipset, Seymour Martin. 1996. *American Exceptionalism: A Double-edged Sword.* New York: W.W. Norton, p. 63.

16. According to C-Span's 2017 Presidential Historians Survey, President Rutherford B. Hayes ranked thirty-second out of forty-three presidents; Hayes dropped six places compared to the 2000 survey. https://www.c-span.org/presidentsurvey2017/?page=overall.

17. H.L. Mencken, quoted in Brinkey, Alan. 1982. Voices of Protest: Huey Long,

Father Coughlin, and the Great Depression. New York: Alfred A. Knopf, p. 73.

18. Grow, Michael. 1990. "Los Estados Unidos y el Paraguay Durante la Segunda Guerra Mundial." In Simón, José Luis G. (editor). 1990. *Política Exterior y Relaciones Exteriores del Paraguay Contemporáneo.* Asunción: Centro Paraguayo de Estudios Sociológicos, p. 58.

19. Mora, F. 1998. "The Forgotten Relationship: United States-Paraguay Relations, 1937–89." *Journal of Contemporary History*, 33(3), p. 460. Retrieved from http://www.jstor.org/stable/261125.

20. Reagan, Ronald. 1985. "Remarks to Community Leaders in Madrid, Spain." May 7, 1985. Ronald Reagan Presidential Library & Museum. https://www.reaganlibrary.gov/research/speeches/50785b.

21. Dinges, John. 2012. *The Condor Years: How Pinochet And His Allies Brought Terrorism To Three Continents.* The New Press. Kindle Edition, p. 200.

22. Data from USAID's Foreign Aid Explorer. https://explorer.usaid.gov.

23. Steinsson, Sverrir and Thorhallsson, Baldur. 2017. "Small State Foreign Policy." 2017. *Oxford Research Encyclopedia of Politics.* Oxford University Press, p. 2. http://uni.hi.is/baldurt/files/2018/09/Small-State-Foreign-Policy-5404.pdf.

24. *Ibid, p.* 10.

25. Última Hora. 2019. "Sindicato cuestiona administración del canciller Castiglioni." July 7, 2019. https://www.ultimahora.com/sindicato-cuestiona-administracion-del-canciller-castiglioni-n2830122.html.

26. Steinsson, Sverrir and Thorhallsson, Baldur. 2017. "Small State Foreign Policy." *Oxford Research Encyclopedia of Politics.* Oxford University Press, p. 20. http://uni.hi.is/baldurt/files/2018/09/Small-State-Foreign-Policy-5404.pdf.

27. Friedman, Thomas. 2000. *The Lexus and the Olive Tree.* New York: Anchor Books, pp. 101–111.

28. Steinsson, Sverrir and Thorhallsson, Baldur. 2017. "Small State Foreign Policy." *Oxford Research Encyclopedia of Politics.* Oxford University Press, p. 20. http://uni.hi.is/baldurt/files/2018/09/Small-State-Foreign-Policy-5404.pdf.

29. Arce, Lucas. 2011. "En la búsqueda de una estrategia global: La Política Externa del Paraguay." *Cuadernos sobre Relaciones Internacionales, Regionalismo y Desarrollo.* Vol. 6. No. 11. Enero-Junio 2011.

30. Steinsson, Sverrir and Thorhallsson, Baldur. 2017. "Small State Foreign Policy." *Oxford Research Encyclopedia of Politics.* Oxford University Press, p. 2. http://uni.hi.is/baldurt/files/2018/09/Small-State-Foreign-Policy-5404.pdf.

31. Nye, Joseph. S. 1990. "Soft power." *Foreign Policy.* Vol. 80, pp. 153–171.

Chapter VIII

1. Data for 2016 GDP per capita based on purchasing power parity and current international dollars. https://data.worldbank.org.

2. The World Bank. 2017. "World Development Indicators." http://data.worldbank.org/indicator/NY.GDP.PCAP.CD.

3. The film titled "Paraguay" was made by the defunct Office of the Coordinator of Inter-American Affairs and produced by Julien Bryan. https://www.youtube.com/watch?v=ZM-aJHmL4NU.

4. Roett, Riordan and Sacks, Richard Scott. 1991. *Paraguay. The Personalist Legacy.* Boulder: Westview Press, p. 65.

5. See Lewis, Paul H. 1993. *Political Parties and Generations in Paraguay's Liberal Era, 1869–1940.* Chapel Hill: The University of North Carolina Press.

6. Pritchett, Lant and Woolcock, Michael. 2004. "Solutions When the Solution is the Problem: Arraying the Disarray in Development." *World Development.* Vol. 32, No. 2, p. 191.

7. Wilkinson, Will. 2017. "Public Policy after Utopia." Niskanen Center Blog, October 24, 2017. https://niskanencenter.org/blog/public-policy-utopia.

8. Robertson, J. P. and J. P. and W. P. Robertson, W. P. 1839. *Letters on Paraguay: comprising an account of a four years' residence in that Republic, under the Government of the Dictator Francia.* v.1. 1792–1843, p. 85. https://hdl.handle.net/2027/hvd.32044011020047.

9. Quoted in Stewart, Dugald. 1829. *Account of the Life and Writings of Adam Smith LLD.* Hilliard and Brown, p. 64.

10. Quoted in Hua, Yu. 2011. *China in Ten Words.* New York: Knopf Doubleday Publishing Group. Kindle Edition. Location 67.

11. González, Teodosio. 1997. *Infortunios del Paraguay.* Asunción: El Lector.

12. Quoted in Corte Suprema de Justicia. 2018. "Acción de inconstitucionalidad: 'Impugnaciones presentadas por Ricardo Herman Pankow, candidato a diputado por capital por el Movimiento Cruzada Nacional c/ las candidaturas de los señores Horacio Cartes y Nicanor Duarte Frutos, por la Asociación Nacional Republicana Partido Colorado, y Fernando Lugo por la Concertación Nacional Frente Guasu, para las elecciones generales de 22/04/2018.'" April 11, 2018. https://www.csj.gov.py/jurisprudencia/home/DocumentoJurisprudencia?codigo=62469.

13. Kaufman, Peter D. (editor). 2015. *Poor Charlie's almanack: the wit and wisdom of Charles T. Munger.* Virginia Beach: The Donning Company Publishers.

14. Quoted in Hart, B.H. Liddell. 2015. *Why Don't We Learn from History?* Philadelphia: R.P. Pryne. Kindle Edition, Location 27–29.

15. Vera, Helio. 2011. *En busca del hueso perdido (Tratado de paraguayología).* Asunción: ServiLibros.

16. *The Economist.* 2007. "The quest for prosperity." Published March 17, 2007. https://www.economist.com/special-report/2007/03/17/the-quest-for-prosperity.

17. Serafini Geoghegan, Verónica. 2019. "Pobreza en Paraguay: crecimiento económico y conflicto redistributivo." Centro de Análisis y Difusión de la Economía Paraguaya (CADEP).

18. Latin America Business Stories. 2018. "Deirdre McCloskey on Liberalism and the Future of Latin America." Published November 16, 2018. https://labs.ebanx.com/en/articles/ecommerce/deirdre-mccloskey-on-liberalism-and-the-future-of-latin-america.

Bibliography

Abente, D. 1988. "Constraints and Opportunities: Prospects for Democratization in Paraguay." *Journal of Interamerican Studies and World Affairs,* 30 (1), 73–104.

Abente, Diego. 2012. *Fortaleciendo la gobernabilidad.* Paraguay Debate, Nota de Politica No. 2. http://www.cadep.org.py/2012/12/fortaleciendo-la-gobernabilidad.

Abente, Diego, and Borda, Dionisio (editors). 2012. *El Reto del Futuro. Asumiendo el legado del Bicentenario.* Asunción: Ministerio de Hacienda.

Abente, Diego, and Masi, Fernando (editors). 2005. *Estado, Economía y Sociedad. Una Mirada Internacional a la Democracia Paraguaya.* Asunción: CADEP.

Abente, Diego (editor), Masi, Fernando, and Gomez Florentín, Carlos. 2017. *Política Exterior Brasileña. Oportunidades y obstáculos para el Paraguay.* Asunción: CADEP.

Achen, Christopher H., and Bartels, Larry M. 2016. *Democracy for Realists: Why Elections Do Not Produce Responsive Government.* Princeton: Princeton University Press. Kindle Edition.

Andrews, Matt, Pritchett, Lant, and Woolcock, Michael. 2017. *Building State Capability: Evidence, Analysis, Action.* London: Oxford University Press.

ARD, Inc. 2009. *Paraguay Democracy and Governance Assessment.* Prepared for the United States Agency for International Development. http://pdf.usaid.gov/pdf_docs/pbaah431.pdf.

Arditi, Benjamin. 1992. *Adiós a Stroessner. La reconstrucción de la política en el Paraguay.* Asunción: RP Ediciones & Centro de Documentación y Estudios.

Benítez González, Victor Raúl (editor). 2017. *La historia del futuro. El Paraguay a partir del 2018.* Asunción: Editorial Libre.

Birch, Melissa H. 2014. "Paraguay and Mercosur: The Lesser of Two Evils?" *Latin American Business Review,* Vol. 15, Issues 3–4.

Borda, Dionisio, and Masi, Fernando (editors). 2010. *Estado y Economía en Paraguay. 1870–2010.* Asunción: CADEP.

Borda, Dionisio (editor), González, Cynthia, and García, Diana. 2015. *Inserción de los Jóvenes en el Mercado del Trabajo.* Asunción: CADEP.

Cantero, José. 2016. *Paraguay: An Economic History.* Kindle Edition. Self-published.

Carver, Robert. 2007. *Paradise with Serpents: Travels in the Lost World of Paraguay.* London: William Collins.

Dinges, John. 2012. *The Condor Years: How Pinochet And His Allies Brought Terrorism To Three Continents.* New York: The New Press. Kindle Edition.

Easterly, William. 2002. *The Elusive Quest for Growth.* Cambridge: MIT Press.

Feliú, Fernanda. 2017. *Los Brasiguayos II. ¿Bandeirantes modernos?* Paraguay: Self-published.

Fernández Bogado, Benjamín. 2010. *¡A Sacudirse! Claves para la construcción de una nueva República.* Asunción: Editora Libre.

Fisman, Ray. 2017. *Corruption. What Everyone Needs to Know?* London: Oxford University Press. Kindle Edition.

Gimlette, John. 2003. *At the Tomb of the Inflatable Pig: Travels Through Paraguay.* New York: Vintage Books.

Lewis, Paul H. 1980. *Paraguay Under Stroessner.* Chapel Hill: The University of North Carolina Press.

Lewis, Paul H. 1993. *Political Parties and Generations in Paraguay's Liberal Era, 1869–1940.* Chapel Hill: The University of North Carolina Press.

The Library of Congress. 2010. *Terrorist and Organized Crime Groups in the Tri-Border Area (BA) of South America. A Report Prepared by the Federal Research Division, Library of Congress under an Interagency Agreement with the Crime and Narcotics Center Director of Central Intelligence.* https://www.loc.gov/rr/frd/pdf-files/TerrOrgCrime_TBA.pdf.

Lipset, Seymour Martin. 1996. *American Exceptionalism: A Double-edged Sword.* New York: W.W. Norton.

Mora, F. 1998. "The Forgotten Relationship: United States-Paraguay Relations, 1937–89." *Journal of Contemporary History,* 33(3), 451–473. Retrieved from http://www.jstor.org/stable/261125.

Mora, F., and Cooney, J. 2007. *Paraguay and the United States: Distant Allies.* Athens: University of Georgia Press.

Morínigo, José Nicolás. 2017. *Prácticas Colectivas en la Sociedad Paraguaya. Mbarete, Tembiguái, Ñembotavy.* Asunción: El Lector.

Neuwirth, Robert. 2011. *Stealth of Nations: The Global Rise of the Informal Economy.* New York: Knopf Doubleday Publishing Group. Kindle Edition.

Nickson, Andrew. 2017. *Diccionario Histórico de Paraguay.* Asunción: Intercontinental Editora S.A.

Nickson, Andrew. R. 1982. "The Itaipú Hydro-Electric Project: The Paraguayan Perspective." *Bulletin of Latin American Research.* Vol. 2, No. 1 (October 1982). pp. 1–20.

O'Shaughnessy, Hugh and Ruiz Díaz, Venerando. 2009. *The Priest of Paraguay: Fernando Lugo and the Making of a Nation.* New York: Zed Books.

Paredes, Roberto. 2017. *Las sucesiones presidenciales post stronistas.* Asunción: Caballo de Troya.

Powers, Nancy. R. 1992. "The Transition to Democracy in Paraguay: Problems and Prospects. A Rapporteur's Report." Working Paper #171. *The Helen Kellogg Institute for International Studies.* https://pdfs.semanticscholar.org/8aae/f34bdbdff7a667908a00a4a487f778d1d798.pdf.

Riquelme, Marcial. 1994. "Toward a Weberian Characterization of the Stroessner Regime in Paraguay (1954–1989)." *Revista Europea De Estudios Latinoamericanos Y Del Caribe / European Review of Latin American and Caribbean Studies* (57), 29–51. Retrieved from http://www.jstor.org/stable/25675638.

Riveros García, David. 2016. *Participacioin Poliitica de la Juventud en Paraguay: Un estudio exploratorio de participacioin en el Siglo XXI.* Ciudad del Este: reAcc!ón. https://drive.google.com/open?id=0Bz4Pnyapc773R01CUE82bjNyNTA.

Roett, Riordan, and Sacks, Richard Scott. 1991. *Paraguay. The Personalist Legacy.* Boulder, CO: Westview Press.

Rose Ackerman, Susan, and Lagunes, Paul (editors). 2015. *Greed, Corruption, and the Modern State: Essays in Political Economy.* Northampton: Edward Elgar Publishing.

Russo Cantero, Carlos Marcial, and Galeano Perrone, Horacio. 2000. *Política Exterior, Cambios e Integración Regional. Un Enfoque Desde la Realidad Paraguaya.* Asunción: Intercontinental Editora.

Scavone Yegros, Ricardo, and Brezzo, Liliana M. 2010. *Historia de las relaciones internacionales del Paraguay.* Asunción: El Lector.

Service, Elman R., and Service Helen S. 1954. *Tobatí: Paraguayan Town.* Chicago: The University of Chicago Press.

Setrini, Gustavo. 2011. "Twenty Years of Paraguayan Electoral Democracy: from Monopolistic to Pluralistic Clientelism." *Tinker Foundation Incorporated and CADEP.* Working Paper No. 3. http://209.177.156.169/libreria_cm/archivos/pdf_1014.pdf.

Simón, José Luis G. (editor). 1990. *Política Exterior y Relaciones Exteriores del Paraguay Contemporáneo.* Asunción: Centro Paraguayo de Estudios Sociológicos.

Telesca, Ignacio (coordinator). 2014. *Historia del Paraguay.* Asunción: Taurus.

Tocqueville, Alexis De. 2007. *Democracy in America, Volume I and II.* Kindle Edition.

Velázquez, Rafael Eladio. 2018. *Una Periodización de la Historia Paraguaya.* Asunción: El Lector.

Velázquez Villagra, Sergio. 2018. *Elegir y no solo votar. Una propuesta para reformar el sistema electoral paraguayo.* Asunción: El Lector.

Index

ABC Digital 113
Abdo Benítez, Mario 53, 128, 182, 189, 194
Abente, Diego 22, 44, 48, 58, 69, 76, 178
abrazo republicano (republican embrace) 67
Acaray Dam 156, 167
Aceros del Paraguay Sociedad Anónima (ACEPAR) 183
Achen, Christopher 73
Act of Iguazú 167–68
Acuerdo Nacional 43
agricultural productivity 157
air-guitar 200
airness 200
Albright, Madeleine 187
Albuquerque, José 150
Alegre, Efraín 51, 53
Ali, Muhammad 25
Alibaba 175
Allende, Salvador 40
Almada, Martín 38–39, 45
Alto Paraná 71
Amado, Jorge 130
Amambay 124
Amazon (company) 106, 175
Amazon basin 10
American Civil War 23, 30, 32
American Convention on Human Rights 43, 189
American embassy *see* U.S. Embassy
American Society of Civil Engineers 156
Anabaptist movement 144
ANDE 166–167
anti-communism 34, 167, 182, 185–186, 188
Apocalypse Now (film) 197
Apple (company) 175
arandu ka'aty (knowledge of the jungle) 140
Arawaks 10
Arce, Lucas 190
Archer Daniels Midland 160

Archives of Terror 39, 45, 185
Argaña, Luis María 45–47, 63
Argentina 5–6, 9–10, 14, 18, 22, 24, 26, 28, 30, 32, 38, 40, 46, 48, 50, 57, 82, 86, 89, 95, 98, 105, 123, 143, 147, 151, 155–158, 161, 164, 167, 169–172, 178–183, 190–191, 195
Armed Forces 31–32, 34, 36–37, 46
Armenian genocide 189
arms trade 124
Artavia, Roberto 80
artificial intelligence 85
Asian Tigers 81, 89, 109
Asociación Nacional Republicana *see* Colorado Party
Asuncenos 11, 16–17, 103, 114, 154
Asunción 1, 9–12, 16–18, 21, 23–25, 28–29, 31–32, 35, 40, 42–43, 47, 59, 61, 63, 67, 75–76, 78, 83–84, 89, 91–93, 96–97, 99, 101–102, 106, 109, 114, 124, 126, 129, 131, 139–140, 154–155, 164, 166, 173–175, 182–186, 188–189, 197; foundation 12, 203
Atatürk, Mustafa Kemal 31
Atyrá 109
Ayala, Eligio 62, 76

Bahamas 58
banking crisis of 1995–98 46
Barreto, Ana 14
Bartels, Larry 73
beef production 160–161
Belyaev, Ivan 29
Benítez González, Victor 70
Bergen, Ernst 74, 90, 108
Berkeley Mafia 58
The Big Lebowski (film) 101
Birch, Melissa 180
Bitcoin 175
Bitex 175
Blair, Laurence 175
Blanco Party (Uruguay) 22
Boccia, Alfredo 51, 69

233

Bogado, Víctor 196
Bogado Tabacman, Eduardo 58
Bolivia 28, 30, 106, 123, 151, 169, 172, 179–180, 195
Borda, Dionisio 46, 48, 50, 78
Bormann, Martin 5–6
Bourdain, Anthony 5
Brasiguayos 128, 135, 147–150, 163, 178, 203
Brasilia 167
Brazil 2, 6, 9, 11–12, 14, 18, 22–24, 26, 28, 30–32, 38, 43, 48, 50, 53, 68, 80, 82, 86, 89, 115, 123, 148, 156–157, 161–162, 172, 178, 181–183
Brazilian Empire 22
Brazilian miracle 167
bribes 75, 107, 110, 162
Brown, Dan 23
Buenos Aires 12, 16–18, 20, 150
Buffett, Warren 199
business-to-business (B2B) transactions 83

Caacupé 99, 135
Caballero, Bernardino 27
Cabaña, Reinaldo "Cucho" 123
CADEP 2, 111, 143
Cali Cartel 124
California 99, 143
Canada 145
Cantero, José 17, 78–79
capability trap 58
Caperucita Roja (Little Red Riding Hood vehicle) 42
Capone, Al 122
Captains of the Sands 130
Cargill 161
Caribs 10
Carlyle, Thomas 155
Carnegie, Andrew 203
Carrefour 176
Carter, Jimmy 36, 186
Carter, Miguel 168
Cartes, Horacio 51–53, 64, 76–77, 84, 111, 189
Cartes Group 94
Casado, Carlos 145
Castro, Fidel 48, 186
Catherine the Great 145
Catholic Church 14, 62, 135, 151, 202
ceaseless agitation 54–55, 193, 197
Cédula Real 12, 18
cemetery of theories 57
Center for International Earth Science Information Network Report 175
Center for International Private Enterprise 87
Central Bank 50, 58, 66, 79

Centro de Análisis y Difusión de la Economía Paraguaya see CADEP
Chaco region 11, 28–29, 123, 140, 143, 146–148, 151, 153–155, 157, 172–173, 176, 185, 197
Chaco War 28–32, 65, 146, 179, 185
Chamber of Publishers and Booksellers 141
La Chacarita 127–128
Charles III of Spain 17
Chaves, Federico 32, 78
Chávez, Hugo 107
Chery 183
Chiang Kai-shek 180, 182–183
Chicago Boys 58
Chilavert, José Luis Félix 2
Chile 6, 58, 82, 107–108, 161, 186
Chilean secret police 40
China 20, 82, 140, 158, 175, 182–183
Choeung Ek 42
Choritzer 146
Church of Jesus Christ of Latter-day Saints 135
Ciudad del Este 71, 84, 91, 102, 104, 128, 175, 180, 194, 197
civil society 54–55, 61–62, 194, 197, 199, 202–203
Civil War of 1947 31, 36, 67, 96
clientelism 51, 58, 71
Clorinda 106
closed lists see listas sábanas
COFCO International 159
cognitive dissonance 71, 73
Cold War 167, 185–186
Colmán, Andrés 5, 170
Colmán, Humberto 82
Colombia 123
Colonia del Sacramento 21
Colorado Party 27, 31–38, 44–46, 48–53, 58, 60, 62–64, 67–68, 70–74, 76–77, 108, 121, 181
Colorado Party (Uruguay) 22
Columbus, Christopher 151
Comisión de Verdad y Justicia (Truth and Justice Commission) 38
Commons Foundation 175
Communist youth 35
Comuneros 16, 18
Congress, burning of 52, 54, 193
CONMEBOL 188, 201
Connecticut 173
Constitution of 1870 26, 30, 58
Constitution of 1940 31
Constitution of 1992 43, 45, 48–49, 51–52, 55, 62, 69–70 74, 115, 121, 135, 141, 151, 154, 193
Cooney, Jerry W. 185

Coppola, Francis Ford 197
Coronel Oviedo 109
Correa, Rafael 50
Corrientes 22, 180
Corruption Perceptions Index 106–107
Costa Rica 94, 120
Costanera 91
COVID-19 53
criadazgo 130
Crimea 178
crony capitalism 113, 200
Cubas, Raúl 46–48
Cuentapropistas 131
cuidacoches 114
cultural landlocked nature 178
Curuguaty 51, 132–133

Dahl, Robert 56
Daily Mail 6
Dávalos, Serafina 65
decoupling 82
Defensores del Chaco (Soccer Stadium) 29
deforestation 163, 171–173, 176, 197
Delaware 146
Democracy, support for 56–57
Democracy Index 69
Democratic Republic of Congo 25
demographic distribution 155
demographic dividend 137–138, 202
derechera 154, 163
de Soto, Hernando 87
Development Centre (OECD) 190
devil's excrement 169
D'Hondt System 69
Diamond, Larry 68
difference between rule *of* law and rule *by* law 118
Dinges, John 187
DNA analysis of Paraguayans 152
Doing Business Report 87, 106, 112, 114
Domínguez, Alejandro 201
Dominican Republic 110, 131, 186
Dónde estará mi primavera? (book) 141
Drexler, Jorge 42
Drug Enforcement Administration 125
Duarte Frutos, Nicanor 48
Duarte-Recalde, Liliana 57, 64
Duck, Donald 63
Duolingo 56
Dutch disease 169

Earthsight 176
Eastern European immigrants 148, 162
eBay 106
economic convergence 86
economic diplomacy 180, 189
Economic Freedom of the World 87, 134

economic growth 31, 37, 52, 65, 76, 78, 81–84, 86, 92, 95, 100, 121, 130–131, 137, 141–142, 161, 167, 174, 179, 187, 193, 201
The Economist 80, 140
Economist Intelligence Unit 69, 213
Ecuador 69, 155
Ejército del Pueblo Paraguayo (EPP) 125–126
El Salvador 90
Election of 1928 28
Electoral Code of 1996 64–65
Electoral Tribunal 64, 71, 74
Empresa de Servicios Sanitarios del Paraguay (ESSAP) 173
Encarnación 91, 197
Encomienda system 13–15, 61, 132
environmental damage 3, 172, 175
Environmental Kuznets Curve 171, 173–175, 201
Environmental Performance Index 175
Erdoğan, Recep 189
Escobar, Pablo 35, 122–123
Estigarribia, Hugo 178
Estigarribia, José Félix 29–31
Ethereum 175
Ethnography Museum (Museo Etnográfico) 11
European Conquistadors 11
European Union 89, 106, 176
Export Diversification Index 82
extractive institutions 101

Facebook 83, 114
FARC *see* Revolutionary Armed Forces of Colombia
Fascism 30, 58
Favero, Tranquilo 149
Feast of the Immaculate Conception 135
Febrerista Party 30–32, 36
February 3, 1989 (end of Stroessner regime) 42, 129, 194
Federación Nacional Campesina 61
Federal Reserve 79
Federales (Argentina) 22
Fédération Internationale de Football Association's (FIFA) 201
femicide 134
Fernández de Kirchner, Cristina 50
Fernheim 146
Ferreira, Amílcar 77
Filadelfia 143, 146
financial markets 26, 80
Financial Times 106, 178
First Command of the Capital (Primeiro Comando da Capital, PCC) 124–125
Fisman, Ray 107
Fitch 80

flood refugees 92
Flores, Venancio 21
FONACIDE 141
Food and Agriculture Organization 172
Ford, Gerald 109
Foreign Affairs 28
foreign aid 31, 36, 38
foreign direct investment 36, 82, 89–90, 161, 177
Foreman, George 25
Forestry Law 173
France 19, 21, 44, 103
Franco, Federico 51
Franco, Julio César 48
Franco, Rafael 50
Franklin, Benjamin 113
Fraser Institute 87
Freedom House 69
Frente Amplio (Uruguay) 50
Friedman, Benjamin 65
Friedman, Thomas 190
Friendship Bridge 103, 148, 181
Friesland 144
Frisen, Ricardo 146
Frost, Wesley 185
Fukuyama, Francis 35, 198, 201–202
Fundación Saraki 139

Garat, Guillermo 123
García, Aleixo 11
Gates, Bill 203
Gdansk 145
Germany 5–6, 103, 143, 148
getting to Denmark 4, 56, 197–201
Giménez, Lea 66
Gini coefficient 94
global cocaine manufacture 124
Global Competitiveness Report 84, 87, 165
Global Emotions report 95
Global Financial Integrity 113
Global Forest Resources Assessment 172
Godfather (film) 179
golden parachute 170
Golden Straitjacket 190
González, Teodosio 199
González Daher, Óscar 75, 196
González Macchi, Luis Ángel 48, 115–116
Good Neighbor policy 185
Governability Pact of 1994 45, 117
governance indicators 117, 195
government procurement 108, 111
Gran Chaco 28, 172
Grapes of Wrath 129
Great Britain 21
Greece 81, 137
Greene, Graham 9
Grow, Michael 185

Grupo Favero 149
Guaraní (indigenous language) 3, 10, 12, 53, 56, 60, 67, 109–110, 119–120, 127, 135, 140, 147, 151–153
Guaraní Aquifer 157
Guaraní currency 31, 79, 106, 181
The Guardian 147, 175
Guatemala 90
guinea grass 157

Harari, Yuval 96
harp (Paraguayan) 203
Hay, James Eston 96–100
Hayek, F.A. 69
Hayes, Rutherford B. 185
Henan Complant Mechanical and Electrical Company 183
Heritage Foundation 87
Hezbollah 122, 126
Hicks, Frederic 61, 110
Hirschman, Albert 128
History Channel 6
Ho Chi Minh 20
Ho Chi Minh City 103
Hoa Lo Prison 42
Hobbes, Thomas 163
Holocaust Museum 42
Honduras 90
Hong Kong 183
Hopkins, Edward A. 184
Huawei 183
Human Capital Index 139
Human Development Index 60, 94
Human Rights Report (U.S. Department of State) 116
hydroelectric energy 156, 175

Iguazú Falls 105
IMF *see* International Monetary Fund
impeachment of Fernando Lugo 179, 189
Independence of Paraguay 14, 16–18, 20, 162, 178
Index of Economic Freedom 87, 117
indigenous linguistic groups 151
indigenous people 10 14, 20, 60, 128, 132, 146, 151–153, 162
industrial policy 90
Industrial Revolution 171
informality 102, 111–115, 122, 131, 134, 152
Instituto de Bienestar Rural 162
Instituto Nacional Forestal 173
Instituto Paraguayo del Indígena (Paraguayan Institute for the Indigenous) 153
Inter-American Court of Human Rights 154, 188
Inter-American Democratic Charter 189

Inter-American Development Bank (IADB) 58, 80, 84–85, 89, 91, 140, 188
International Monetary Fund 36, 48, 79, 81, 111–112, 188
internet use 82–83
inversion 199
island diplomacy 177, 187, 192
island surrounded by land 152, 177, 179
isolationism 20, 177–181, 188, 191
Israel 161, 189
Itaipú Barons 45–46, 86
Itaipú Dam 37–38, 53, 86, 98, 141, 148, 156, 167–171, 191
Itaipú Treaty 168, 171
Italy 137, 148

Japan 138, 163
Japanese immigrants 128–129, 151, 162, 203
Jerusalem 177, 189
Jesuits 14–17
Jesús de Tavarangué 67
Johnson, Lyndon 167, 186
Jopará 56, 127, 154
Juncker, Jean-Claude 200
Jurado de Enjuiciamiento de Magistrados (JEM) 75
Jury for the Prosecution of Magistrates *see* Jurado de Enjuiciamiento de Magistrados (JEM)

Kennedy, Joe 122
Keynes, John Maynard 20
Khmer Rouge 23
Kirchheimer, Otto 62
Kirchner, Néstor 50
Kirzner, Israel 103
Kirznerios 103, 105–106, 126
Kissinger, Henry 186
Korean immigrants 128–129, 162, 203
Kundt, Hans 29
Kuznets Environmental Curve 171–175, 201

labor unions 61, 89
Lachi, Marcello 71, 73
laissez-faire 27, 148
land ownership 18, 154, 162–164
land tenure 131–132, 172
lapacho tree 37, 91
Las Carmelitas neighborhood 44
The Last Dictator (film) 194
Latin America & the Caribbean 1–2, 5, 11–12, 14, 21, 37, 48, 54–58, 60, 62, 65, 69, 79–97, 106, 110, 117, 119–120, 128–129, 131, 134, 139–41, 151, 165, 172, 183, 187, 191, 195
Latinobarómetro 56–57, 95, 119, 135, 174
Lava Jato (Car Wash) 111
Lebanese immigrants 126, 128

Lee Kuan Yew 37, 109
legal chicaneries 116, 118, 162
Leninist political structure 34, 42
Leoz, Nicolás 188, 201
lesbian, gay, bisexual, and transgender rights 191, 202
Letelier, Orlando 40
Lewis, Paul 30, 61, 63, 99
Liberal Party 27–28, 30–31, 44, 48–49, 51–53, 61–63, 67–68, 71–72, 74, 181
Liberty Bells 123
Lima 16, 87
Lincoln, Abraham 32
Lipset, Seymour Martin 185
listas sábanas 64, 70
Livi-Bacci, Massimo 15
Lloyd, William Forster 107
Loire Valley 44
Loizaga–Cotegipe Treaty 167
Loma Plata 146
Long, Huey P. 185
López, Carlos Antonio 20–21, 181, 184
López, Magui 67
Lopiztas 27
The Lorax 156
Louis XIV of France 19
Lugo, Fernando 49–51, 55, 133, 169, 179, 189, 191
Lula da Silva 50, 169, 191
Luque 75
Luther, Martin 144
Luxembourg 173, 201
Lynch, Eliza 21

Macintyre, Ben 6
Mad Men (TV series) 171
Maeder, Ernesto 15
Magna Carta 12
Malthusian Trap 10
Mao Zedong 20, 182
Maquilas 89, 106
March to the Sea 23
marijuana production 123
Martínez-Escobar, Fernando 70
Martini, Carlos 141
Marzo Paraguayo (the Paraguayan March) 47, 49
Masi, Fernando 58, 63, 78, 80
Mato Grosso 22
McCloskey, Deirdre 201
McDonald, Ronald 2
McDonald's 110, 127
McDuck, Scrooge 150
McLeod, Sandra 71, 196
mechanization of agriculture 86, 130–131, 149
Medellín Cartel 122, 124

Medina, Leandro 111
Melià, Bartomeu 152
Mencius 199
Mencken, H.L. 185
Méndez, Epifanio 50
Menem, Carlos 170
Mengele, Josef 5–6
Mennonites 108, 126–128, 134, 143–147, 162, 203
Mercado Cuatro 101–102, 113
Mercantilism 16
Mercosur 2, 89–90, 105–106, 179–180, 189–191
Mercosur Economic Research Network 2
Messi, Lionel 171
mestizaje 14
Metric Conversion Act 109
Mexico 103, 110, 146
MF Economía 80
military coup 30, 32, 42–43, 46, 55, 121, 167, 186–187
millennials 140
millennium development goals 60
Miranda, Carlos 73
Mobutu Sese Seko 25
Monte de López, Mary 10
Moody's 80
Mora, Frank O. 185
Morales, Evo 49–50
Morínigo, Higinio 31–32, 36, 186
Morínigo, José Nicolás 71
Mossad 6
Mugabe, Robert 37
Multilateral Convention on Mutual Administrative Assistance in Tax Matters 190
Munger, Charlie 199

Napoleon 17
narcopolítica 122
Nation, Carrie A. 54
National Accord see Acuerdo Nacional
National Administration of Electricity see ANDE
National Farmers Federation see Federación Nacional Campesina
National Forestry Institute see Instituto Nacional Forestal
National Fund for Public Investment and Development see FONACIDE
National Industry of Cement (Industria Nacional de Cemento, INC) 90
National Mechanism for the Prevention of Torture 133
National Public Radio (NPR) 92
Nazis 5–7, 30, 126
Neufeld, Alfred 153

Neuland 146
Neuwirth, Robert 105
New York City 108
New York Times 3, 44, 48, 54, 124
Nichols, Byron 61, 70–71
Nickson, Andrew 1, 35–36, 170
Nietzsche, Elisabeth 6
ninis (neither study nor work youth) 140
Nixon, Richard 184
North, Douglass 107
Nueva Germania 6
Nye, Joseph 191

Olimpia 2
Oregon 97
Organisation for Economic Co-operation and Development (OECD) 84, 134, 190
Organization of American States 188
O'Rourke, P.J. 77
Ortega, Daniel 186
Orwellian legislation 34
Ottoman Empire 145, 189
Ovandoy, Fernando 111
Ovelar, Blanca 49
Oviedo, Lino 46, 49, 55, 121, 187
Oxfam 163

Paiva, Félix 30
Palacio de López (Lopez's Palace) 21–22
Palestine 163
Panama 16
Paraguay River 28, 92, 127, 155, 157, 172–174
Paraguayan Association of Political Scientists 57
Paraguayan Institute for the Indigenous see Instituto Paraguayo del Indígena
Paraguayan People's Army see Ejército del Pueblo Paraguayo (EPP)
Paraguayans living in the U.S. (2016) 143
Paraguay's Woes (book) 199
Paraná River 105, 156, 170
Paris Agreement 272
Partido Liberal Radical Auténtico (PLRA) see Liberal Party
Patria contratista, La 114
patrimonial regime see patrimonialism
patrimonialism 35
patronage 34–35, 37, 58, 66–67, 71, 75
Peace Corps 96, 99
Pedro Juan Caballero 124
peicha nte 110
Perón, Juan Domingo 38, 181
Peru 12, 87, 103, 123
Petróleos de Venezuela (PDVSA) 107
Pew Research 135
Pinochet, Augusto 37–38, 58, 186

Pisani, Michael 111
Pizarro, Francisco 11
Plan Condor 39–40, 182
Planck, Max 196
planilleros 59
political identity 72
polka 39, 67, 203
polyarchy 56
Polybius 199
polygyny 13
Pompeo, Mike 186
population growth 131, 133, 173
Por orden superior (by superior order) 34
Prebisch, Raúl 79
predatory state 101
pre-trial detention 133, 199
the price of peace 37
primary elections of 1992 43, 72
primary elections of 2017 76
prisons, state of 133
Pritchett, Lant 56, 58, 198
Pro Desarrollo Paraguay 111
Programme for International Student
    Assessment 139
Prohibition Era 113, 122
Prussian Kingdom 145
Przeworski, Adam 76
public notaries 114
public schools 139, 142, 145, 152
public teachers' union 141
Puerto Presidente Stroessner 103
Pynandi 67

Qatar Airways 161
Quyquyhó 9

Rachid, Leila 177
Rafaat, Jorge 124
Ramírez Boettner, Luis María 188
reAcción 141
Reagan, Ronald 186
Recuerdos de Ypacaraí (song) 174
Red Command (Comando Vermelho) 124
régimen de turismo 105
Religious Freedom Report (U.S.
    Department of State report) 135
renewable energy 165, 194
rent-seeking 35, 67, 176, 101, 108, 120–121
report on worst forms of child labor (U.S.
    Department of Labor) 130
Revolts of the Comuneros *see* Comuneros
Revolutionary Armed Forces of Colombia
    125
Rhode Island 146
Rio de Janeiro 91, 124, 164
Rio de la Plata Viceroyalty 16
Riquelme, Marcial 34

Rivarola, Milda 9, 28
Roa, María Esther 54
Roa Bastos, Augusto 152, 177
road infrastructure 28, 149, 202
Robertson, John Parish 155, 198
Rockefeller, John D. 203
Rodríguez, Andrés 42, 44–46, 129
Rodríguez de Francia, José Gaspar 18–19,
    162, 178, 200
Roett, Riordan 28, 196
Romero, Aníbal 153
Roosevelt, Franklin Delano 185
Ruíz Díaz, Estela 75
rule of law 16, 45, 49, 51, 56, 102, 109, 114–
    119, 121–123, 133, 193, 195, 198, 201–202
rural migrants 127, 131, 136
rural population ·93, 129
Rural Welfare Institute *see* Instituto de
    Bienestar Rural
Rusk, Dean 167, 186
Russia 82, 116, 145, 161
Russian Revolution 145

Sachs, Jeffrey 166
Sacks, Richard Scott 28, 196
sale of public lands 26–27
Saltos de Guairá 167–168
San Bernardino 6
San Lorenzo 127–128
Sánchez, José Tomás 63
Sao Paulo 164, 169
savings rates 138–139
Schneider, Friedrich 111
Scotland 98
Semillas para la Democracia 66
September Revolution of 1930 (Argentina)
    30
Service, Elman 13, 61, 96, 157
Service, Helen 61, 96, 157
Service, Robert 187
Setrini, Gustavo 58
Seven Wonders of the Modern World 156
Sherman, William Tecumseh 23
Sienra, Carlos 29
Simon, Julian 157, 201
Simons, Menno 144–145
The Simpsons (TV series) 3
Singapore 89, 109
Sinohydro 183
slave population 14, 130, 148, 151
Slovakia 103
small farmers 149, 162–164
Smith, Adam 98, 102, 198–199
Sobchak, Walter 101
Social Progress Index 166
Social Services 60, 136, 146, 150
Society of Jesus *see* Jesuits

soft power 191–192
Solano López, Francisco 19, 21–23, 178–179, 181
Solow, Robert 83
Solow Model 83–86
The Sopranos (TV series) 59
Soto, Lilian 65
South Africa 137, 183–184, 186, 189
South American Football Confederation *see* CONMEBOL
South Korea 140, 175
Soviet Union 145
soybean production 106, 131, 149, 158–161
Spain 11–12, 16–18, 137, 143, 177
Spanish conquerors 13, 162
Spanish Crown 11–14, 16–18, 162
Standard & Poor's 80
state capacity 58
state-owned enterprises 32, 36, 59, 75, 90, 107, 148, 166, 183
Steinsson, Sverrir 187–191
Steward, Julian 2
Stroessner, Alfredo 2, 27, 32–39, 42–45, 50, 62, 68, 73, 77, 95, 101, 108, 109, 117, 129, 181–184, 186–187, 191–192, 203; regime 32–39, 43–45, 48, 51, 57–58, 63, 68–70, 73–74, 77–78, 81, 95, 101, 109, 115, 117, 132, 148–149, 162–163, 167, 178–179, 181–182, 186, 188, 192, 194, 196
Stroessner, Alfredo, Jr. 35
Stroessner, Gustavo 35, 42
El Stronato *see* Stroessner regime
subsistence farming 130–131
Suharto 58
sultanism 34–35
Sun Myung Moon 163
Supreme Court 46, 49, 51, 55, 60, 71, 110, 117, 121–122, 133, 170, 180, 196
El Supremo *see* Rodríguez de Francia, José Gaspar
Susnik, Branislava 10
Sutton, Willie 126
Swann, Chester 62
Switzerland 144, 111
Syria 103

Taiwan 103, 177, 180, 182–183, 186
tax rates 38, 88
Taylor, Alonso 21–23
Técnica, La 40, 42
Tekoporã Program 60
Tel Aviv 189
Telesca, Ignacio 14
Tencent 175
Tereré 53, 83, 122, 127
terra de ninguen (no man's land) 123–124
Thompson, Hunter S. 63, 91

Thorhallsson, Baldur 187–191
Three Gorges Dam 168
Tobateños 98–100
Tobatí 96–100
Tocqueville, Alexis 54–55
total factor productivity 84–85
tourism pass *see* régimen de turismo
Tovaja (brother-in-law) 13
trade 2, 12, 16–17, 20, 31, 36, 82, 89–90, 105–106, 114, 180, 185, 190
trade arbitrage 95, 102–103, 113, 115, 122
traffic accidents 131
Tragedy of the Commons 107
transition to democracy 43–46, 68, 71, 108
Transparency International 106–107, 110
Tri Deal 105–106, 126
Triffin, Robert 79
TripAdvisor 99
Triple Alliance War 22, 24–27, 167, 178–179, 181, 185; death toll 23–24
Tupi-Guaraní 10
Turkey 30, 103
Twin Anchors of Macroeconomy 79
tyranny of the majority 55

Ukraine 145–146, 148
Última Hora 51, 71
UNESCO World Heritage site 17
Unification Church 163
Unitarios (Argentina) 22
United Nations Office on Drugs and Crime (UNODC) 124
United Nations Peacekeeping Operations ("blue helmets") 190
United Nations Special Rapporteur on contemporary forms of slavery 130
United Nations Special Rapporteur on the rights of indigenous peoples 153
United Nations Sustainable Development Goals 195
United States 30–31, 36, 40, 53–55, 59, 66, 69, 82, 106, 109, 113, 120, 122, 124, 138, 143, 160–161, 164–165, 171–172, 178, 184–188, 191
U.S. Agency for International Development 1, 66, 117, 172
U.S. Census ·143
U.S. Embassy 1, 3, 74, 176, 185, 187
U.S. government 1, 31, 36, 39, 42, 102, 124–125, 167, 184–187, 195
United States National Film Registry 5
Universidad Nacional de Asunción 57
urban population 129, 194
urbanization 130, 173, 197
Uruguay 2, 6, 9, 11, 18, 21, 46, 66, 69, 86, 97, 105, 157–158, 161, 181, 183, 190

USAID *see* U.S. Agency for International Development

value added tax 88, 105
Vanderbilt University 56
Vargas, Getulio 30, 38, 181
Vargas, Manuel 181
Velázquez, Rafael 13
Venezuela 55, 69, 107, 164, 184, 201
Vera, Aidé 54
Vera, Helio 13, 57, 72, 118, 200
Viceroyalty of the Río de la Plata 16–18
Vierci Group 94
Vietnam 20, 155, 161, 186
Vistula river delta 145
Vorster, B.J. 184

Wall Street Journal 87
War of the Pacific 28
Wasmosy, Juan Carlos 43, 45–46, 121, 187
Water & Sewer Company *see* Empresa de Servicios Sanitarios del Paraguay (ESSAP)
Water Witch vessel 184
Weber, Max 34–35
WeChat 83
WhatsApp 54, 83, 97
Whicker, Alan 194
Wilkinson, Will 198
Willy Wonka and The Chocolate Factory (film) 5
women's employment 65, 98, 130, 133–134, 140, 203

women's political participation 26, 65–66
Woolcock, Michael 56, 58, 198
World Anti-Communist League 182
World Bank 85, 87, 112, 130, 137, 141–142, 163, 172, 188
World Drug Report 124
World Economic Forum 87, 111, 131, 165
World Health Organization 60, 131
World Trade Centers (WTC) Association 91
World War I 27, 45
World War II 2, 5, 10, 24, 31, 82, 128, 145–146, 178, 181
World Wildlife Fund 174

Yacyretá Dam 38, 156, 167, 170–171
Yale Center for Environmental Law & Policy 175
Ybycuí National Park 21
yerba mate 12, 16–17, 27, 78
yerno (son-in-law) 13
Ynsfrán, Oscar Facundo 199
youth unemployment 137
Ypacaraí Lake 174

Zacarías, Alejandro 71
Zacarías Clan 71, 196
Zacarías Irún, Javier 71, 196
Zacarías Irún, Justo 71
Zaire *see* Democratic Republic of Congo
Zero Deforestation law 172–173
Zucolillo, Aldo 94
Zucolillo Group 95